A Grim Almanac of
Leicestershire

A GRIM ALMANAC OF
LEICESTERSHIRE

NICOLA SLY

The
History
Press

First published 2013
The History Press
The Mill, Brimscombe Port
Stroud, Gloucestershire, GL5 2QG
www.thehistorypress.co.uk

British Library Cataloguing in Publication Data.
A catalogue record for this book is available from the British Library.

ISBN 978 0 7524 8744 1

Typesetting and origination by The History Press
Printed in India.
Manufacturing managed by Jellyfish Solutions Ltd

CONTENTS

ALSO BY
THE AUTHOR

INTRODUCTION & ACKNOWLEDGEMENTS

I have now written several books for The History Press in their *Grim Almanac* series but, for me, this one was especially enjoyable to write, since it is about Leicestershire, the county where I was born and where I spent the first twenty-nine years of my life. (It even features two of my ancestors.)

The true stories within are sourced entirely from the contemporary newspapers listed in the bibliography at the rear of the book. However, much as today, not all reporting was accurate and there were frequent discrepancies between publications, with differing dates, names and spellings. There are also some Leicestershire villages, such as Quorndon / Quorn, which have changed their names over time. I have used whichever version was current at the time of the featured incident.

I would like to thank Matilda Richards, my editor at The History Press, for her help, encouragement and enthusiasm in bringing this book to print. As always, my husband Richard remains a constant source of support, as does 'Harris' – a great friend for more than forty years – who corrected my memory of the county of Leicestershire on more than one occasion.

Every effort has been made to clear copyright; however, my apologies to anyone I may have inadvertently missed. I can assure you it was not deliberate but an oversight on my part.

Nicola Sly, 2013

JANUARY

Loughborough Market Place and Town Hall, 1960s. (Author's collection)

1   JANUARY 1899 Peter Hubbard lived and worked with his uncle, sixty-eight-year-old Josiah Hubbard, at the village bakery in Bitteswell. On 2 January, their assistant, Thomas Church, reported for work at 6.30 a.m. and was greeted by Peter, who asked him to fetch some brandy as he didn't feel well. On his return to the bakery, Church was appalled to find a large pool of blood on the floor and, when he questioned Peter, he was told that Josiah had fallen. The elderly man lay dead in the bake house with extensive injuries, apparently caused by a blunt instrument, although when blood and grey hairs were found on Peter Hubbard's boots, the doctors concluded that he had kicked his uncle to death.

An inquest held by coroner George Bouskell returned a verdict of wilful murder against twenty-eight-year-old Peter, who was committed for trial at the next assizes. Peter claimed to have knocked his uncle down and kicked him during an argument on 1 January about Peter's desire to get married. However, the medical superintendent of the Leicester Borough Asylum and the prison surgeon were both of the opinion that Peter was 'feeble-minded' and deficient in understanding.

Both Peter's parents had spent time in a lunatic asylum and he was found guilty but insane. He was ordered to be detained during Her Majesty's pleasure and died in November 1926, while still in custody.

Leicester County Police were heavily criticised for allowing Church to get on with the day's baking after the body was found, having moved the corpse into the next room.

2   JANUARY 1899 Intending to wash his knives and tools, Leicester pork butcher Joseph Henry Hillyer filled a tin bath with boiling water and placed it in his back yard. He momentarily left the bath unattended while he went to collect something from indoors but rushed back when he heard screaming. He was horrified to find that his four-year-old son had climbed into the bath. Joseph Henry Hillyer junior was badly scalded from the waist down and died from shock that night in the Leicester Infirmary.

At an inquest on 4 January, coroner Robert Harvey recorded a verdict of 'accidental death'.

3   JANUARY 1907 Kate Morley of Loughborough woke to find all three of her sons dead in their beds. An inquest was opened and adjourned for post-mortem examinations on the boys, who were aged five, three and one year old.

When the inquest concluded on 11 February, doctors stated that the boys died from 'carbonic oxide gas poisoning', due to the inhalation of fumes from the coal fire in their bedroom. The police testified that the chimney was so caked with soot that there was no draft at all until a chimney sweep was brought in to clear it.

The coroner stressed that Kate was a good mother and the jury returned verdicts in accordance with the medical evidence.

4   JANUARY 1886 Selina Mary Redfin was playing in a field in Snarestone, which was used as a public recreation ground. The canal ran through a tunnel beneath the field and, at the tunnel's end, only an 18-inch high parapet protected the children from a 24-foot drop into the canal below.

When nine-year-old Selina toppled into the water, another girl tried to reach her with a stick, while two more children ran for help. Two men raced back to the canal with them but, by the time they got there, all they could see was Selina's hat floating on the water.

Coroner George F. Harrison recalled another fatal accident at the same place a few years earlier, at which time a request was made to the canal company to do something about the dangerous parapet. However, shortly afterwards, ownership of the canal passed to the Midland Railway Company and the coroner's recommendations were not acted upon.

In returning a verdict of 'accidentally drowned', the jury asked the coroner to write to the railway, calling their attention to the danger and recommending that the parapet should be at least 4 feet high, with narrow coping on top to prevent children from walking on it.

5   JANUARY 1823 Joseph Hurst and William Peet had a trifling dispute at Hinckley, which they resolved to settle by fighting. It was obvious that Peet was getting the worst of the bout and spectators separated the two youths after just a few blows had been exchanged. The men shook hands and Peet was taken into a nearby cottage, where he expired within seconds. Horrified, Hurst handed himself in to the police to await the coroner's inquest.

Fortunately for Hurst, the inquest found that Peet 'died from excessive passion and not by blows received from his antagonist'. No criminal charges were brought against Hurst in connection with Peet's death.

6   JANUARY 1897 A rent collector visiting a property in Loughborough found the tenant dead. Seventy-year-old Harriett Rushden (or Rushton) lay on a heap of rags on the floor, naked apart from a bodice. Her emaciated body was filthy and verminous and her house so disgusting that coroner Henry Deane ordered it to be cleaned before he would allow the inquest jury inside.

Having been ill with bronchitis, Harriett had been of concern to her neighbours for many months – according to Ann Dickens, she was destitute and had to pawn things to survive. Mrs Dickens had supplied her with food and coal and had also lent her money, although she could ill afford to do so.

Harriett was well known to the local relieving officer but when Francis J. Rowbotham visited, she refused to allow him into the house, telling him to mind his own business. Neighbours believed that Harriett would be better off in the Workhouse, but having been rebuffed, Rowbotham washed his hands of her and said that he could not intervene unless Harriett herself asked him to.

The inquest jury returned a verdict of death from natural causes but asked the coroner to investigate Rowbotham's conduct. Accordingly, Mr Deane asked the Board of Guardians to carry out a thorough enquiry.

When the clerk to the Guardians reported back, he advised the coroner that there was plenty of food in Harriett's house including bacon, bread, tea, sugar, oatmeal and a roast duck, as well as jars of beef extract. There were also seventeen rabbits, although these had been kept for so long that they were unfit for eating. Harriett had lots of clothes and bedclothes, which were folded and wrapped in tissue paper. She also had two shillings in cash and several valuable pieces of jewellery.

7 JANUARY 1943 An inquest held by coroner Mr E. Tempest Bouskell into the deaths of five soldiers concluded in South Croxton. When an army lorry carrying twenty soldiers crashed in the village on 7 December 1942, four men were pulled from the wreckage dead, a fifth dying in hospital on 29 December.

During the blackout necessitated by the Second World War, the lorry was driving without headlights. The vehicles had a tendency to pull to the left and the country lane was bordered by high hedges and trees, which gave the impression of travelling along a tunnel. Driver J. Stoddart stated that he was driving very slowly owing to the fact that he had no lights. He felt a bump and suspected that he was on the grass verge, so braked and then released his brakes to avoid skidding, at which point the lorry hit a tree.

The inquest returned five verdicts of 'accidental death' on Privates Leslie John Oliver (32), Edwin Dare (19), George Sharples (25), Leslie Robertson (30), and Martin Kelly (23).

8 JANUARY 1900 A new kiln was under construction at a brickyard in Loughborough. The outside walls were finished and the framework supporting the arched inner roof had been removed three weeks earlier but, on 8 January, while several men were working on the top of the kiln, it collapsed. James White shouted a warning to his colleagues, who scrambled clear, but White himself didn't make it and was buried by debris, dying instantly from crushed chest walls.

The kiln had been inspected several times after the timber supports were removed and was judged safe – indeed, it had supported up to twelve men, more than double the number on the roof when the collapse occurred. The only possible explanation

Baxter Gate, Loughborough. (Author's collection)

was that the incident occurred on Monday morning and it had rained heavily since the men finished work on Saturday, possibly softening the clay and weakening the unsupported ceiling.

At the inquest into White's death, the coroner advised the jury to consider whether there was any negligence or if this was a totally unforeseeable accident. The jury returned a verdict of 'accidental death', although they recommended that the supports should be left in any future kilns until construction was complete.

9   JANUARY 1886   Although Millington's Pit in Leicester was private property, it was close to a recreation ground and when it froze over, people flocked to skate and slide on it.

On 9 January the ice broke, sending two men and six boys into the water. The men and three boys were rescued but Joseph Winterton Bennett (10), William Alton (11), and Harry Swingler (13) drowned.

Coroner George F. Harrison held an inquest, at which witness Alfred Sarson claimed to be a member of an organisation called The Railway Ambulance Society. Sarson was fully trained in artificial respiration and was convinced that he could have saved the boys had he been permitted to do so, but told the coroner that members of the public refused to let him assist, insisting on trying their own methods of resuscitation, which were completely ineffective.

The three deaths were not the first to have occurred at the pit, which was referred to as 'a mantrap'. The jury returned verdicts of 'accidental death', adding a rider that the pit should be filled up or fenced. They asked the coroner to severely reprimand the owner, who had been warned about the dangerous state of the pit and had failed to take action.

10 **JANUARY 1893** Three boys decided to walk across the frozen River Soar but the ice broke when they reached the middle. Two young boys saw the accident and heard one of those in the water shout 'Come and get me out,' but neither witness was able to swim and there was nobody else in sight who might have attempted a rescue. By the time Thomas Dawson and Joseph Tarry had raced home and told their parents what had happened, there was no possibility of recovering anyone from the river alive. At an inquest held by coroner Robert Harvey, the deaths of eight-year-olds Joseph Manship and William Ward and seven-year-old William Burton were deemed 'accidental drowning'.

11 **JANUARY 1876** The Groby Granite Company had a three-mile-long railway line to their works and, on 11 January, eight men were riding on an engine, pulling three waggons laden with granite to the weighing machine (six were quarrymen, going for their dinners).

Without warning, the train derailed and overturned, trapping four men beneath it. One scrambled out with only minor injuries but James Gamble, William Grimes and Ralph Richards were all more seriously injured. Grimes and Richards are believed to

Central buildings, Leicester Infirmary. (Author's collection)

have survived the accident but, on 14 January, Gamble was still complaining of terrible pain and was taken to the Leicester Infirmary, where he died from internal bleeding.

An inquest held by coroner George F. Harrison learned that the track and engine were well maintained, although there was one place on the line where the ground had sunk slightly. Nobody considered this a serious safety issue and the train had progressed at least 10 yards past the defective section of line when it left the rails. The most likely explanation for the accident was the frosty weather and, having heard this, the jury returned a verdict of 'accidental death'.

12 JANUARY 1892 Coroner Mr G.A. Bartlett held an inquest into the death of five-year-old Alfred Barrowcliffe.

When George Biggs went to Syston on 9 January, his landlord's son, Alfred, begged to be allowed to go too. Once George completed his business, they went to Syston Station to catch the train back to Leicester. George sat Alfred on a seat in the weighing shed and made him promise to stay there while he went to buy their tickets. Alfred had an orange and some biscuits and George left him eating them and went to the booking office on the opposite side of the line. He was gone for less than three minutes but when he returned, Alfred had disappeared.

There was only one other person on the platform, a Mr Morris, who told George that he had not seen Alfred since the express train went through a minute or so earlier. George alerted station staff then began searching for Alfred but was interrupted by Morris, who shouted that Alfred had been found. His terribly mutilated body lay on the railway line and footprints in the snow on the platform suggested that he had walked off the edge.

Nobody had actually seen the accident but it seemed probable that Alfred became anxious on his own and tried to find Biggs. The inquest jury returned a verdict of 'accidental death'.

13 JANUARY 1862 Farmer Edward Dunmore of Staunton Wyville hired a steam-driven threshing machine from Henry Butcher, which proved far from satisfactory. It had numerous leaks, the pump was faulty, the water gauge was broken, it kept stalling and, at midday, it broke down yet again. Twelve men gathered round, watching Butcher repair a pipe with string and red lead, grumbling all the while about how unreliable the machine had become, when the boiler suddenly exploded.

Thomas Lee was blown 40 yards into a ditch, dying instantly. William Woolman's body parts were scattered far and wide, his head travelling 30 yards in one direction, his leg 15 yards in another, and the rest of his body flying more than 50 yards.

Samuel Ashby was struck on the chest by a boiler part and died instantly, while George Woolman was seriously injured and died within hours. Five more were injured, although all eventually recovered.

An inquest deemed that the deaths were 'owing to the culpable negligence of Butcher and his partner William Bloxam'. When the coroner pointed out that this was manslaughter, seven of the jury baulked and eventually the coroner agreed to receive the verdict as delivered and leave the magistrates to decide if the two men should be formally charged.

Both were committed for trial at the Leicestershire Assizes, although the Grand Jury found no bill against Bloxam, leaving Butcher to face a charge of 'feloniously killing and slaying' the four men. His defence counsel blamed the tragedy on Samuel Ashby, who was feeding the boiler with water. It was suggested that, observing the leakage, Samuel screwed down the safety valve as far as possible, thinking it would prevent too much water flowing into the boiler. Unfortunately, this prevented the escape of steam and the pressure caused the boiler to explode. The fact that the safety valve was found screwed to within two threads of the bottom convinced the jury to give Butcher the benefit of the doubt and he was acquitted.

14 JANUARY 1895 Coroner Robert Harvey held an inquest at Leicester on the deaths of a father and son.

On 12 January, policemen were posted along the canal banks, warning people not to venture onto the highly dangerous ice, but most people ignored them. Thus there were numerous people on the canal when eleven-year-old Frank Arthur Perkins fell through the ice near Walnut Road Bridge. His fifty-two-year-old father, William, went to his assistance but he too fell in. Other skaters flocked to help and before long there were six people in the water, only four of whom were saved.

People tried to throw ropes but they proved too short, as did a ladder that was pushed across the ice. Someone fetched a life buoy but it broke on entering the water. Eventually, somebody placed a gate in the water, sliding it underneath the two casualties. Perkins and his son were dragged to the bank but were pronounced dead at the scene.

The inquest jury returned a verdict of 'accidental death' on both father and son and asked the coroner to commend PC Harvey. Although wearing a uniform, complete with greatcoat, leggings, heavy boots and ice skates, Harvey managed to tread water for almost twenty minutes, holding Perkins under the armpits and keeping his head above water.

15 JANUARY 1897 Lettice and George Lee lead almost separate lives. Lettice worked as a charwoman and shared one bedroom at their home in Leicester with their seven children, while George lived on an allowance from his sister, bought and cooked

his own food, and had his own bedroom. However, the couple must have enjoyed a relationship of sorts, since on 3 January, Lettice suffered a miscarriage.

A neighbour nursed Lettice for a few days, until twelve-year-old Maud told her that she would be caring for her mother in future. The neighbour told George Lee that he must get medical help for his wife, which he agreed to do. However, it wasn't until 15 January, when Lettice was at death's door, that he fetched a doctor and, even then, he failed to stress the severity of her condition and she was dead when the surgeon arrived. The doctor was certain that, had he been called earlier, he could have saved her life and an inquest returned a verdict of manslaughter by gross and wilful neglect against Mr Lee.

When he appeared before magistrates, George made a statement, against the advice of his solicitor. He said that he had not known how ill his wife was, claiming that she was terrified of going into hospital and refused to allow him to call a doctor, continually reassuring him that she was fine and he should not worry. 'There was no wilful negligence, only negligence through ignorance,' concluded Mr Lee.

The magistrates committed him for trial at the assizes, where he was found guilty. However, since one of George Lee's daughters confirmed hearing her mother say that she did not want a doctor, the judge sentenced him to just nine months' imprisonment, with hard labour.

16 JANUARY 1899 As baker's wife Mary Ann Barnett of Somerby prepared bread and cheese to be sent out to a boy working in the fields, she suddenly gave a strangled cry.

Her husband caught her as she collapsed but was unable to ascertain what the matter was and sent for a doctor, who realised that Mary Ann had something lodged in her gullet and was choking. With assistance from the village constable, the doctor tried unsuccessfully to clear the obstruction, keeping up artificial respiration for some time, but Mary Ann never regained consciousness and died from suffocation. An inquest held by coroner Mr A.H. Marsh returned a verdict of 'death from misadventure.'

17 JANUARY 1891 Josiah Dakin (23), Thomas Porter (18), and Edward Hull (17) decided to go skating on the River Soar at Sileby. Job Bailey was spearing eels in the river and, when they asked him about the condition of the ice, he replied that it was safe enough at that particular spot but he couldn't vouch for its condition up or downstream. After Edward tested the ice by jumping on it, the three skated off towards Cossington Mill.

Clifton Bunney was putting on his skates when his friends suddenly vanished from view. He and Bailey ran to where the men had fallen through the ice but Josiah and Thomas had already disappeared, while Edward clung to edge of the broken ice, begging for someone to get him out. Bailey tried to reach him with his eel spear but it was too short. He also tried to walk across the ice but it cracked and he was forced to retreat. He and Bunney watched helplessly as Edward grew too exhausted to hold on and the water closed over him.

The three men were recovered with drags and an inquest ruled that they had accidentally drowned. The ice on the sides of the river was around 5 inches thick and the inquest jury spent some time pondering why it was so much thinner in the middle. They concluded that chemicals and sewage flowing from Leicester, coupled with a fast current, were unlikely to make 'good ice'.

18 **JANUARY 1899** Shortly after midday, two-and-a-half-year-old William Pryor fell into a brook at the rear of his parents' house in Leicester. The brook was swollen and fast-flowing after recent heavy rain and the toddler was swept away. He was spotted downstream by construction workers who managed to get him out, but by then, William had drowned.

There had been numerous complaints about the low brick wall separating the brook from gardens in Cottesmore Road, which had completely collapsed in places. William had already fallen in twice before and been rescued but, even so, no attempt was made to fence off the water and this occasion proved third time unlucky for the child.

19 **JANUARY 1899** Deputy-coroner Mr W.A. Clarke held an inquest into the death of Eliza, the newborn daughter of Henry Barradale and his wife of Leicester.

According to Mrs Barradale, her husband refused to fetch the midwife when she went into labour, telling her, 'I hope you die.' By the time a neighbour realised that Mrs Barradale needed assistance, it was too late. Midwife Mrs Plumb arrived to find the baby drowned in the 'night commode' and sent for Dr Lewitt.

At the inquest, Dr Lewitt stated that he saw the baby shortly after midday on 18 January. He was sure that she was born alive and asked Mrs Barradale why she had not sent for someone earlier.

Barradale actually walked past Mrs Plumb's house on his way to work. At the inquest, he denied having been asked to fetch her, saying that although his wife had been ill all night, he hadn't realised that her confinement was imminent. He insisted that all that she asked for that morning was a cup of tea, which he made for her.

Unfortunately, Mrs Barradale's testimony before the coroner was hearsay evidence and although Clarke told the jury that he had not the slightest doubt that she was speaking the truth, there was no legal redress for Barradale's gross misconduct.

The jury returned a verdict of 'accidental death', adding that mere words were not strong enough to express their opinion of Barradale, who they described as 'an inhuman monster'.

20 JANUARY 1895 Fifty-year-old Elizabeth Sharman appeared at Leicester Borough Police Court charged with cruelly ill-treating Percy Ambrose Tollington between 1 October 1894 and 1 January 1895.

One-year-old Percy was an illegitimate baby, whose mother paid Mrs Sharman 3s a week to look after him. However, Miss Tollington was in arrears and Mrs Sharman seemed to think she could just stop feeding Percy until she was paid. A doctor called by the NSPCC found that Percy weighed around 12lbs, when he should have weighed more than 20lbs. He was emaciated, filthy and malodorous, and covered from head to foot in running sores.

On her first appearance before magistrates, Mrs Sharman complained that Percy's mother owed her 22s and she could not afford to keep the child for nothing. She insisted that Percy had plenty of food, suggesting that he had inherited consumption from his father as the more he ate, the thinner he got. Mrs Sharman detailed Percy's diet, including patent baby food, milk and boiled bread, but her milkman was called as a witness and insisted that she only spent 1d a day on milk, far less than she claimed to give Percy.

At Mrs Sharman's request, the hearing was adjourned so that she might call more witnesses. However, when proceedings resumed on 20 January, the only new witnesses were Mrs Sharman's daughter and neighbour.

Hearing that Percy had gained 2lbs in three weeks in the Workhouse, magistrates found that Mrs Sharman had neglected him and imposed a fine of £2 or fourteen days' imprisonment in default.

21 JANUARY 1934 Four young boys were playing on the canal bank at South Wigston when one fell in. Seeing his four-year-old brother, Belmont, floundering in the water, eight-year-old Eric Sharp stripped off his clothes and jumped in, even though he couldn't swim. Meanwhile, five-year-old Royston Dilks went to two men fishing nearby and told them that there were two little boys in the water but the men quickly packed up their fishing gear and bicycled away, leaving the Sharp brothers to drown.

At the inquest held by coroner George Bouskell, Royston was the chief witness and Bouskell informed the jury that, so far, the police had been unable to trace the men. If Royston's story was true – and Bouskell had no reason to doubt it – then, in direct contrast to Eric's bravery, the anglers had been callous and un-English in allowing the children to drown. The jury returned two verdicts of 'accidental death'.

22 JANUARY 1883 Italian Dominic Mossorella appeared at the Leicestershire Assizes charged with the wilful murder of James Green on 5 November 1882.

Green died during a street fight in Leicester between two Italians and two Irishmen. According to witnesses, five Italians walked past the Irishmen and, after an exchange of words between the groups, two doubled back and challenged Michael Gavin and James Allen to a fight. After being knocked down, Mossorella got to his feet and stabbed Green, an innocent bystander, severing his femoral artery and causing him to bleed to death.

At Mossorella's trial the judge stated that, had Gavin or Allen been killed, Mossorella would have been charged with manslaughter, since the fight would have 'excited his passion' and temporarily prevented him from having full control of himself. The judge suggested that, in the dark street, it was not unreasonable for Mossorella to mistake Green for one of the party by whom he had been knocked down and instructed the jury that they should only find him guilty of murder if they believed that he was aware that Green had taken no part in the quarrel.

The jury found Mossorella guilty of manslaughter and he was sentenced to ten years' imprisonment. He was followed into the dock by Giuseppe Valvona, who was charged with maliciously wounding Gavin, with intent to do grievous bodily harm. Valvona was found guilty and sentenced to eighteen months' imprisonment.

23 JANUARY 1880 William Swain Antill appeared at the Leicestershire Assizes charged with shooting with intent to murder.

On 30 September 1879, Rothley farmer Samuel Priestley Simpson was walking to Mountsorrel and caught up with twenty-two-year-old Antill. The men walked on together and, when Simpson had concluded his business, he saw Antill shivering in a doorway. Antill told Simpson that he was planning to walk into Leicester and, seeing how cold the young man was, Simpson invited him to warm himself at his home on the way. When they arrived at Simpson's farmhouse, he went into the parlour to light a fire and, as he was doing so, Antill entered the room. Suddenly, a shot was fired, the bullet passing through Simpson's coat collar and lodging in his jaw. Antill told Simpson that he had fired the pistol for a lark and meant to hit the ceiling. He then left hurriedly, but was apprehended the next day in Loughborough.

Even at his trial, Antill continued to insist that he intended only to play a practical joke on Simpson, but nobody found his actions amusing and he was sentenced to twelve months' hard labour.

24 JANUARY 1948 Frank Timson's taxi was called to The Grand Hotel, Leicester, to take a couple to Kitchener Road. As they got into the car, the man handed the driver £1, saying that it would cover the fare plus a generous tip, but, as Frank turned to thank him, he realised that the man was holding a gun to the woman's head.

The Grand Hotel, Leicester. (Author's collection)

Ordering Frank to drive, the man handed him a further £7. 'When we get there, fetch the police,' he instructed, asking Frank to mention that there were letters in his pocket. When they reached Kitchener Road, the woman climbed out of the car. 'I don't care. I'm not frightened,' she said, before her companion fired several shots at point-blank range, fatally injuring her before turning the gun on himself.

Frank asked the occupant of a nearby house to send for the police and an ambulance and, when he returned to his cab, the shooter was struggling to reload his automatic pistol. The police disarmed him and he was taken to hospital, as was the woman, who was identified as Joan Henson. Her killer was Polish Air Force Squadron Leader Josef Zadawski.

Joan was married, but met and fell in love with Zadawski while her husband was serving abroad. Zadawski was also married but before long he and Joan were living as man and wife. Joan gave birth to their son in 1946 but left Zadawski the following year, when he was about to be sent back to Poland. He had hoped to take Joan and their son with him, so he invited her to The Grand to try and get her back, but, although he showed her his gun and threatened to kill them both if she wouldn't return, she refused to change her mind.

Josef survived to be tried for wilful murder at the Leicester Assizes on 15 March. His defence counsel plumped for an insanity defence, suggesting that Joan's behaviour had pushed the already mentally troubled Zadawski over the edge. It was a persuasive argument and, when the jury found him guilty but insane, he was ordered to be detained during His Majesty's pleasure.

25 JANUARY 1863 When Mr Flaville and his family returned to their home in Ashby Folville from church, they were alarmed to find their servant, William Harvey, slumped over the kitchen table, dead from a gunshot wound under his right ear. The family's other servant, Thomas Buswell, was apprehended in Leicester the next morning, when he told the police that his name was Thomas Brown and denied ever having visited Ashby Folville. However, when searched at the police station, a letter addressed to Thomas Buswell, Ashby Folville, was found in his pocket, along with Harvey's prayer book.

His cover blown, Buswell admitted to shooting Harvey but swore that he intended only to scare him. While making up the fire, he saw Flaville's gun standing in a corner and loaded it with a cap. He crept up behind Harvey, who was writing a letter, and pulled the trigger, expecting nothing worse than a loud bang. Unfortunately, the gun was loaded.

Fifteen-year-old Buswell was tried for wilful murder at the Leicestershire Assizes in March. He and Harvey shared a room and even a bed at their place of work and, since there was no suggestion of any quarrel between them, the jury seemed to accept the defence's explanation that Harvey's death was the tragic result of an ill-advised practical joke and found Buswell guilty of manslaughter only. The judge stated that he was taking into account Buswell's youth, while at the same time awarding a sentence that would give a warning to those who were wicked or insane enough to take up a gun to frighten anyone, without first checking to see if it was loaded. He decided on two years' imprisonment, with hard labour.

Ashby Folville. (Author's collection)

26 JANUARY **1897** An inquest at Leicester Town Hall returned verdicts of 'accidental death' on three boys, who died after falling through ice.

On 24 January, people began skating and sliding on the canal at Aylestone, ignoring warnings from the police that it was unsafe. (Witnesses later stated that the ice was so thin that it rocked as people passed over it.) Between Boundary Road and Batten Street, the ice gave way beneath James Boot (14), Matthew Henry Barratt (14) and George Edward Narroway (10), who all fell into the water. One boy managed to scramble onto the ice but was pulled back into the water by his terrified friends. Bystanders held out a pole to the boys and several people locked hands and tried to reach them, while George Herbert walked across the ice, but he too had to be rescued when it failed to support his weight.

Men from the local gasworks helped drag the canal but it was ninety minutes before the first body was recovered, and the third was not retrieved until the following morning. PC Dixey told the inquest that he personally had warned hundreds of people about venturing onto the ice that day but was largely ignored.

Note: Even within the same newspaper article, there is variation in the boys' names and ages. Barratt is referred to as both Matthew Henry and Alfred Henry, aged 12 or 14. James Boot's age is variously given as 13 and 14.

27 JANUARY **1827** Mary Measures, the landlady of The Queen's Head Inn at Ashby-de-la-Zouch, sent her servants to bed at around midnight, saying that she would follow shortly. Sometime later, Ann Hill was concerned that her mistress still hadn't come to bed and went downstairs to check on her.

She found Mrs Measures lying on the hearth, the kitchen full of acrid smoke. With the sole exception of her corset stays, all of her clothes had been burned from her body and her torso and limbs were badly scorched. Ann gave a terrible shriek and Mrs Measures told her, 'Don't make a noise; I shall be better presently.' Ann threw some water over Mrs Measures then, at her request, assisted her upstairs to her bed, where she languished until her death on 4 February. She remained lucid until the end but had no memory of how she came to be on fire, other than remembering holding a lighted candle. Mrs Measures did not cry out for help so it was assumed that she was unconscious when the fire started and an inquest jury surmised that, since a candle was found underneath her, she had probably suffered a fit or stroke and fallen onto the flame, setting her clothes on fire. A verdict of 'accidental death' was recorded.

28 JANUARY 1897 Six-year-old Elizabeth Thompson of Leicester came home from school sobbing and revealed that Charles Stenton had given her an apple, before taking her into a stable and sexually assaulting her.

The NSPCC got wind of the case and Inspector Ritchings took it upon himself to visit Stenton and take him to Elizabeth's home, where he questioned him about her allegations. Stenton admitted taking Elizabeth into the stable but denied assaulting her in any way. He was charged with criminal assault and appeared at the Leicestershire Assizes in February. When Ritchings was admonished for exceeding his authority and asked if his actions were sanctioned by the society, he admitted to acting on his own initiative. He was then asked if he thought that Stenton was 'of particularly bright intellect' and replied, 'His manner appeared guilty,' which the judge deemed a highly improper remark.

With or without the testimony of Inspector Ritchings, the jury found eighteen-year-old Stenton guilty of criminal assault but recommended mercy on account of his youth and lack of intelligence. He was sentenced to four years' penal servitude, at which his mother went into hysterics and had to be removed from the court.

29 JANUARY 1870 Frederick Bennett was employed as an under-shunter by the Midland Railway Company and, at around midday, he and Thomas Foster were shunting waggons, which they intended to couple to an engine.

Foster signalled for the engine to come a little closer and, as it did, nineteen-year-old Bennett slipped on a patch of ice and one of the wheels ran over his left foot. The train was moving so slowly that driver Dick Bryan was able to stop immediately, before any further damage was done. Bennett was taken to the Leicester Infirmary, where he was found to have a crushed foot and a 3-inch long wound across his instep. Within days, the wound was swollen and suppurating, causing Bennett a great deal of pain, and he grew gradually weaker until 5 March, when he finally succumbed to his injuries.

Throughout his spell in hospital, Bennett continually stressed that nobody was to blame for his injury, saying that he had simply slipped. Coroner John Gregory recorded the jury's verdict of 'accidental death' at the subsequent inquest.

30 JANUARY 1868 As thirteen-year-old Mary Ann Quenby and her friend walked through fields at Shepshed, they were overtaken by a man, who grabbed Mary Ann's friend and sexually assaulted her. The girl managed to escape but as she ran away, the man turned his attentions to Mary Ann. By the time help arrived he had fled, leaving Mary Ann to limp home, where a medical examination confirmed that she had been brutally assaulted.

Both girls were confident that they could identify their attacker and gave an excellent description of the clothes he was wearing. However, when twenty-four-year-old Samuel Wain was arrested, the most compelling evidence against him was that he was suffering from a venereal disease, which he transmitted to Mary Ann while attempting to rape her.

Found guilty at the Leicestershire Assizes of 'feloniously assaulting and ravishing', Wain was sentenced to two years imprisonment with hard labour.

31 JANUARY 1894 After labourer George Remington beat his wife with a chair, Esther, who had been married to him for fourteen years and borne him five children, finally left him. Two days later, George tracked her down and asked her to come back. When she refused, he punched her in the face, knocking her down, and kicking her as she lay on the ground.

One week later, George was brought before magistrates at Leicester Borough Police Court charged with assault. When magistrates heard that Esther had not seen a doctor, they stopped the hearing and sent for one, who found that she was black and blue all over and told magistrates that her extensive bruising could well have been caused by a chair.

Remington had a long string of previous convictions, mostly for assaults on the police or on women, and his wife was adamant that she would never live with him again. Magistrates granted her a separation order, giving her custody of the three youngest children and ordered Remington to pay 7s 6d a week maintenance, before sentencing him to six months' imprisonment with hard labour for the assault. 'I shall not pay it. I would sooner be hung,' vowed Remington, as he was led from the dock to start his sentence.

FEBRUARY

Leicester city police station, 1946. (Author's collection)

1 **FEBRUARY 1868** As Joseph Rudkin stood talking near the Abbey Meadow Gate in Leicester, a woman walked past carrying a little girl in her arms. Rudkin knew her as Emma Jane Crofts, an alcoholic who led a very dissolute life, and there was something about her manner that disturbed Rudkin so much that he followed her.

He passed his own home, where his wife was standing at the gate. 'I believe that woman is going to drown herself,' Rudkin told her. He almost caught up with Emma and shouted, 'What are you going to do?' at which she ran to the canal, hurled the child into the water and jumped in herself.

Rudkin raced to his house for drags and, when he returned to the canal bank, Emma had been swept 20 yards towards Belgrave. Rudkin threw the drag towards her but it fell short and, in his excitement, he let the rope slip through his hands. He fetched his boat and managed to rescue the child, passing her to neighbours, then retrieved his drag with a rake and began dragging for Emma, who had now disappeared. She was eventually pulled from the water dead and, sadly, it proved impossible to revive her nineteen-month-old daughter, Amy Preston Crofts.

An inquest held on 3 February heard that Emma took to drink after her husband left and went to America. Amy was the result of a relationship after Emma's marriage ended, but that too broke down. Since then, Emma had threatened suicide numerous times and had previously been prevented from drowning herself and from taking an overdose of laudanum. The inquest determined that 'the deceased woman drowned herself and child when in an unsound state of mind, brought on by excesses of alcohol.'

2 **FEBRUARY 1894** Twelve-year-old Norman Colson and his fourteen-year-old brother, Douglas, were playing in a field with pupils from Milton College, Countesthorpe, when a sudden landslip left the brothers buried up to their waists in sand and earth. Neither boy was hurt but as they struggled to free themselves, a further fall buried them completely.

Their companions raised the alarm and several men quickly began digging. Douglas was rescued, exhausted but unharmed, but it took more than half an hour to find Norman, by which time he had suffocated.

At an inquest held at the college the following day, the coroner recorded a verdict of 'accidental death'.

3 **FEBRUARY 1898** Deputy Coroner Mr A.H. Marsh held an inquest at Croxton Kerrial into the death of farmer George Cobley.

The day before, sixty-four-year-old Cobley was working on a threshing machine. His farm labourer, Albert Bailey, was passing corn to Cobley, who was feeding it into the machine but Cobley asked to change places with Bailey and, as they switched, Cobley stumbled. His arm went into the machinery and was ripped off at the shoulder.

A doctor was in attendance within minutes but Cobley died from shock and blood loss. The inquest jury returned a verdict of 'death from misadventure'.

4 FEBRUARY 1891 At Sketchley Dye Works in Hinckley, seventeen-year-old Charles Payne and his workmate, Mr Hogg, were asked to clean out a benzine tank.

Payne entered the tank through a manhole at the top, climbing down a ladder to the bottom. A few minutes later, Hogg heard a strange noise and, looking into the tank, saw Payne fall over. Hogg called foreman Mr Dillon and the two went to fetch Payne, but were badly affected by fumes and had to get out before they were completely overcome.

Almost an hour elapsed before Payne was removed from the tank, by which time he was long dead. An inquest held by coroner George Bouskell returned a verdict of 'death from suffocation', finding that nobody was to blame for Payne's death.

5 FEBRUARY 1895 As collier Harry Holt and two workmates, Aldridge and Davis, were walking between Ibstock and Hugglescote, they came across a man slumped against a gate. They lifted him up and he managed to walk a few steps, remarking how cold it was. Holt asked the man his name and he replied that he was Edward Smith from Heather.

Holt and his companions then continued their journey, leaving Smith in the middle of the road, where he was found by two colliers nearly five hours later. George Cox spoke to Smith but he could only groan in reply, so Cox sent his friend for help then fetched some hot tea, but Smith was unable to swallow it. When the police arrived, Smith was carried to a nearby public house, where he died within minutes. A post-mortem examination showed that he was practically frozen solid and his death was due to exposure.

Returning a verdict in accordance with the medical evidence, the inquest jury pointed out that had Holt, Aldridge and Davis acted as most humane persons would have done, Smith's life might have been saved. The coroner reprimanded them, saying, 'If you three men were all drunk, I could see how it might come about, but how anyone who was sober could leave a poor man to his fate in such a manner is past comprehension.'

6 FEBRUARY 1863 Charles Mollard Randall, the landlord of The Craven Arms public house on Humberstone Gate, Leicester, was larking about with some of his regular customers. Randall was sitting on the back of a chair, with his feet on the seat and one man made a bet that he could lift his leg over Randall's head, but when he tried to do so, he accidentally kicked Randall and knocked him to the floor.

Humberstone Gate, Leicester (the Craven Arms Hotel is on the left). (Author's collection)

The fall broke a small bone in Randall's hand and precipitated an attack of *delirium tremens*, to which Randall was predisposed. In the past, such attacks had been successfully treated with chloroform but on this occasion, when the chloroform was administered, Randall suddenly went rigid and died.

An inquest jury later returned a verdict of 'accidental death'.

7 FEBRUARY 1898 Kate Danvers of Shepshed appeared at Loughborough Police Court charged with cruelly neglecting her four children in a manner likely to cause them unnecessary suffering and injury to health.

Kate's husband, William, worked as a collier at Whitwick and, each day, walked more than five miles to work, leaving home before 4 a.m. and returning late at night. A steady, industrious man, he handed his wages over to his wife, who spent the money drinking with other men, rather than on caring for Elizabeth (12), Annie (9), Emma (6) and John (2).

Alerted to the children's condition by their school, NSPCC Inspector Barnes visited the house with PS Darby. The children were inadequately clothed against the cold weather and were infested with fleas and lice. Their bedroom was caked in excrement, while their scant bedding was urine-soaked and alive with vermin – the room stank so badly that both Barnes and Darby had to leave the house to vomit.

Before the magistrates, Kate claimed that all of the evidence against her was false. She then admitted that she had done wrong but promised to improve if she could be

Market Place, Shepshed, 1930. (Author's collection)

let off 'just this once'. When magistrates sent her to prison for one month, she went into hysterics and was removed from the court in a very distressed condition.

8 **FEBRUARY 1893** Croueste's Circus was in Leicester and the show's climax was an extremely daring trapeze act. A young French woman was swinging on a trapeze near the roof of the big top when she missed her hold and tumbled screaming towards the ground. A safety net was in place but seventeen-year-old Blanche Gentil, who was professionally known as Mademoiselle Blanche Blanchard, just caught the edge of it, landing heavily on the back of her head. She was picked up unconscious by her father and rushed to the Infirmary, but was dead on arrival from a fractured skull and broken neck.

Blanche had been a professional trapeze artist for three years and a gymnast and acrobat since early childhood. However, those spectators familiar with her skills thought that she appeared a little 'off colour' before her fall, which occurred as Blanche balanced with the trapeze across the middle of her back, aiming to drop head downwards and catch the bar behind her knees.

At the inquest, presided over by coroner Robert Harvey, the jury returned a verdict of accidental death, recommending the provision of larger safety nets in future. Blanche was buried in Leicester, before the circus moved to its next destination.

9 **FEBRUARY 1847** When Frances Hurst's husband was transported, she took up with seventeen-year-old John Clark (or Clarke). The couple lived together at Hinckley but theirs was a violent relationship and they frequently quarrelled.

On the morning of 9 February, John beat Frances. She managed to escape but John told numerous people during the day that he would 'get her' later and when she went home that evening, he was as good as his word. Frances became seriously ill as a direct result of Clark's ill-treatment and developed a 'formation' (abscess) on the back of her neck. When she died, it was clearly shown that the injuries inflicted by Clark were responsible for the abscess that ultimately killed her and the inquest into her death returned a verdict of 'manslaughter' against him, although magistrates were later to commit him for trial for wilful murder.

When he appeared at the assizes in Leicester on 20 March, the question for the jury was whether Clark intended to murder Frances when he assaulted her. The judge told the jury that he believed that there was considerable doubt on the matter and they found Clark guilty of the lesser offence. He was sentenced to transportation for life and sailed for Van Dieman's Land aboard *Eden* on 30 September 1848.

10 FEBRUARY 1893 On an exceptionally windy day, forty-one-year-old Henry Scotton left his workplace to go for lunch. As he walked along Belgrave Road on his way back to work, a wall and advertising hoarding blew down, burying Scotton in the rubble. People scrabbled through the debris with their bare hands but although Scotton was quickly located, he was already dead from a fractured skull.

The section of wall that collapsed was built in 1879 and was around 18 yards long and 10 feet high. The hoarding in front of the wall was more than 9 yards long and 14 feet high. The posts supporting the hoarding had rotted where they were driven into the ground, leaving the entire advertising board supported mainly by nails driven into the wall. These nails had weakened the wall's structure and the 4 feet of hoarding above the top of the wall acted like a sail. While the wall was strong enough to support itself, it could not cope with the additional force and leverage of the wind on the hoarding.

An inquest held by coroner Robert Harvey recorded a verdict of 'accidental death', with a recommendation that someone in authority should be responsible for checking the safety of hoardings.

11 FEBRUARY 1829 Servant Judith Buswell spent the day doing laundry at High Cross Street, Leicester and was last seen at 11 p.m., when she wished her employers, Mr and Mrs Biggs, 'Good night'. When she didn't come downstairs the following morning, Mrs Biggs checked her bedroom and found her dead.

A small, half-empty bottle of Prussic Acid was found amongst her bedclothes, along with an apron and six napkins, and a post-mortem showed that Judith's death was caused by ingestion of the irritant poison. The examination also revealed that she was six months pregnant.

High Cross Street, Leicester, 1890. (Author's collection)

Mr Biggs was a chemist and druggist and suspicion quickly fell on his apprentice, Richard Freeman. In the past, Freeman had bragged that he had been intimate with Judith and had told people that he had given her 'stuff' to enable him to take liberties with her. He also claimed to know what to use to bring about an abortion.

Freeman was tried for Judith's wilful murder at the Leicestershire Assizes and he was also separately charged with being an accessory in Judith's death, which, if proved, would also be a capital offence. There was some question about whether or not Judith would have been able to replace the cork in the Prussic Acid bottle after drinking half the contents and several experiments were performed on dogs, to see how quickly they were affected by the poison.

The presence of the napkins and apron in Judith's bed suggested that she was preparing for an abortion but drugs from the shop were routinely stored in the cellar of the house and it was not clear whether she had appropriated the acid herself, if it had been procured for her, or if someone else had given it to her. In the face of conflicting evidence at the trial, the jury needed only five minutes' deliberation before pronouncing Freeman 'not guilty'.

12 FEBRUARY 1895 Seventeen-year-old George Statham Mansfield appeared at the Leicestershire Assizes charged with committing an unnatural offence with a sheep at Ratcliffe Culey on 25 November 1894. The only witness against him stated that he

saw Mansfield driving sheep across a field, became suspicious of his conduct and so observed the offence actually being committed.

Mr Justice Hawkins submitted the witness to a thorough interrogation and seemed unable to comprehend why he had not stopped the offence, saying that his inaction reflected badly on his humanity and intelligence and that it was lamentable that he hadn't acted to prevent a young person getting into trouble.

The jury found Mansfield guilty of attempting the alleged offence and he was sentenced to six weeks' imprisonment with hard labour.

Mr Justice Hawkins.
(*London Illustrated News*)

13 FEBRUARY **1892** John Hobson died at Hinckley and much sympathy was expressed for his wife of only three weeks.

The funeral was fixed for the afternoon of 18 February, when a group of Hobson's friends arrived from Leeds to pay their last respects. Suddenly, one respectably dressed woman flung herself across the body and began sobbing bitterly, claiming that the deceased was her husband. The former Mrs Hobson was devastated when her husband left her and had placed advertisements in the newspapers begging him, 'Return and all the past will be forgiven.' Although Hobson was aware of the advertisements, he chose to ignore them, having already bigamously married his new wife in Hinckley.

The funeral was eventually cancelled and Hobson's body taken to Leeds, where it was buried by his first wife.

14 FEBRUARY **1887** Sixty-two-year-old Thomas Bloxham was executed at Leicester Prison, having been found guilty of the wilful murder of his wife on 26 November 1886.

Thomas and Ann Bloxham's marriage had produced eleven children but their relationship deteriorated after Thomas suspected his wife of being unfaithful. Before witnesses, he threatened numerous times to shoot her or cut her throat and on 25 November, he visited a gunsmith's shop in Gallowtree Gate, Leicester and purchased a large pistol, telling the shop owner that he wanted it for starting dog races.

The following day, he shot his wife in the head, before cutting her throat with a knife.

At his trial at the Leicestershire Assizes, a statement made by Bloxham was read out to the court. He first claimed that his wife represented herself to him as a widow when they married, whereas in reality she still had two living husbands. According to her husband, Ann began drinking heavily six years into the marriage and ran the family into debt. She also slept with other men.

To try and get her to live a decent life, Bloxham intended to take out a warrant on her for bigamy, but Ann threatened to kill herself. Bloxham stated that he and his wife made a suicide pact but when Bloxham tried to honour his side of the agreement after Ann's death, the gun jammed and, since his children were crying, he was unable to cut his throat.

When the judge recalled a medical witness to reiterate that none of Ann Bloxham's wounds could possibly have been self-inflicted, the jury found him guilty.

Note: Some sources give the date of Bloxham's execution as 11 February.

15 FEBRUARY 1867 Harriet Ayto of Leicester went to work, leaving her son George Mortimer in the care of his fifteen-year-old stepbrother, Wilson. Before leaving, Harriet gave George a dose of 'Godfrey's Cordial' – a proprietary concoction containing opium, treacle, water and spices, which was widely used to keep children quiet. Wilson was told that if George was 'cross' before she got home, he was to fetch a halfpenny-worth of the mixture from Mrs Billson's grocer's shop.

When George grew fretful, Wilson went to the shop as instructed. Mrs Billson was a little distracted, since some boys had just broken her shop windows, but she reached into the glass case behind the counter and measured out half an ounce of liquid for Wilson, who gave some to twenty-month-old George. Soon afterwards, George seemed thirsty and after having a drink, was exceptionally drowsy. Wilson became concerned, especially when he tasted the contents of the bottle and realised that it was far too bitter to be Godfrey's Cordial.

He went to a neighbour, who thought the bottle contained laudanum. On hearing that, Wilson returned to the shop and showed the bottle to Mrs Billson, who examined it and immediately sent for a druggist and a doctor. George was given an emetic but sank into a coma, broken only by occasional convulsions, and died early the next morning.

An inquest held by coroner John Gregory established that Mrs Billson kept Godfrey's Cordial and laudanum next to each other in the glass case and, although clearly labelled, the bottles were similar in size and shape. Mrs Billson admitted to being 'in a confused state' on account of the broken shop windows. The inquest jury returned a verdict that 'the child was accidentally poisoned, arising from exciting circumstances through which Mrs Billson was passing on the afternoon in question', asking the coroner to officially reprimand her for keeping the bottles together. Mrs Billson was so upset by the tragedy that she announced that she was giving up selling laudanum altogether.

16 FEBRUARY 1898 Having been found guilty of manslaughter at the Leicestershire Assizes the day before, Henry Moore was brought before Mr Justice Hawkins to learn what his punishment would be.

The case was a controversial one, arising from a football match between Enderby Granite Reserves and Aylestone United. After the match on 16 October 1897, twenty-year-old John Boyd Briggs described the Enderby players as 'brutes', saying that they had cruelly ill-treated him and complaining particularly of a tackle by Henry Moore.

As Briggs dribbled the ball towards the goal, he passed Moore, the opposing full back. Goalkeeper Thomas Yeomans ran to meet Briggs and kicked the ball out of play but, as he did so, Moore pushed Briggs hard in the back and he fell, landing with his stomach on the goalkeeper's upturned knee. He later died from a ruptured bowel.

The match was said to be rough and, since many spectators thought that Moore deliberately launched himself at Briggs, the inquest found a verdict of manslaughter against him and he was sent for trial at the Leicestershire Assizes. When the jury found him guilty, Mr Justice Hawkins, who admitted to knowing absolutely nothing about football other than the fact that people gathered together in fields, ran about and did all sorts of things with a ball, deferred sentencing until the next day.

Moore had been given excellent character references and Hawkins stated that he intended to treat him differently to the way in which he would have dealt with a 'drunken, idle, riotous, cruel, offensive person.' Hawkins believed that Moore's actions arose from lack of thought rather than from malice and, since it was obvious that Moore exhibited sincere sorrow and regret for what the judge referred to as 'a gross mistake', Hawkins stated that he intended to release him on his own recognisances in the sum of £50. Providing that Moore continued to deserve the excellent character that had been given for him, he would hear no more about the matter. If, on the other hand, Moore committed any future acts of violence, on the football pitch or off, he would bear the full brunt of the law.

17 FEBRUARY 1893 Although twenty-six-year-old hawker Albert Ernest Harris of Leicester had been married for only three weeks, he and his wife had already separated four times. Yet Albert, who was deaf and dumb, seemed keen to reconcile and on the evening of 17 February, his wife ate supper with him and agreed to stay the night.

Mrs Harris was woken by a tremendous blow on her head and, opening her eyes, found her husband bending over her, holding a revolver. Realising that she was awake, Harris tried to strangle her, before throwing her down the stairs. Fortunately, Mrs Harris managed to escape and ran out into the street, where she found a policeman, who took her to hospital. Doctors found that she had been shot in the side of the head, although the bullet rebounded when it struck her skull.

When Harris was arrested, police found a five-chambered revolver in his bedroom, which had recently been fired. Charged with attempted murder, he appeared before Mr Justice Vaughan Williams at the Leicestershire Assizes on 3 July.

Mr Justice Vaughan Williams.
(Author's collection)

The defence argued that Harris and his wife were quarrelling about money and the gun went off accidentally as they fought. The jury eventually found Harris guilty of attempted murder but recommended leniency on account of his infirmity. The judge promised to take that into account and sentenced Harris to five years' imprisonment.

18 FEBRUARY 1871 Heyman Balsam and Simon Hettle worked as tailors for Mr Whitehead in Leicester but were about to leave for London and invited the staff to the pub for a farewell drink.

A gallon of ale was consumed then Balsam ordered another half-gallon, asking for a clean glass. When it arrived, he picked up the glass and turned away from the table, saying something in Yiddish to Hettle as he did. The glass was filled and given to eighteen-year-old Amelia Westbury. 'Drink our health,' Balsam told her and she obediently took a swig of beer, passing the glass on to the next girl.

Before long Amelia, Mary Jane Fowkes and Sarah Ball, who had all drunk from the glass, began to feel very ill and Mary Jane fainted. Balsam helped her friends take her outside, where he kissed her and Sarah.

The girls made their way back to Mary Jane's house and her worried father immediately called a doctor. Surgeon Mr E. Robinson found all three girls near death and determined that they had ingested some kind of irritant poison. He gave them an emetic and, once they had vomited, arranged for their admission to the Leicester Infirmary. The vomit was bottled and sent to an analytical chemist in London, who found it consisted of beer, with traces of aconite and strychnine, both of which were deadly poisons.

Hettle and Balsam were arrested on suspicion of having poisoned the girls' drinks and appeared at the Leicestershire Assizes in July, having been incarcerated since their arrest in February. The defence maintained that the girls were drunk rather than ill and, after hearing all the evidence, Mr Justice Byles interrupted to ask the prosecution what was the motive? He pointed out that the poison was administered – if it was administered at all – in a crowded public room and it seemed unlikely that nobody had seen anything. Where did the poison come from and how did the prisoners obtain it?

The prosecution insisted in continuing with the trial, saying that they wished the jury to decide but, in his summary, Byles exposed even more holes in the case, querying why traces of two poisons had been found rather than one. The judge stated that he was well aware that his observations were entirely in favour of the prisoners but the responsibility ultimately rested with the jury. Both prisoners were acquitted.

19 FEBRUARY 1897 George Henry Stanley, aged thirty-nine, appeared at the Leicestershire Assizes charged with unlawful and malicious wounding.

Stanley had lodged with Mary Ann Clarke and her husband at Hinckley for two weeks when, on 4 January, Mary Ann went to change his bed linen and found his bedding absolutely crawling with vermin. When she pointed out what she had found to Stanley, he grabbed her by the hair and shook her, calling her ignorant and impudent. Mary Ann slapped his face and Stanley promptly picked up a fork from the table and stabbed her nose with it. When Mr Clarke rushed to his wife's defence, telling Stanley to pack his bags and leave, the lodger snatched up a heavy frying pan from the fire and swung it at Clarke's head, burning his face with the boiling fat. Immediately afterwards, Stanley shook Clarke violently, threw him into a corner and stood over him, menacingly waving the fork.

Although Stanley claimed to have been trying to defend himself against a vicious attack by Mrs Clarke, the jury found him guilty. Bearing in mind the fact that he had already served one month in prison while awaiting his trial, Mr Justice Charles sentenced him to a further two month's imprisonment.

20 FEBRUARY 1877 Charles James Pyne died at the Leicester Infirmary from the effects of a hammer blow to his head. He had been hospitalised since 22 November 1876, after being hit by workmate Thomas Bennett.

Coroner George F. Harrison was told that Pyne worked as a turner and Bennett as an apprentice blacksmith. It was Bennett's job to finish off Pyne's work and he had previously complained to his supervisor about the poor quality of a job that Pyne had done. Since then, Pyne had constantly needled and threatened Bennett, who was physically a much smaller man.

When Bennett made another complaint about Pyne's work on 22 November, Pyne pushed him hard in the chest, sending him sprawling over a workbench. Bennett picked up his hammer and told Pyne that if he did that again he would hit him, but Pyne snatched the hammer from him and knocked him over. Sensing that tempers were becoming frayed, foreman Ambrose Hobson intervened. 'I'll have no quarrelling here,' he said, leading Pyne away so that the two men could cool down. As he did, Bennett stood up, picked up his hammer again and swung at Pyne, knocking him senseless.

The inquest returned a verdict of wilful murder against Bennett, who had already been brought before magistrates numerous times but released on bail. Now he was arrested and committed for trial on the coroner's warrant. The Leicestershire Assizes commenced just four days later, and twenty-two-year-old Bennett appeared before Mr Justice Denman.

The court was told that Bennett was a peaceable, even-tempered man, while Pyne was a quarrelsome individual. Bennett deeply regretted his moment of madness and, throughout his stay in hospital, Pyne readily acknowledged that the incident was his fault from first to last and expressed a wish that Bennett should be dealt with leniently.

Denman pondered the peculiarities of the case, saying that Bennett had used a deadly weapon and had therefore been rightly charged with wilful murder, although it was arguable whether the blow was struck in self-defence or in hot blood. When the jury found Bennett guilty of manslaughter rather than murder, Denman took the victim's wishes into account and sentenced him to just one week's imprisonment.

Mr Justice Denman (later Lord Denman). (Author's collection)

21 FEBRUARY 1840 The body of Joseph Mason was removed from the River Soar at Littlethorpe.

Mason had been suffering from smallpox and, on 19 February, was so delirious with fever that it took six men to hold him down. Eventually, he was swathed in sheets and tied to his bed with strong cords.

Neighbour Thomas Cramp volunteered to sit with Mason and, at around midnight, he gave him one of the powders prescribed by the doctor, after which Mason seemed much calmer. Cramp risked leaving him alone for a few minutes, while he went to make a drink, but when he returned to the bedroom, Mason had freed himself from his bounds and threw a wild punch at Cramp, before running downstairs. Clad only in his shirt, he climbed out of a window and, with Cramp in pursuit, fled down the main street and through fields towards Croft. Mason stopped periodically to turn and threaten Cramp with violence, before breaking through a hedge. Cramp ran down the other side of the hedge, expecting to meet Mason at the end. However, Mason never appeared and, unable to find him, Cramp organised a search party.

Mason drowned in the Soar, at a place where the water was just 18 inches deep. Medical evidence at the inquest suggested that he was 'delirious due to an excitement in the brain, consequent upon the disease of smallpox' and the inquest jury returned a verdict of death from insanity.

22 FEBRUARY 1928 Coroner George Bouskell held an inquest into the death of Doris Geary. On 18 February, she and Dorothy Nowell arranged a double date with two men they met in a pub. After an enjoyable evening, the men offered the women a ride on their motorbikes and, after arranging to meet up again outside Trinity Hall in Hinckley, Dorothy went off on the pillion of one bike, Doris on the other.

Dorothy arrived back first and waited a long time for Doris, before finally giving up and going home. Meanwhile, unbeknown to her friend, Doris had been found by a bus driver, lying in a gutter between Hinckley and Nuneaton. She was rushed to Hinckley Hospital, where she died the following morning from a fractured skull and brain damage, consistent with having fallen onto a hard road.

The police appealed in the local press for the motorcyclist to come forward and eventually Pierce Albert Humphries contacted them. He told the police that he had taken Doris for a ride, explaining that his motorbike suddenly wobbled, causing him to swerve across the road. Doris fell off and, although he stopped and tried to get her to stand up, she was deeply unconscious. Being a married man with a child and fearful of the consequences of being caught with a twenty-two-year-old woman, he left her to her fate and rode home.

Cottage Hospital, Hinckley, 1939. (Author's collection)

Coroner Bouskell berated Humphries for his callous conduct, claiming not to understand the mentality of someone who could have done such a thing and saying that Humphries couldn't have behaved worse if Doris were a dog.

'If I had been a single man, I would have stuck to the girl and got her to hospital,' explained Humphries. Returning a verdict of 'accidental death', the jury asked the coroner to severely reprimand Humphries for his behaviour.

'I fear it would be a waste of words,' replied Bouskell.

23 FEBRUARY 1890 Tramp Mary Spencer was charged with sleeping out at Queniborough with no visible means of support. Her children, Annie (10) and Frederick (7), were with her and, when asked if she had any other children, she hinted that there was a third child, who died and was left in a field near Kegworth. A search was made and the body of a baby girl was found under a pile of rubbish. A post-mortem examination confirmed pneumonia as the cause of death but suggested that the baby had been starved and neglected.

Mary told the police that the baby died a natural death at Ilkeston and she had carried the body with her for two days. However, she was seen with three living children at Shardlow Union Workhouse in Derbyshire on 10 January, from where she apparently tramped to the Model Lodging House at Loughborough.

An assistant there recalled Mary's baby being very hungry and staff insisting she bought arrowroot for it. 'I wish the little ****** was dead,' Mary told them petulantly, before storming off with her children, even though she had paid for a bed for the night.

She was brought back and, the next morning, the assistant offered her some baby clothes, but Mary left while she was fetching them.

Mary was charged with the manslaughter of her unnamed daughter on or around 30 January but, by the time her case came to the assizes in July, she was judged unfit to plead and confined in a lunatic asylum.

24 FEBRUARY 1894 Twelve-year-old Walter Tyrrell had been employed by a wagoner since June 1893 and on 24 February he and John Scores, were carting stone at Stoney Stanton Quarry. Scores asked Walter to lead the horse and cart out of the quarry, a job he had done many times before. The horse was a very quiet animal and as soon as the cart was fully loaded, Scores went to do something else, leaving Walter alone.

Carter George Hextall watched from a distance as Walter turned the horse around. As he did, the horse tossed its head, nudging the boy into an empty cart and knocking the wind out of him. Before Hextall could react, the horse moved, crushing Walter between itself and the empty cart. Hextall yelled to Scores, who came running to see what the matter was. When they moved the horse, Walter dropped to the ground, where he lay unresponsive for several minutes before breathing his last. A doctor later found that he had several broken bones, including a broken neck.

An inquest held by coroner George Bouskell on 26 February recorded a verdict of 'accidental death', the jury adding a rider that, in their opinion, boys under the age of fourteen should not be in charge of loaded carts at the quarry.

25 FEBRUARY 1871 As twenty-nine-year-old William Benford walked along Humberstone Gate, Leicester, a man suddenly rushed up and stabbed him in the chest, killing him almost instantly. A crowd gathered and the knifeman lashed out wildly, wounding four more people before he could be restrained.

Twenty-six-year-old Jonathan Barrow was a respectable butcher, with a hitherto irreproachable character. However, on the night in question, he was absolutely blind drunk. At the time of the stabbing, he was carrying almost £70 on his person and apparently believed that he had been robbed.

Barrow was charged with wilful murder and appeared at the Leicestershire Assizes in March, where witnesses gave conflicting evidence, some convinced that Barrow knifed Benford at random and others sure there was an altercation between the two men prior to the stabbing. In summing up the evidence, the judge suggested that the contradictory testimony could mean the difference between a verdict of guilty of murder or guilty of manslaughter.

The jury plumped for a verdict of 'guilty of manslaughter' and Barrow was sentenced to fifteen years' penal servitude.

26 FEBRUARY 1840 Six youths were amusing themselves by sliding on a frozen pit in Hinckley. When they retired to the bank for a rest, John Osborn suggested that they should try out a clear piece of ice in the centre of the pit that was surrounded by weeds.

The others thought it looked unsafe but John would not be dissuaded. He ran to the patch of ice and attempted to slide across it but as he reached the middle, the ice shattered. Although the water only came up to his chin, he was unable to get out. Every time he grabbed the edge of the ice it broke. As he grew colder and weaker, his brother Thomas tried to rescue him but he too fell into the water and sank.

By now, the other boys had run for help but the bodies of the Osborn brothers were not located for some time. A later inquest returned verdicts of 'accidental death' on both boys.

27 FEBRUARY 1875 When baby Frederick Arthur Payne of Leicester failed to thrive, his mother consulted a chemist, who sold her a proprietary medicine known as 'infants' preservative', which claimed to prevent and cure a wide range of maladies including 'convulsions, flatulency, affections of the bowels, difficult teething, the thrush, rickets, measles, hooping-cough, cow-pox, or vaccine inoculation' [sic].

Frederick's father had hurt his knee and was prescribed a liniment, which came in a very similar bottle, although the liniment was clearly labelled 'Poison'. The Paynes stored the bottles together in a cupboard and when Mrs Payne asked her husband to pass her the baby's medicine he mistakenly gave her his liniment. Without checking the label, Mrs Payne gave Frederick six drops and immediately realised her mistake when he began to wheeze. A doctor was called but could do nothing to reverse the effects of the liniment and Frederick died. At the inquest on 27 February, the coroner recorded a verdict of 'accidental death' and stressed the necessity of exercising the utmost care when administering medicine to children.

28 FEBRUARY 1933 When Thomas W. Wilson disappeared from home, there was great concern for his welfare, as he was known to be depressed following the death of his beloved pet cat.

His employers took the controversial step of asking a water diviner to help in the search. One of Wilson's waistcoats was delivered to John Clarke at his home in

Kettleby and, using a forked twig and a map, he pinpointed Wilson's location in the river at Thurmaston.

Taken to the river bank, Clarke was blindfolded and spun round several times. 'He could not possibly have known in which direction he was facing,' commented an onlooker but each time, Clarke's forked twig indicated a particular line across the river by dipping and bending and Wilson's body was found just a few feet from where Clarke divined it to be.

An inquest jury returned a verdict of 'found drowned', finding it impossible to determine how or why Wilson came to be in the river.

29 FEBRUARY 1896 Bricklayer Thomas Jayes appeared at Leicester Borough Police Court charged with assaulting his wife on 28 February. Mary Ann Jayes was present in court, sporting two black eyes.

When questioned, she explained that her husband took some boots and a handkerchief to the pawn shop to get money for drink. Thomas had already spent his week's wages on alcohol and Mary Ann reminded him that without his boots he wouldn't be able to work, saying that she would give him a shilling if he didn't pawn them. Thomas told her that wasn't enough.

In the pawn shop, Mary Ann managed to snatch one boot off the counter and threw it into the street, running out after it. Her husband caught her and punched her, cutting her forehead. Passers-by intervened and Thomas was taken to the police station, but Mary Ann was afraid to leave him there and went to get him. She refused to press charges and he was consequently released, after which he punched her in the face again for having him locked up.

Magistrates sentenced Jayes to three months' imprisonment for the assault on his wife, who immediately applied for a separation order. It was granted, with magistrates ordering Jayes to pay ten shillings maintenance each week.

MARCH

Station Road, Hinckley. (Author's collection)

1 **MARCH 1925** Reverend William George Clement Bettison, the vicar of Hungerton, celebrated Communion then ate breakfast. Hearing a scream shortly afterwards, his housekeeper, Mrs Tulsingham, went to investigate and saw the vicar's sister, Dorothy Violet Bettison, coming from her brother's study.

'Oh, dear, Mr Bettison has shot himself. I must run down and phone for the doctor,' said Dorothy, which she did before returning to the study. Another shot rang out and Mrs Tulsingham rushed to see what was happening. Once again she met Dorothy coming out of the room and this time Dorothy told her, 'He asked me to do it.'

Dr Edward Williams found the left-hand side of the vicar's head and face shot completely away and he also had a chest wound. The head injury would have proved fatal – although not necessarily instantly – and it was possible that Bettison was dead when he was shot in the chest. Williams also found Dorothy completely insane and arranged for her immediate admission to the County Lunatic Asylum.

Reverend Bettison was known to have been depressed and had a family history of insanity and suicide. Coroner George Bouskell stated at the inquest that the truth would never be known but intimated that the balance of probability was that Miss Bettison fired the second shot. Dr Williams thought that, given his head wound, it was unlikely that Bettison would have been able to ask his sister to shoot him but suggested that he may still have been alive when she returned from calling for a doctor, leading her to 'put him out of his misery'. The jury returned a verdict of 'suicide while temporarily insane'.

2 **MARCH 1868** John Sleath was tried at the Leicestershire Assizes for the manslaughter of George Peet on 24 November 1867.

Peet was a travelling hawker and, on the night in question, he was driving his horse and cart between Whitwick and Thringstone. Outside Whitwick parish church, Peet's cart was hit by another, which was being driven at a rapid rate by Sleath, who was very drunk and was apparently on the wrong side of the road. Peet and his friends were thrown from the cart by the collision and Peet died two days later from punctured lungs, penetrated by his broken ribs.

At the inquest into Peet's death, there was so much conflicting evidence that the jury returned an open verdict, a situation that the police found so unsatisfactory that they instigated a prosecution against Sleath for manslaughter. He was allowed bail until his trial, at which he was found guilty and sentenced to one calendar month's imprisonment.

Whitwick parish church. (Author's collection)

3 MARCH **1893** Thirty-year-old Kate Hopewell appeared before magistrates at Leicester Borough Police Court charged with threatening to murder Father Henry Ceslaus Fletcher, the Prior at the Holy Cross Priory Roman Catholic Church, Leicester.

Since April 1891, Kate had written more than a hundred letters to Fletcher, most of which had been put aside unopened until it was decided to bring the case to court. One of her grievances against Fletcher was that he would not dismiss Mr Simon, the porter at the Priory, who was under strict instructions to refuse to admit her when she called. A letter dated 20 February read: 'Fletcher, you set your foot in Leicester again while Simon is here and I will murder you. I will murder you, I swear I will. You will not send him away – you will die.'

Father Fletcher told the magistrates that he had known the defendant since she was a child and had no wish to see her harshly dealt with. Nevertheless, she had accosted and molested him several times – in the church and in the streets – and he lived in fear of violence from her.

Magistrates committed Miss Hopewell to the Leicestershire Assizes, allowing her bail until her trial. There she pleaded guilty to sending threatening letters and the court was told that she was under treatment from a doctor for hysterical mania, who was prepared to state that she was insane when she wrote the letters. She was discharged from court with an order to come up for judgement when called upon – in other words, her offence was held on record, to be dealt with should she offend again.

4 MARCH 1868 Grocer and druggist Alfred Peberdy was tried at the Leicestershire Assizes for the manslaughter of James Henry Herbert at Leicester.

On 14 August 1867, Ann Herbert was left in charge of her grandson and noticed that James seemed poorly. She went to Peberdy and asked for a pennyworth of tincture of rhubarb, which he measured into the teacup she took with her. Peberdy recommended a dose of seven or eight drops of the tincture but Ann gave James ten drops, mixed with water.

When the baby's mother came to collect him at lunchtime, she found James stupefied, his eyes rolling in his head. She sniffed the remaining medicine and declared that it was laudanum. Ann took the cup straight back to Peberdy, who assured her that it contained tincture of rhubarb, although he admitted that his measure had previously been used for laudanum. He emptied the cup, rinsed it out then measured another dose of tincture into it, also giving Ann 'a sup of antimony wine' for baby James.

Meanwhile, Hannah Herbert rushed her son to a surgeon, who thought that his symptoms were indicative of an overdose of laudanum. He treated James but the baby declined rapidly, dying within the hour.

An inquest returned a verdict of manslaughter against twenty-seven-year-old Peberdy, who was committed for trial. In summing up the case for the jury, the judge said that it was for them to determine if there had been any negligence, either on the part of the defendant or by Ann Herbert in administering the preparation to the baby. Peberdy was still convinced that he sold Ann tincture of rhubarb, saying that if there had been a mistake, he had no idea how it happened.

If Peberdy made an honest mistake, the death of baby James was a tragic accident, whereas if Peberdy was negligent, he was guilty of manslaughter. The jury gave him the benefit of the doubt and he was acquitted.

5 MARCH 1870 In Leicester, eight-year-old William Mansfield Frisby and his six-year-old sister Ada Eliza went for a walk with their younger brother. They were specifically told not to go into Abbey Meadows, since there was a brisk wind and their mother was afraid they would be blown into the water.

The children disobeyed their mother and a little later, the youngest boy walked home alone and casually told his parents that his brother and sister were 'in the cut', adding that the wind blew Ada in and Willie walked in to get her.

Meanwhile, the attention of a man working in a nearby field was attracted by a child's shout and as James Sutton looked up he saw a boy jump off the plank bridge into the water. Sutton raced to the bridge and saw the boy being carried along by the current, which was faster than normal following recent heavy rains. Sutton could also see a little girl further downstream but, since he could not swim, he was unable to attempt to rescue the children. Instead he ran to the sewage works, towards which the children were drifting.

Unfortunately, there were no drags or other life-saving equipment at the sewage works and both children drowned. Coroner John Gregory recorded two verdicts of 'accidental death' at the inquest and noted the jury's recommendations to permanently site drags at the sewage works and to fence both sides of the plank bridge, rather than having a barrier on one side only.

6 MARCH 1894 James Brown appeared at the Leicester Borough Police Court charged with neglecting his six children between 1 September 1893 and 24 February 1894, in such a manner as to cause them unnecessary suffering. He was further charged with assaulting his wife, Emma, but after he promised to behave better in future, she refused to give evidence against him, so that charge was dropped.

Mr Simpson prosecuted the first charge on behalf of the NSPCC, informing the Bench that Brown's children ranged from two to ten years old. Emma was a hard-working, respectable woman, who did her best for the children, but her husband was often dismissed from jobs for drunkenness and, when he did work, spent most of his pay on alcohol. The family depended on charity and hand-outs for food and the children were malnourished and poorly clad.

Even after hearing that Brown served two months in prison for a similar offence in 1892, the magistrates could not agree on whether to send him back there again or give him another chance. They eventually bound Brown over for six months to see if he would mend his ways.

7 MARCH 1857 Collier Edward Laley was tried at the Leicestershire Assizes for the wilful murder of William Fullilove at Whitwick on 20 December 1856.

Fullilove was a very sprightly seventy-four-year-old and, in spite of his age, he still worked occasionally for the Surveyor of Highways. On 20 December, he was drinking in Whitwick and was rather drunk by the time he headed for home, accompanied by a colleague named West. They had not gone far when they met a group of five Irish labourers. Without any provocation, eighteen-year-old Laley stepped forward and grabbed Fullilove by the neck, throwing him down onto the pavement. His head struck the kerb and began to bleed heavily, at which four of the Irishmen fled. (The fifth stayed behind to help West take Fullilove home.)

Fullilove lingered for several days before dying, when Laley was charged with wilful murder. The trial jury found him guilty of manslaughter and he was sentenced to one year's imprisonment, with hard labour.

8   MARCH   1894   Coroner Henry Deane held an inquest at Sileby into the death of thirty-six-year-old Arthur Russell at his place of work.

Russell walked with a limp and had a slightly deformed left hand. His duties at the Phoenix Brick Works included oiling the machinery, which was always done when the men stopped for meal breaks and their machines were halted.

At 8.45 a.m. on 7 March, the foreman noticed one machine running at half speed. He went to the stoke hole and found that the steam pressure was very low and there was no sign of Russell, who was supposed to be stoking the engine. Nobody had seen Russell for some time, so the foreman went to look for him, eventually finding him dead under a milling machine, his oil can close at hand.

The men operating the milling machine admitted to having called Russell to attend to it because it wasn't working quickly enough. The engine was stopped and restarted again at 8.30 a.m., after which time Russell was clearly seen by several people in the engine house.

It was obvious that Russell had met his death by getting caught in the machine's cog wheels, which were covered in his blood, but Deane was anxious to discover why he was *under* the machine. Russell knew not to try and oil the machines when they were working and it seemed impossible that someone else had started the machine, unaware that Russell was working underneath it. The inquest jury were unable to solve the mystery and returned a verdict of 'accidental death'.

9   MARCH   1900   An inquest on collier Joseph Curl concluded four months after his death on 9 November 1899. The reason for the delay was that witness John Upton was severely injured in the incident that claimed Curl's life and the inquest was adjourned several times in the hope that he would be able to attend.

Upton told the inquest that he was an 'onsetter' in charge of the pit bottom at No. 2 Pit at Ibstock Colliery. Part of Curl's job was to remove empty tubs from the cage and, on the day of the accident, he was waiting for it to descend. Lewis Cooper brought two full tubs of coal to Upton, wedging a piece of wood into a wheel to stop them rolling away. Unfortunately, the wood broke and the tubs continued moving, ending up directly beneath the descending cage.

Upton signalled for the cage to be halted, so that the tubs could be moved, and it stopped roughly 9 yards from the pit bottom. Curl and Upton climbed onto the trucks and began shovelling coal out of them, only to see the cage resume its descent. Both men were crushed and Curl later died from his injuries in the Leicester Infirmary.

The banksman, who controlled the cage from the surface, should not have given the engineman permission to restart the descent without a specific signal from Upton. Engineman George Noon was therefore formally cautioned by the coroner before giving his evidence. The system of signalling between the pit bottom and the surface was not written down but had simply evolved throughout history and Noon was convinced that Upton had given the signal to restart.

Upton was recalled and explained that the agreed signal to stop the cage was one rap and to restart was two raps. At the pit bottom, Upton was unable to see the cage descending but relied on vibration to alert him to its movement. The mechanism sometimes vibrated when the cage was not moving and Upton thought that he may have given a second single rap, under the impression that his first signal had not been received and the cage was not stopping. Meanwhile, at the surface, Noon interpreted this as a signal to resume the cage's descent.

The inquest jury returned a verdict of 'accidental death', commenting on the laxity of the signalling system and recommending the application of stricter rules in future.

10 MARCH 1894 Nine-year-old Robert Garfield and his six-year-old brother, Frank, were playing with John Henry Richardson near Thorpe Satchville. The boys were amusing themselves by throwing sticks into a pond but as Frank tried to pick up a stick from the water's edge, he slipped and fell in. Robert tried desperately to reach his younger brother but neither boy could swim and when Robert also fell into the water, John ran back to the village to raise the alarm.

Louise Lander (or Saunders) probed the pond with her clothes prop but was unable to locate the boys. Eventually, labourer George Loddington waded in and retrieved them but the brothers were dead. An inquest later recorded two verdicts of 'accidentally drowned'.

Thorpe Satchville. (Author's collection)

11 MARCH 1897 Carpenter John William Stevenson hired mason Francis John Reeve to help him clean out a well at Belton.

Having pumped water from the well all morning, Reeve climbed down to see how much remained. Stevenson offered to go but Reeve insisted that he would do the job, since he was wearing an old coat. When Reeve got about halfway down the 30-foot-deep well, he suddenly tumbled off the ladder. Finlay McGlachan went in after him but the air in the well was so foul that he got only a few feet before he was forced back to the surface. William Jacques then volunteered to go down but was soon slumped against the ladder unconscious. A fourth man had a rope tied around his waist, but got only about 8 feet down the well before signalling to be pulled up.

Reeve and Jacques were eventually retrieved using a hook on a rope. Both were long dead from 'suffocation by carbonic acid gases'.

Belton. (Author's collection)

12 MARCH 1829 Having been found guilty at the Leicestershire Assizes (with William Warburton) of stealing rum, brandy, peppermint, silver spoons and other sundry items, William Collins of Loughborough was sentenced to death. His sentence was later commuted to one of transportation for fourteen years and, on 12 March 1829, he sailed for New South Wales on board the ship *Waterloo*.

William's wife was described as a most honest and industrious woman, for whom her husband's transportation was just the latest in a spell of misfortunes and tragedies. Four years earlier, one of the couple's children was accidentally scalded to death and, shortly afterwards, a second child died in a fire. In July 1828, a third child fell out of a cart and was killed when the wheel passed over its body. 'It was feared that the poor woman would lose her senses from the last melancholy circumstance,' reported the contemporary newspapers.

13 MARCH 1879 An inquest was held at Barrow-upon-Soar into the death of eleven-year-old John Powe.

John was captivated by the recent trial of cat burglar and murderer Charles Joseph Peace, who was hanged on 25 February at Armley Gaol, Leeds. He was especially fascinated by a graphic representation of Peace's execution in a newspaper. John fashioned a noose from a length of window cord and placed a mirror on a table. His mother was out of the room for less than ten minutes but when she came back, John was dead.

Charles Peace.

The coroner surmised that John wanted to look at himself with a noose around his neck but in posing, his feet accidentally slipped from under him. The jury concurred; returning a verdict that John accidentally strangled himself.

Armley Gaol, Leeds. (Author's collection)

14 MARCH 1941 Thomas William Thorpe's violent behaviour eventually drove his wife of twenty-six years to leave him and on 14 March, Nellie moved out of their marital home to live with workmate Elizabeth Ann Parsons. On 14 July, as Nellie and Elizabeth were among a group of women leaving a Leicester factory, Thomas suddenly leaped on Nellie from behind, shouting, 'I'll give you going about with other men.' Then, before anyone could stop him, he cut her throat with a razor before cutting his own.

Nellie bled to death but her husband recovered to stand trial for her wilful murder. When Nellie was killed, the area was crowded with workers heading home and there were numerous witnesses to her untimely death, so the fact that sixty-one-year-old Thorpe killed her was never in doubt. Thorpe swore that he only intended to frighten Nellie and, before jumping out at her, carefully made sure that the blunt side of the razor would be facing her throat. Unfortunately, Nellie knocked his arm, the blade turned and Thorpe was so dismayed by what he had done that he tried to kill himself.

His story wasn't believed by the jury, who found him guilty of wilful murder. He was hanged by Thomas Pierrepoint at Leicester Prison on 23 December 1941.

15 MARCH 1897 When Anne Broughton of Leicester died from breast cancer, she left a husband and six children aged between eleven and twenty-six years old, four of whom still lived at home.

Anne's husband, Samuel, was a drunkard and thus it fell to twenty-one-year-old William Henry 'Harry' Broughton to take care of his siblings. Harry grew increasingly frustrated as his father drank away all of the family's money and, on 15 March, when Samuel arrived home drunk yet again, his son snapped. When he scolded his father for his dissolute habits, Samuel made an unkind remark about Harry's mother, to whom the young man had been exceptionally close. Harry punched him in the eye and angrily told him to go to bed until he was sober. Later that evening, as Samuel slept, Harry crept into the room with a coal hammer and battered him to death.

Harry was appalled at what he had done, telling the police that he did not know what he could have been thinking about. He freely admitted to hitting his father, who died in hospital from a fractured skull and brain damage. When an inquest later found a verdict of wilful murder against Harry, he fainted as the coroner committed him for trial at the Leicestershire Assizes.

Harry initially pleaded guilty but was persuaded by his counsel to change his plea to not guilty and face his trial. Universally known as a quiet, inoffensive man, who was described by neighbours as 'everything a son should be', Harry was found guilty but recommended to mercy.

His mandatory death sentence was later repealed to one of life imprisonment, which he served in Parkhurst Prison on the Isle of Wight.

Note: Some newspaper reports state that Broughton's prison sentence was ten years, rather than life.

16 MARCH 1895 John Richard Towers left his home in Leicester for a walk with his girlfriend, Maud. Twenty-one-year-old John was a pipe smoker and was puffing away as the couple walked along the canal banks. As they neared the Mill Lane Bridge, he suddenly turned to Maud and said, 'If I smoke, I shall be done,' before falling into the canal. Maud held her hand out to him but he was unable to reach it. A passer-by held out his walking stick but John sank and did not surface again until his dead body was dragged from the water.

At the inquest held by coroner Robert Harvey, Maud testified that John was sober and was acting perfectly normally before his sudden plunge into the water. John's father was also questioned and stated that John was in good spirits when he left home. However, John was used to smoking a mild 'shag' tobacco and had only been able to purchase stronger 'twist', which he smoked for the first time while out with Maud.

Confirming drowning as the cause of John's death, Dr Jacques told the coroner that it was highly probable that the exceptionally strong tobacco had induced a fit of giddiness and caused John to stumble into the canal. The inquest jury returned a verdict of 'accidental death'.

17 MARCH 1871 Fourteen-year-old Oliver Cure of Hinckley was playing leapfrog with his friends when he fell flat on his face after vaulting over another boy. With all of the breath knocked out of him, he lay on the ground groaning for some time. Eventually, he was able to get up and hobble home but claimed to have stomach ache, which grew worse overnight.

Early the next morning his parents sent for a doctor, but Oliver was dead before he arrived and a post-mortem examination showed that he died from a ruptured bladder.

An inquest held by coroner John Gregory returned a verdict of 'accidental death'.

18 MARCH 1895 Phrenologist David Ball appeared at Leicester Police Court charged with pretending to tell fortunes.

Magistrates heard from Emily Smith, the wife of a police constable, who described a visit to Ball's home on 7 March with a friend, made at the request of Police Superintendent Hawkins. The door was opened by a woman, who told them 'Master' was in the front room. By gazing into a crystal ball and reading a pack of cards, Ball promised both ladies a glowing future. Emily was told that a young man who 'looked well after her' would soon make himself evident, while her friend Mary Ann could expect to meet a 'tall, smart gentleman' and was told not to cross water, which looked bad for her. Each consultation cost 6*d*.

In February 1894, Ball was brought before magistrates for pretending to tell the future of two female detectives. At that time, he was bound over for six months and promised to give up fortune telling. At his current appearance before the Bench, his solicitor insisted that no deception or attempted deception had taken place. The magistrates disagreed and accused Ball of being a rogue and a vagabond, fining him £10 or one month's imprisonment in default.

19 MARCH 1896 During the construction of the new Leicester Reservoir at Swithland, four men were uprooting a tree stump, situated at the top of a 25-foot deep quarry. Foreman William Gulliver had given strict instructions that nobody was to go into the area below the tree but twenty-nine-year-old Thomas Adkin was working in another part of the quarry and was not aware of this.

Nobody noticed him approaching the danger zone as, having loosened the stump, the men shouted a warning and pushed it into the quarry. A crane driver, working on the opposite side of the quarry, saw it bouncing towards Adkin, who had obviously heard the warning shouts and tried to run away but was bowled over by the mass of earth and roots, weighing more than 10cwt.

He died instantly and an inquest held by coroner Henry Deane determined that sufficient precautions were taken in removing the tree root and that his death was accidental.

20 MARCH 1930 John George and Edith Lucy Mills shared their home at Thurmaston with their two children and a lodger, George Henry Brackenbury.

The front room served as a hardware shop and, on 20 March, John Mills was awakened by the smell of smoke at 1 a.m. and found the shop on fire. He shouted to alert the other inhabitants, before running 200 yards to the police station to raise the alarm.

When he got back, the staircase was ablaze and he was unable to get in. He put a ladder up to the window of the children's bedroom and his wife passed his little girl out to him but, when he got back to the window after carrying his daughter to safety, there was no sign of his wife. Mills climbed into the bedroom and groped around until he found his son. Having carried him down the ladder, he then went back for his wife but was unable to lift her and eventually had to leave, as he couldn't breathe. Sadly, Mrs Mills perished in the fire but her husband seemed more concerned about the fate of his cashbox and his best suit.

At the inquest into her death, it emerged that Mills was in dire financial straits and held insurance policies on his house, stock and his wife's life. Then a witness came forward who claimed to have seen Mills through the shop window, bending over a small flame. The inquest was adjourned several times to allow the police to investigate but the witness eventually retracted his statement, admitting that he made up the whole story.

When the inquest concluded on 4 April, coroner Mr Fowler criticised Mills for leaving his wife and children in a burning house, saying that they could all have escaped together. Fowler also remarked that he found the circumstances of the fire suspicious, especially in view of the extensive insurance held by Mills. 'Charges cannot be founded on mere suspicion alone,' Fowler told the jury, adding that the Thurmaston fire was a mystery destined to remain unsolved. The jury returned a verdict that Mrs Mills died in the fire but they had no evidence to show how it started. They added that they were far from satisfied with Mills, saying that they believed he could have done more to rescue his wife.

At the Leicester Assizes on 11 June 1930, nineteen-year-old John William Lewin Ward was sentenced to six months' imprisonment for perjury, after admitting fabricating his evidence. The judge remarked that his lies had the effect of blackening the character of a respectable and innocent fellow citizen.

21 MARCH 1846 William Hubbard appeared at the Leicestershire Assizes charged with the wilful murder of his wife, Hannah.

The couple had been married for less than three years and lodged with William's brother and his wife in Leicester. Some accounts state that William was bone idle and refused to work, others suggest that he had been unwell and was hospitalised for several weeks. Either way, the lack of his wage packet left the Hubbards impoverished and Hannah wanted to move to Birmingham, to be nearer her mother.

Twenty-three-year-old William was a mild, inoffensive man but Hannah was rather fiery and the couple often quarrelled. On occasions, Hannah hit her husband and she had even thrown hot tea in his face. Now she was adamant that she was going to leave William and live in Birmingham and refused to listen to her husband, who tried his hardest to persuade her not to go. Having sold much of the couple's furniture to raise money, William moved back to his father's house, although he continued to visit his wife and daughter

As he lay in bed early on 11 August 1845, William's brother, John, heard voices in the back yard. Then William's baby began crying and William came upstairs to her. When he went back into the kitchen, John heard William say, 'She's asleep,' but the next thing John heard was the sound of scuffling and groaning from downstairs. John and his wife ran down to see what was happening, finding Hannah bleeding from a deep gash on her throat. She bled to death before a doctor could reach her.

'I've done it and I intended to do it,' William said as he waited for the police to arrive but, when asked to make a statement, he said, 'I am not prepared to say anything.'

Although he pleaded 'not guilty' at his trial, the jury found him guilty and he was sentenced to death. He was executed at Leicester Prison on 1 April 1846.

22 MARCH 1832 William Wildbore appeared at the assizes in Leicester charged with committing a felonious assault upon a female child not five years of age. It was alleged that while the child's mother was attending a funeral at the parish church in Hinckley, Wildbore enticed the child into the belfry and 'offered gross violence to her person', severely injuring the child and himself in the process.

Witnesses for his defence described twenty-three-year-old Wildbore as 'nearly but not altogether an idiot' and to illustrate his simplicity, described to the court a practical joke, of which Wildbore was the butt. Wildbore was told that a ladder had been placed on top of a building in Hinckley, for the purpose of fetching down the moon, and worked especially hard all day so that he could have time off

Hinckley parish church. (Author's collection)

to go and watch; returning disappointed to complain that he had walked three times round the town and not found the ladder.

On hearing this, the jury acquitted Wildbore on the grounds of insanity and he was ordered to be confined at the King's pleasure.

23 MARCH 1801 John Massey was executed at a specially-erected gibbet post at Red Hill, less than a quarter of a mile from the spot where he brutally murdered his wife.

Massey was walking between Congerstone and Barlestone with his wife and daughter when a quarrel arose between them. Massey was accustomed to settling arguments with his fists and, having beaten his wife severely, he threw her and his daughter into a mill dam. Although both were rescued, Massey's wife died six weeks later and doctor's believed that her death was caused by the brutal treatment she received at the hands of her husband. He was found guilty of wilful murder at the Leicester Assizes, where the chief witness against him was his daughter.

Sentenced to be hanged and gibbeted, Massey kept delaying the inevitable by repeatedly asking for 'just one more prayer', until officials refused to allow any further procrastination.

24 MARCH 1895 Throughout the afternoon, a fierce gale blew across most of Leicestershire, causing extensive damage to property throughout the county.

There were three fatalities as a result of the extreme weather conditions. Nine-year-old Ethel Beadman died from a fractured skull, after a yard wall collapsed on her as she ran an errand in Leicester. In Aylestone, neighbours John Thomas White and Henry Joyce died when a massive elm tree fell onto them as they were collecting sticks. The men's wives watched in anguish as villagers tried to extricate their husbands from beneath the tree, but so severe were the men's injuries that they were thought to have died instantly.

The field in which they were killed was commonly used as a recreation ground by the local children, although fortunately the bad weather had driven them indoors. At the inquest into the deaths of White and Joyce, the jury returned two verdicts of accidental death, donating their fees to the widows.

25 MARCH 1895 Coroner George Bouskell held an inquest at Branston into the death of farmer Joseph Mount.

Returning home after a shooting trip with his fifteen-year-old brother on 22 March, Mount spotted a sheep that was in need of attention. Placing his double-barrelled shotgun on the ground while he took care of the animal, Joseph realised that the gun was loaded and called to his brother to move the trigger to half cock. As the youth picked up the gun, it went off, shooting Joseph in the back.

Twenty-eight-year-old Joseph died before medical assistance could reach him and at the inquest his distraught brother was the chief witness. Having described what

happened, the youth admitted that he had never fired a gun in his life and had no idea how he came to shoot his brother.

When Joseph's wife confirmed that the brothers normally lived on affectionate terms and that she knew of no quarrel between them, the inquest jury returned a verdict of 'accidental death'.

26 MARCH 1870 Elijah Cliff was a sawyer and corn grinder, who had a yard in Leicester, where he worked with his fourteen-year-old nephew.

The grinding machine and saw were both operated by an eight horsepower steam engine and to transfer power from one machine to the other, the user had to move a strap between two pulley wheels.

On 26 March, Elijah and his nephew were grinding corn until 4 p.m., when Elijah ordered some more coal to be put onto the boiler to raise more steam so that he might saw some wood. Elijah was a skilled engineer, who had designed and constructed all of the machinery himself. His familiarity with the mechanics seemed to have made him careless, since he attempted to change the belt from the grinding pulley to the sawing pulley without first stopping the machinery.

His nephew heard a crash and found his uncle wrapped around the shaft between the two pulleys. The boy called for help and a carpenter who had a workshop nearby managed to liberate Elijah, who was suffering from a broken leg, broken back and a broken collar bone among other injuries, from which he died later that night in Leicester Infirmary.

An inquest held by coroner John Gregory returned a verdict of 'accidental death', saying that if he had stopped the engine even momentarily to change the belt, his life would not have been endangered.

27 MARCH 1833 Seventeen-year-old Thomas Birch and twenty-one-year-old Robert Wilson appeared at the assizes in Leicester charged with manslaughter.

Birch had a grievance with Thomas Pembleton and, although Birch was willing to shake hands, Pembleton insisted that they should fight. The fight took place in November 1832, with Wilson acting as Birch's second. After ninety minutes of combat, Pembleton suddenly collapsed and, although Birch and Wilson joined Pembleton's friends in trying to revive him, he died from bleeding on the brain from a burst blood vessel, undoubtedly caused by a blow.

The jury found both defendants guilty but, since it was said to have been a fair, stand-up fight, instigated by the victim, the judge treated them leniently, sentencing each man to just three months' imprisonment.

28 MARCH 1894 George Henry Perkins had lodged at Mary Ann Payne's lodging house in New Buildings, Hinckley, for more than two years and, on 28 March, he asked if she could lend him a shilling. When Mrs Payne refused, Perkins picked up a carving knife and attempted to cut her throat. Mrs Payne struggled and screamed and when neighbours rushed in they found her suffering from a large but superficial wound in her throat and a cut on her cheek, while Perkins was in the wash house, having slashed his own throat. He was taken to Hinckley Cottage Hospital, where he survived for almost a week before succumbing to bronchitis.

Perkins was said to be bone idle and a very heavy drinker. At the time of the stabbing, he had not worked for many months but earned his board and pocket money by doing odd jobs at his lodgings. At the inquest into his death, the jury ruled that he took his own life in a state of temporary insanity, brought about by his heavy drinking.

Ironically, when forty-four-year-old Perkins was undressed at the hospital, two 6d coins were found in his pocket. He was able to make a brief statement expressing his

New Buildings, Hinckley, 1933. (Author's collection)

contrition for his actions but claiming to remember nothing at all about the attack on his landlady.

29 MARCH 1896 John Wells purchased a 1*d* ticket at the Leicester Corporation Baths and, minutes later, attendant Walter William Dickman saw a man's clothes in one of the cubicles, although there was no sign of anybody bathing. Dickman looked around for some time, before spotting a body lying on the bottom, at the deep end of the pool.

A post-mortem examination revealed congestion in the veins of Wells's face and neck, suggesting that he may have had a fit on entering the water. Since he was the only bather, there was nobody to raise the alarm and consequently Wells drowned.

Although an inquest jury returned a verdict of 'accidental death', they questioned why there was no attendant present. Attendants were only expected to check the baths periodically rather than supervise all bathers but, hearing that there had been two previous drownings, the coroner suggested changing this practice so that an attendant was always present whenever there was a lone bather.

30 MARCH 1825 Abraham Billson was hanged at Leicester, having been convicted of wilfully murdering his wife at Broughton Astley on 7 December 1824.

Billson had a long history of spousal violence and his wife had taken him before magistrates to have him bound over to keep the peace towards her. On 7 December, having spent the afternoon in a public house, Billson hit her on the side of the head, knocking her over, then began sawing at her throat with his razor. Mrs Billson fought desperately, almost severing two of her fingers as she tried to pull the blade away from her throat. Amazingly, she escaped Abraham's clutches and ran nearly 50 yards to a neighbour's house, before collapsing and dying. She was found to have a seven-inch long, two-inch deep cut across her throat and died from exsanguination, leaving four children under the age of eleven motherless.

Billson locked himself in the house but when neighbours forced an entry, he went through the back door and ran away across the fields. When apprehended, he denied any knowledge of his wife's death, until his eleven-year-old son, who had witnessed the murder, stated that his father had killed his mother.

Before being taken to prison, Billson asked to see his dead wife, falling to his knees at her side and kissing her several times. 'Although he didn't shed a tear, he was apparently in the deepest anguish,' reported the local newspaper.

Note: Billson's wife is believed to have been named Catherine.

31 MARCH 1878 At the Great Northern Railway Works near Melton Mowbray, a train was being driven very slowly along the line.

Thinking that he was giving the child a treat by allowing him to have a ride, a young man named Brothwell pulled nine-year-old Arthur McKay onto the front of the train. As the train was stopping, Brothwell, whose father-in-law was driving it, jumped off. Arthur followed but fell onto the line and the train amputated both of his legs near the hips.

Although he was taken straight to the Workhouse Infirmary, he was too badly injured to survive. At the inquest on 1 April, the jury returned a verdict of 'accidental death', asking the coroner to censure Brothwell and to warn contractors to be more cautious about allowing people to ride on the engines.

APRIL

Interior of Leicester's old Town Hall. (Author's collection)

1 **APRIL, 1863** After drinking steadily for several days, Quorn publican and hosiery manufacturer Joseph Webster drove his horse and cart to the top of Mountsorrel Quarry. He unharnessed the horse and let it go, before pushing the cart off the top of the precipice to fall 90 feet into the quarry below.

There were almost 600 men at work at the time and fortunately some saw the cart falling and were able to shout a warning. Sadly, Henry Pidcock did not move quickly enough and the cart landed on him, causing such serious spinal injuries that he died within hours.

Webster ran away after backing the cart over the cliff but was later apprehended and seemed very remorseful. Coroner John Gregory held an inquest at The Exhibition public house in Mountsorrel, at which the jury returned a verdict of manslaughter against Webster, who was sent for trial at the next Leicestershire Assizes.

His defence counsel related that forty-one-year-old Webster had merely set his horse free to graze, for the purpose of asserting his common rights, and, unfortunately, the weight of the cart pulled it off the top of the quarry. Why would Webster wantonly destroy his own property, questioned the defence? The prosecution answered by telling the court that Webster was a perfect maniac when under the influence of alcohol.

The jury found the prosecution's explanation more plausible and, after they found Webster guilty, Mr Justice Williams sentenced him to eighteen months' imprisonment.

2 **APRIL, 1878** Laws in England restricted the sale of alcohol on Sundays, although licence holders were permitted to sell to residents and to supply refreshments to bona-fide travellers, providing they were not less than three miles from the place where they slept the previous night.

On 2 April, coroner Mr Deane held an inquest at Whitwick on the death of thirty-six-year-old collier Samuel Jarvis, who died from 'pressure on the heart, excited by drink and the shock of a fall.'

It was revealed that Jarvis and his friends had spent most of Sunday walking from one pub to the next and had no difficulty in representing themselves as bona-fide travellers in order to obtain drinks. The coroner remarked that just because people chose to walk three miles it did not make them bona-fide travellers. It was not sufficient for the landlord to enquire where the men came from, stated Deane, but he must take reasonable precautions and 'be careful as to the class of people who asked to be served.'

3 **APRIL, 1837** When fifteen-year-old Hannah Robinson died in Leicester's All Saints' Workhouse, a post-mortem examination showed that almost every single one of her organs was diseased. The girl was emaciated to the point of being skeletal and,

although the doctor found that her death was from natural causes, it was greatly hastened by neglect and cruelty.

Hannah had been ill since Christmas 1836 and, much to her mother's displeasure, had barely left her bed since. Neighbours who visited found the girl lying in her own excrement, covered by a filthy blanket, in pain and ravenously hungry, and, when they remonstrated with her mother, Mary Robinson assured them that Hannah could get up perfectly well when she wanted to.

When the girl's deplorable condition was finally brought to the attention of the district Medical Officer, Hannah was removed to the Workhouse, but the nourishing food she received there came too late to save her life. At the inquest into her death, several neighbours described Mary's inhuman treatment of her daughter, although Hannah's thirteen-year-old brother told a different story. According to Charles, Hannah was given the only bed in the house and the rest of the family went without food so that she could eat. Although no doctor was called to attend Hannah, his parents obtained medicine for her but she was unable to take it.

The inquest jury found a verdict of manslaughter against Mary Robinson for her neglect and cruelty towards her daughter but, on 29 July, she was acquitted at the Leicestershire Assizes.

4   APRIL 1896   Although they were not legally married, Henry Lett lived with his partner for more than twenty years, fourteen of which were spent at Oadby. Mrs Lett,

London Road, Oadby. (Author's collection)

as she was known, kept a small general shop, while her 'husband' worked for a builder. Late in 1895, her brother, Henry Crossland, moved in with the couple, securing a job with Lett's employer.

After a few weeks, Crossland fell ill and lost his job. Once he recovered, he was only able to get occasional work and so stopped paying his sister the ten shillings a week he contributed towards his keep.

The fact that Crossland was living in his house rent free irritated Lett and on 4 April, after an evening's drinking, he came home in an angry mood. In a fit of temper, he threw a paraffin lamp towards Crossland, which fortunately missed, hitting the fireplace and filling the room with smoke and flames. Lett stormed out, leaving Crossland to deal with the after-effects, although he returned minutes later carrying the coal hammer, which he took to bed with him, threatening to 'kill the first ****** that comes up those stairs.'

Shortly afterwards, Mrs Lett heard her brother on the landing, asking Lett what his grievance against him was. Lett made no reply and the next thing Mrs Lett heard was somebody tumbling down the stairs. It was her brother, and he died the following day from a fractured skull.

Henry Lett was charged with his wilful murder but insisted that, although he might have pushed Crossland down the stairs, he had not hit him with the hammer. He was found guilty at the assizes and sentenced to death, although the jury recommended mercy and his sentence was later commuted to one of life imprisonment, served at Portland Convict Prison.

Portland Convict Prison. (Author's collection)

Interior of Portland Prison. (Author's collection)

Note: Both Lett and Crossland are referred to as Henry and Harry. In each case, Henry appears to have been their given name.

5 APRIL, 1877 Coachman John Henry Starkey turned up at work two hours early. He explained that one of the horses needed shoeing and, while eating breakfast with the other servants, he talked about his wife and family for the first time ever. Starkey said that his wife had been 'very strange' for the past fortnight and complained that she had been lending money to one of the couple's two lodgers.

Meanwhile, back at Starkey's house in Cedar Street, Leicester, one of the lodgers returned home from the nightshift. Unusually, there was no breakfast waiting for him and the house was silent, so Mr Bates made himself something to eat and went upstairs to bed. Between 9 and 10 a.m., Starkey arrived home, riding one of his master's horses. He called to neighbour Mrs Chamberlain to ask his wife to fetch him his scarf and watch and, when Mrs Chamberlain got no answer, he went into the house himself.

'It's no wonder she did not hear; she's lying on the floor with her throat cut,' he announced.

At Mrs Chamberlain's suggestion, Starkey summoned the police and a doctor. However, when the doctor examined Alice Ruth Starkey, he was adamant that she had been dead for at least six hours and could not possibly have inflicted her dreadful throat wounds herself. Since Starkey claimed to have eaten breakfast with his wife that morning, he was charged with Alice's murder. 'If I never speak in my life again, I never did it,' he insisted.

Twenty-six-year-old Starkey was tried at the Leicester Assizes, but the solicitor he had paid to defend him absconded with his money and the court appointed a replacement. It emerged that Starkey was having an affair with a young woman and had promised to marry her. Starkey's defence counsel tried to argue that Alice had found out about the affair and committed suicide, but the medical evidence negated that explanation and Starkey was found guilty. He made a full confession to the murder before his execution by William Marwood on 31 July.

6 APRIL, 1837 An inquest was held at Moira on the death of Thomas Ellis, an engineer at the Hastings and Grey Pit at the Moira Colliery.

On 4 April, Ellis was preparing to go below ground to repair a pump. The mouth of the pit was near the engine house and steam from the engine swathed the area in thick clouds, concealing the fact that one of the folding doors had inadvertently been left open. Ellis walked into the pit and was heard screaming as he fell, bumping off the walls of the shaft, before landing on a wooden platform 70 yards down. A labourer sent down to retrieve his body found very little left of the thirty-six-year-old engineer.

The inquest jury returned a verdict of 'accidental death'.

7 APRIL, 1899 Three performances of a show called 'The Mandarin: A Chinese Cantata', were put on at Oadby School, during which there was a re-enactment of a skirmish between the British and the Chinese. The soldiers carried muskets and organiser James Myatt thought that it would add authenticity to the performance if the guns went bang.

The guns were loaded with caps and test fired. Everything went according to plan for the first two performances but on the third, one of the guns was accidentally exchanged for one that hadn't been tested and had been put away loaded. Eight people were injured and eleven-year-old Ernest Edward Bates, whose bottom jaw was completely shot away, went on to die from his injuries, his death almost robbing Myatt of his reason. Myatt was too ill to appear at the inquest, at which the jury returned a verdict of 'accidental death', saying that they attached no blame to anybody.

The other seven casualties are assumed to have survived. Five had minor injuries only, but Ernest's brother, Harold, had twenty-seven shots in his face and neck and there were fears for his eyesight. Another boy had his nose shot clean off.

8 APRIL, 1925 The coroner for North Leicestershire held an inquest into the death of eighty-four-year-old widow Emma Wainwright, who died in hospital on 6 April, having been found on 21 March lying unconscious in the back yard of her house in

Coalville. She was wearing just her nightdress and was bitterly cold and quite stiff, dying without ever having fully regained consciousness.

The inquest jury deduced that Emma met her death by falling onto the brick-paved yard while sleepwalking, and returned a verdict that she died from 'exhaustion and shock from injuries sustained through accidentally falling from her bedroom window.'

9 APRIL 1898 Francis William Ward, an auctioneer's porter from Syston, appeared at the Leicester County Police Court charged with neglecting his six children, aged between one and eight years old. The one-year-old suffered from spinal disease, anaemia and bronchitis, all exacerbated by neglect.

Ward earned good wages, plus tips, but since the death of his wife twelve months earlier he had hired no less than eleven housekeepers to take care of his children while he was at work. Every housekeeper left, either because Ward didn't pay her wages or because he refused to give her any housekeeping money. One woman was engaged on a promise of 3s a week but left after a month without having been paid a penny and was actually 3s worse off, after using her own money to buy food for the children. Ward was often away for days at a time and, more often than not, returned home drunk.

Magistrates found Ward guilty and sentenced him to two months' imprisonment with hard labour. The children were sent to the Workhouse.

10 APRIL 1890 John Burns appeared at the Leicestershire Borough Quarter Sessions charged with the theft of a pair of boots, which were the property of the Chief Constable of Leicester.

On 1 April, twenty-four-year-old ex-convict Burns went to collect a payment from the Discharged Prisoners' Aid Society and, when he left the Town Hall, a pair of policeman's boots left with him. Burns later gave the boots to a man named Strong and asked him to pawn them, but when the pawnshop owner grew suspicious and contacted the police, Strong immediately revealed the name of the 'owner' of the boots. When Burns was arrested, he was carrying tools that could be used for housebreaking, although he swore that he actually used them to make bone toothpicks.

At his appearance at the Quarter Sessions, the Recorder pointed out that Burns had been released on licence from a five-year prison sentence, which commenced in 1885. Since that sentence had not yet expired, Burns was sentenced to a further seven years' penal servitude for the theft of the boots.

11 APRIL, 1868 James Lovett of Quorn was quarrelling with a man named Morley when John Darker stepped between them. As he did, Lovett sprang at him and bit off a piece of his nose.

Lovett appeared before magistrates at Loughborough on 5 May charged with assault. There were several witnesses to the event but Darker generously insisted that he had no desire to 'press the case'. However, the magistrates were appalled by what they deemed 'a most savage assault' and fined Lovett £1 plus costs, or twenty-one days' hard labour in default.

Note: Some sources give the date of the fight as 13 April.

12 APRIL, 1842 An inquest in Leicester concluded with a verdict of 'wilful murder' against eighteen-year-old Mary Barnes and twenty-year-old Charlotte Barnacle.

Their victim was Mary Waring, an elderly woman who lodged with Mary's family. On 7 April, a doctor was summoned to the house by Mary's father, Stephen Barnes, who was himself stricken with a bout of severe vomiting. When surgeon John Penfold Stalland arrived at the house, Mary Waring was already dead and Stephen's wife was terribly ill, although she is believed to have survived. A post-mortem examination revealed that the deceased had ingested arsenic and the poison was found in the kettle and teapot, which the dead woman used to make tea.

Charlotte and Mary had been giggling conspiratorially between themselves for days, telling a young apprentice that they had put some 'jalap' into Mary Waring's kettle. Both were positively identified by chemists in the area as having attempted to purchase arsenic, which they stated that they wanted for killing fleas. (They eventually succeeded at a shop in Market Place.)

The young women appeared at the Leicestershire Assizes on 28 July, where they were found guilty of manslaughter and ordered to be transported for the rest of their natural lives. They set sail for Van Dieman's Land on board the ship *Garland Grove* on 7 September.

13 APRIL, 1889 By midday, nobody in Stapleton had seen any sign of life at the cottage shared by Henry and Elizabeth Shaw and, at 1 p.m., their next-door neighbour realised that she could smell burning. The Shaws' blinds were still drawn down and no amount of knocking on the door or windows roused them, so labourer Thomas Pride fetched a ladder and climbed up to the bedroom window. On opening it, he found the house on fire. Neighbours broke down the door but were too late to save seventy-one-year-old Henry or his seventy-three-year-old wife, both of whom had been dead for several hours.

The cause of the fire was uncertain. The dressing table and a beam were both burned and there was a box of matches on the floor, along with a candlestick that appeared to have fallen off the table. At an inquest held at The Nag's Head, Stapleton by coroner Mr Harrison, the jury returned two verdicts of 'accidental suffocation'.

14 APRIL 1930 An inquest was held into the death of sixty-nine-year-old Frederick Barton.

At 11.20 p.m. on 12 April, a waiter walking through Victoria Park, Leicester, spotted Barton slumped on a park bench and telephoned for an ambulance. Edward Hyman drove the ambulance from Leicester Fire Station to Victoria Park, and spoke to a police sergeant there, who knew nothing of any emergency. The ambulance went to the telephone box from where the call was made, where the crew found a drunk, and when they asked him if he had called for an ambulance, he said that he had, because he wanted to be taken home.

The drunk refused to take no for an answer and became so obnoxious and violent that the ambulance crew eventually did as he wanted – however, instead of taking him home, they dropped him off at the police station, before returning to base. When they were told that there had been more calls to attend Victoria Park, they went straight back, this time managing to find their patient.

Barton had drunk a large quantity of disinfectant and was beyond medical help. At the inquest, the jury were told that he was unlikely to have survived, even without

Fire Station, Leicester. (Author's collection)

Victoria Park, Leicester, 1928. (Author's collection)

the delay of more than an hour in getting an ambulance to him, caused by the crew having to deal with the drunk. The jury returned a verdict of 'suicide while temporarily insane'.

15 APRIL, **1877** Drinkers in The Eight Bells public house, Melton Mowbray, heard John Whittaker banging on a table with an empty jug and calling for it to be filled with beer but the barmaid refused to serve him any more alcohol. Whittaker immediately began to sing very loudly and tunelessly and when the landlord, Charles Curtis, politely asked him to be quiet, he responded with a rude word.

Curtis seized Whittaker by the collar and propelled him towards the pub door, ejecting him down the three steps leading to the street. Unfortunately, Whittaker fell over backwards, hitting his head on the pavement. He was picked up unconscious and taken by cart to the police station, where he died from a fractured skull.

Charles Curtis was charged with manslaughter and appeared at the Leicestershire Assizes in July 1877. There was no argument that Curtis had both a right and a duty to eject rowdy customers from his premises, but the question for the jury was whether he had used excessive or unnecessary force in doing so.

Having listened to the prosecution's case, the jury acquitted Curtis without finding it necessary to hear the defence counsel or the judge's summary of the case. The verdict was greeted with spontaneous applause.

16 APRIL, 1872 Edwin Dutton appeared before magistrates at Leicester Town Hall charged with a violent assault on Elizabeth Scott Burgess.

Seventy-five-year-old Miss Burgess lived alone and employed Dutton's wife as a charlady. Thus Dutton was well aware that Miss Burgess had recently received a £5 note in a letter and, on 30 March, he rang her doorbell and inveigled his way into the house. Once inside, Dutton hit the old lady over the head then tried to force her to drink from a bottle, the contents of which eventually spilled down the front of her dress. Dutton then tried to strangle Miss Burgess, who managed to bite his hand as he thrust it into her mouth.

Neighbours drawn to the house by screams of 'Murder!' saw Dutton leaving and found Miss Burgess lying in the hall, bleeding from her nose and mouth and from a six-inch cut on her head. Dutton was quickly arrested and found to have bite marks on his fingers, although he insisted that the blood on his hands came from handling veal and that he had been nowhere near Miss Burgess's house that night.

Magistrates committed Dutton for trial at the Leicestershire Assizes on 6 July, where, in spite of his insistence that he remembered nothing at all about it, he was found guilty of committing a murderous outrage and sentenced to twenty years' penal servitude.

17 APRIL, 1817 The Industrial Revolution brought about increasing mechanisation in the textile industry, much to the chagrin of the workforce, who believed that the changes were robbing them of their livelihoods. A group of rebels, who became known as Luddites, set out to destroy the machines that they believed were jeopardising their futures.

On 17 April 1817, six Luddites were hanged close to Leicester House of Correction, at a gallows in Infirmary Square, for their part in an attack on the lace machines at a Loughborough factory. During the attack on 28 June 1816, a number of guards and workmen were forced at gunpoint to lie on the floor and one was shot and wounded.

Gang leader James Towle was recognised and he and two other men, Benjamin Badder and John Slater, were tried at Leicester Assizes in August 1816. The jury dismissed the seventy-one witnesses who were called by the defence to establish an alibi and Towle was found guilty. (Slater was acquitted and the case against Badder was dropped.) Towle's appeal against his death sentence was unsuccessful and he was hanged on 20 November 1816.

Some sources state that Towle died without betraying his fellow Luddites, others state that he named them to bargain for his life. Whichever was the case, twelve men subsequently appeared at the Leicestershire Assizes charged with firing a pistol with intent to kill. Two of the defendants, Blackburn and Burton, gave evidence against the others, as a result of which two men were sentenced to be transported for life and

Joshua Mitchell, John Crowder, John Amos, William Withers and Thomas Savidge were sentenced to death, along with Towle's younger brother, William.

Descriptions of the mass execution suggest that it was witnessed by many thousands of spectators, who joined the condemned men in singing hymns. Some of the prisoners addressed the crowd from the gallows, professing their innocence and publicly forgiving Blackburn and Burton. The six Luddites died while singing a hymn, leaving more than thirty children between them to mourn their loss.

Note: Another man was hanged at the same time, although his details are sketchy, since the newspapers seem to have focused on the Luddites. He is variously named as Thomas Beavington or Babington and his reported crimes vary from highway robbery to arson. He too protested his innocence to his last breath.

18 APRIL 1865 Boorn's Circus paraded through the streets of Leicester, announcing their arrival in the city. As the procession made its way down Humberstone Gate, preceded by a crowd of excited children, seven-year-old John Moore ran in front of a horse-drawn carriage and was knocked down. All of the eight horses stepped over the child without touching him but the wheels of the carriage passed over his back. He was carried to a nearby doctor's surgery but died from shock and internal bleeding.

At a later inquest, coroner John Gregory recorded a verdict of 'accidental death' but there were rumours that John's father had accepted a large sum of money from Mr Boorn as compensation for his son's death. Moore later wrote to the local newspaper putting the record straight.

He admitted that Boorn had offered to cover John's funeral expenses, promising to pay the funeral director before the circus left town. When no payment was forthcoming, Moore wrote to Boorn and, receiving no reply to his letter, he followed the circus to Derby.

According to Moore, it took him all his time to get the promised payment from Boorn, who handed over the money begrudgingly, telling Moore he was lucky to get it. 'I got the funeral expenses but not a farthing more,' wrote Moore.

19 APRIL 1898 A 'gob fire' – a spontaneous combustion of pit waste – broke out below ground at No. 5 Pit, Whitwick Colliery, and spread rapidly along the roof timbers. The outbreak was located between the miners and their way out and, after a brief discussion, some decided to risk rushing through the flames in an attempt to escape. Their passage was hindered by the bodies of dead and dying pit ponies, and most were forced back by the presence of choke damp gas. Only five men actually escaped, leaving thirty-five entombed by the blaze.

Rescuers worked tirelessly, until they were forced to abandon any hope of finding survivors. Of the thirty-five victims, twenty-seven were married, each leaving an average of six children. Patrick O'Mara was found on his knees with his rosary beads in his hands, while the youngest victim, John Albert Gee of Thringstone, was only thirteen years old and was thought to have sacrificed his life going back to warn his colleagues of the extent of the fire.

It was to be many months before the last bodies were recovered and inquests later ruled that the deaths were accidental.

20 APRIL, 1885 Reverend Samuel Ingle appeared at the Derbyshire and Leicestershire Assizes charged with a total of sixteen indictments, including inciting a young man named George Henry Needham to commit an unnatural offence, indecent assault and attempted indecent assault.

Ingle was the vicar at Breedon-on-the-Hill church and lodged with parishioner Samuel Needham. Samuel's son, George, was serving an apprenticeship at Burton-on-Trent and visited his family once every four or five weeks. The cottage at Breedon had only three bedrooms, one of which was occupied by George's parents and one by his sister, so necessity dictated that George would share a bedroom (and indeed a bed) with Ingle on his visits home.

Breedon-on-the-Hill church. (Author's collection)

Soon, Ingle was writing frequent letters to George Needham, asking him to burn them after having read them, as they were 'silly'. However, on one occasion, Ingle mistakenly addressed the letter to Derby, rather than to Burton-on-Trent. The letter was sent to the Dead Letter Office, where it was opened and, once staff had read the contents, they forwarded it to the Home Office, who in turn passed it to the Public Prosecutor.

Although the letter was read out at Ingle's trial, its contents were deemed unfit for publication. However, George Needham was called as a witness and denied any impropriety with Ingle, pointing out that the walls between the bedrooms in his parents' cottage were paper-thin and the other occupants of the house could not have failed to hear anything that took place in Ingle's room.

George Needham was twenty-four years old and there were questions in court as to whether or not he was a truthful witness, since, according to the defence, he was clearly an accomplice in Ingle's 'unnatural perversions'. George made no complaint to anyone about Ingle's conduct and had continued to sleep in the same bedroom, so the judge instructed the jury that they must decide on the degree of Needham's complicity and also must determine the purpose of the letter – was it a love letter and were the contents passion or mere idle nonsense?

After retiring for a few minutes, the jury gave their verdict, finding Ingle guilty of both indecent assault and of the attempt to incite. He was sentenced to eighteen months' imprisonment, with hard labour.

21 APRIL, 1891 At the Stafford family's home in Leicester, thirteen-year-old nursemaid Sarah Sharpe heard two of the children playing in their bedroom. There was a sudden thump, after which thirteen-year-old Cecil asked, 'Has it hurt you, Roy?' Although she heard no response from nine-year-old Roy, Sarah never imagined that there was anything wrong, even after hearing a second loud noise.

A little later, their mother called to the boys that it was time they were up and dressed. When there was no reply, their father went upstairs, finding them still in bed. As he stepped forward to rouse them, John Thomas Stafford discovered that his sons were wounded. Cecil was already dead but Roy was still breathing, although unconscious, and was rushed to the Leicester Infirmary, where he died that evening.

Both boys died from bullet wounds to the head and a search of their room revealed a revolver under the bedspread. Cecil had swapped a sword for a gun a few weeks earlier, but his father made him give it back. Thus, when Cecil got hold of another revolver, he kept it very quiet, although he couldn't resist showing it to Sarah Sharpe, after first swearing her to secrecy. Several of his school friends also knew of the gun's existence, and one had even been with Cecil to buy cartridges for it the day before the shootings.

An examination of the revolver by a gunsmith showed it to be a cheap, mass-produced Belgian pistol, which was broken and thus in a very dangerous state, even in the hands of an adult.

At an inquest held at the Staffords' home by coroner Robert Harvey, the jury were most concerned that Cecil was allowed to buy cartridges unchallenged. The assistant gunsmith who sold them to him stated that it was extremely common for people to send children to buy bullets and he wouldn't have supplied them if Cecil hadn't taken in a cartridge and asked to buy some the same.

The inquest jury eventually returned a verdict that 'both boys died from bullet wounds inflicted by misadventure and that Roy received his wound earlier than his brother.'

22 **APRIL, 1882** Father and son Arthur and Herbert Smith of Leicester had been playing draughts for two hours, when Herbert grew tired of the game and announced that he didn't want to play anymore. Arthur was keen to carry on and during the argument that followed, nineteen-year-old Herbert stabbed his father several times.

He appeared at the Leicestershire, Derbyshire and Rutland Assizes on 1 May, charged with malicious wounding, but was found guilty of the lesser offence of unlawful wounding. In sentencing him, the judge pointed out that although Arthur Smith's wounds were minor, one of them was just above his heart and Herbert could very easily have found himself on trial for his life. Mr Justice Stephen noted that the jury obviously believed that Herbert had no malicious intent but, even so, he intended to pass a serious sentence as a deterrent to all those who used knives to settle arguments. Adding that he hoped that Smith would learn a valuable lesson, Stephen sentenced him to six months' imprisonment, with hard labour.

23 **APRIL, 1886** Mr Morley's servants had a holiday on Good Friday and met with friends at Abbey Park in Leicester, taking five-year-old Kenneth Herbert Morley with them.

The party took out a rowing boat, with Joseph Whiting and Emily Hadman each taking an oar. They rowed along the River Soar almost as far as the sewage works when Joseph insisted on taking over the rowing. Emily handed over her oar and Joseph took just a couple of strokes before suddenly standing up, causing the boat to dip to one side. It rapidly filled with water and overturned.

Unable to swim, the boat's seven occupants struggled in the water, although luckily for them, Charles Green was walking over the river bridge. When his wife

Abbey Park, Leicester, 1906. (Author's collection)

noticed the accident, Green vaulted a fence and sprinted along the river bank, stripping off his clothes as he ran. Marshalling people in pleasure boats to assist him, Green succeeded in rescuing three of the female servants and directed two youths in a boat to pull Kenneth out of the water, although it proved impossible to revive him. Another boatman rescued William Henry Oakland, but Whiting and Amelia Bunton both drowned.

Coroner George F. Harrison held an inquest at the Town Hall in respect of Kenneth's death, before moving to The Abbey Hotel, to conduct the inquest into the deaths of the two servants. In all three cases, verdicts of 'accidental death' were returned by the juries, who recommended that Charles Green should be nominated to the Royal Humane Society for an award.

24 APRIL 1870 Seventeen-year-old Arthur Henson died at his home in Barrow-upon-Soar after an accident at work two days earlier.

On his first day of employment at a lime works, Henson was asked to push a wheelbarrow along some planks. He successfully negotiated the planks with a loaded wheelbarrow and was returning to refill it when the wheel wandered off the edge of a plank. Seeing his difficulties, the other workers shouted at him to let go of the barrow, which he did. Unfortunately, he overbalanced and followed the falling barrow almost 25 feet to the ground below. He was picked up semi-conscious and struggling to breathe, a state in which he remained until his death two days later, when a post-mortem examination showed that both of his lungs had collapsed, after being perforated by his broken ribs.

An inquest held by coroner John Gregory heard from the plant foreman that Henson had misrepresented his ability to do the job, having stated at his interview that he was accustomed to 'wheeling over high runs'. The jury returned a verdict of 'accidental death'.

25 **APRIL, 1865** The village of East Farndon was buzzing with the news that a plumber had found the remains of two children in an attic at the home of the Herbert family. On 25 April, the Herberts' cook, Ann Clarke, walked into the police station at Little Bowden and confessed to having concealed one of the children.

An inquest was held by coroner Mr T. Marshall the next day, at which the first task for the jury was to view the bodies. One was little more than a collection of bones but the second was a heavily decomposed male infant and the jury were charged with deciding whether it was born alive and, if so, what caused its death.

After hearing evidence about how the bodies were found, two doctors gave their opinions about the remains. The child was said to be a fully grown, newborn baby, with a knitted worsted garter twisted tightly around his neck and doctors estimated that he had been dead for about six months.

The inquest jury found that Ann Clarke was indisputably the mother of both children but found insufficient evidence to determine whether or not the babies were born alive. Ann was charged with concealment of birth in respect of her most recent pregnancy and appeared at the Northamptonshire Assizes on 17 July 1865. Found guilty, she was sentenced to four months' imprisonment.

26 **APRIL, 1927** At 6.35 a.m., stud groom George Braddock heard a gunshot at Witherley Hall and found sixty-one-year-old farm bailiff Thomas Bull lying on the ground, with forty-year-old estate gamekeeper Walter Goldsmith pointing a gun at him and threatening, 'I will give you another, you ＊＊＊＊＊＊.' Noticing Braddock, Goldsmith reassured him, 'It's all right, George,' before walking off into a spinney, where he shot himself.

There had long been bad blood between Bull and Goldsmith. The two men were at constant loggerheads and when Goldsmith was given notice to quit his job and his tied cottage by 1 May, he was convinced that Bull was to blame.

When Goldsmith's body was recovered, two notes were found in his pocket. The first, addressed to his wife, read: 'I cannot bear it any longer. Say goodbye to the children.

My heart is broken.' The second letter, which seemed to indicate that Goldsmith had intended only to kill himself, read: 'Bull won't get any more the sack. It's all through Bull. He may consider himself lucky he is alive.'

Coroner George Bouskell held an inquest into the two deaths, at which the jury were told that Goldsmith had been rejected by the Army because he suffered from fits. When the jury were told that Goldsmith's doctor believed that he was 'mentally unbalanced', they returned a verdict of wilful murder against Goldsmith, who then committed suicide while of unsound mind.

27 APRIL, 1882 William Burley appeared at the Leicester Borough Police Court charged with assaulting his wife Sarah on 25 February, when he first tried to strangle her, then punched and kicked her, before throwing her out of the house. Sarah had been in the Infirmary since the assault and was only now fit to give evidence in what her solicitor described as 'one of the grossest cases I have ever engaged in.'

The couple married on Christmas Day 1881 and within two weeks, William was kicking or punching his wife almost every day. He constantly swore at her and told her that he didn't want her anymore but instead wanted a wife who would earn sufficient money so that he didn't have to work. The couple lodged with William's mother, who managed to completely ignore her son's brutal treatment of her daughter-in-law.

Although William pleaded guilty and said that he was very sorry, magistrates sentenced him to six weeks' imprisonment with hard labour for the aggravated assault on his wife. They also granted Sarah a separation order and one third of her husband's weekly wage as maintenance.

28 APRIL, 1880 The fall of a large boulder at the Mountsorrel Granite Quarries knocked thirty-five-year-old Joseph Hewitt off the platform on which he was working, sending him plummeting to the bottom of the quarry, where it landed on him, killing him instantly.

When his body was extricated from beneath the massive stone both of his legs had multiple fractures, both arms were broken and he had numerous shattered ribs and a fractured skull.

At the inquest held by coroner Henry Deane, witnesses stated that Hewitt was a skilled and experienced workman, who had examined the quarry face immediately before the accident. The inquest jury returned a verdict that Hewitt was 'crushed to death by the accidental fall of stone.'

29   **APRIL, 1874** The body of two-year-old Mary 'Polly' Newby was found in a ditch, approximately 350 yards from her home. Her throat had been cut and there was a large stab wound in her abdomen.

Polly's mother, Sarah, lived in Sileby with four of her five illegitimate children. On 27 April, she put them to bed, three upstairs and the baby in a cradle downstairs. She then went to sit with a neighbour, who was about to give birth. While she was there, the neighbour asked her to fetch the midwife and she also called at the pub a couple of times for a glass of beer.

At 10.30 p.m., she collected the baby, listening at the foot of the stairs for any sounds from the other children, before going back to her neighbour. At midnight, when Sarah went home, Polly was missing.

Villagers and police began searching for the little girl, who was one of twins. She was described as 'constitutionally weak' and was unable to walk, so it was obvious that someone had taken her from her bed.

After the body was found, a search of Sarah's house revealed traces of blood on the upstairs walls, as well as fresh blood spots on her clothes, which Sarah claimed had been there since the birth of her baby five weeks earlier. Polly was seen alive and well at 7 p.m., so the time before Sarah went to her neighbour's house was unaccounted for and, although Sarah spent most of the evening with her neighbour, her alibi wasn't continuous and she was arrested on suspicion of having murdered her daughter.

Barrow Road, Sileby. (Author's collection)

The inquest, held by coroner Mr Deane, returned a verdict of 'wilful murder by person or persons unknown'. Although Sarah was in custody, she was eventually released due to a lack of evidence against her and Polly's murder went unsolved.

30 APRIL 1928 An inquest at Thurmaston on the death of eleven-year-old Betty Morecambe heard that the child's clothes accidentally caught fire when she was alone in the house. With great presence of mind, Betty climbed into the bath and turned on the taps to extinguish the flames, but was so extensively burned that she didn't survive.

Betty's neighbour, Mrs Whiteman, heard her screaming but didn't bother to check on her welfare. At the time, Mrs Whiteman's husband was out and, on his return, his wife told him about the dreadful screams from next door but he too chose not to check whether Betty was all right.

In returning a verdict of 'accidental death' the coroner censored Mrs Whiteman for her apparent indifference, saying, 'I cannot understand any woman hearing a child scream and not going to investigate.'

MAY

Narborough Road, Leicester, 1916. (Author's collection)

1 MAY 1895 Joiner William Coles lodged with Rebecca Gent in Charles Street, Leicester and, on 1 May, he found himself briefly alone in the house with her ten-year-old daughter, Alice Ethel.

When she returned home, Alice's mother thought her daughter looked unwell but it took five days before the frightened little girl revealed that Coles had lifted her onto the kitchen table and tried to rape her, causing her severe internal injuries and infecting her with a venereal disease. Mrs Gent confronted Coles, who offered her money not to say anything and, when she refused and told him that she intended to take proceedings against him, he quickly left the house, never to return.

He was arrested on 5 September and, when charged with having attempted to have carnal knowledge of Alice, he responded, 'I don't remember anything about it. I was under the influence of drink at the time.' He continued to deny the offence at his appearance at the Leicestershire Assizes in November, claiming that he had not run away from Leicester in fear of any impending proceedings against him but had simply left to take up a job in Nuneaton.

When the jury found forty-four-year-old Coles guilty, the presiding judge commented that he would like to have him flogged. Unfortunately, he had to content himself with a sentence of two years' imprisonment with hard labour, the maximum the law would allow.

Charles Street, Leicester. (Author's collection)

2 MAY 1882 Twenty-nine-year-old labourer George Brown appeared at the Leicestershire, Derbyshire and Rutland Assizes charged with stabbing his wife, Mary Jane, with intent to murder her. The counsel for the prosecution offered to accept a guilty plea for the lesser offence of unlawfully wounding, which was immediately agreed by the defence.

The chief witness against Brown was his wife, who told the court that her husband returned home to New Humberstone after working away for a month to find her living with another man. After going to the pub for a few drinks, Brown attacked his wife with a knife, stabbing her in the neck and face until she agreed to live with him again.

The presiding judge called Mary Jane 'a wicked woman', before directing the jury to find her husband guilty of unlawfully wounding. Addressing Brown, the judge told him that even though he had undoubtedly been greatly provoked, he had still broken the law in a most dangerous way and must be punished accordingly. He was sentenced to one month's imprisonment, with hard labour.

3 MAY 1862 Frederick Clarke was walking home to Narborough when he met John Southam on the road. Clarke asked Southam if he intended walking to Leicester and Southam replied rather drunkenly, 'No, I'll be damned if I do. I'll throw myself into this cart which is coming along the road.'

The cart was driven by John Higginson and carried a cow, along with two passengers. Southam ran into the road and waved his coat about and, as the pony slowed down, he jumped onto the shafts and told the driver that he wanted a ride.

'You're not riding in this cart,' Higginson protested, as Southam tried to scramble from the shafts into the cart.

'Stop the horse,' Southam ordered before falling backwards into the road, where the cart wheel passed over him. Higginson helped Southam to the verge, while Clarke ran into Narborough for a doctor and the police. It was obvious that Southam had a compound fracture of his right leg, which was bleeding heavily. The bone was set but Southam complained of pain in the abdomen and, when he died the following day, a post-mortem examination revealed a perforation in his small intestine, which the doctor believed had been caused when the cart wheel ran over him.

Before his death, Southam made a statement to the police accusing Higginson of striking him several times and of whipping the pony on, rather than stopping when he was asked to allow Southam to get safely down off the shafts.

At the inquest held by coroner John Gregory, Higginson admitted to pushing Southam backwards to prevent him getting on the cart, but added that the pony then travelled 10 or 12 yards further before Southam fell. He denied whipping the pony, his two passengers confirming that he didn't even have a whip. Higginson explained that Southam was a stranger to him and also very drunk and, had he simply asked for a lift rather than trying to barge his way onto the cart, he would have gladly obliged.

The inquest jury returned a verdict of manslaughter against Higginson, who was committed for trial at the next assizes, where the Grand Jury found no bill against him and he was discharged.

4 MAY 1860 Samuel Wells died at his farm in Seagrave, after an illness that began after eating a bowl of gruel on 27 April. Sixty-year-old Wells habitually ate gruel before retiring to bed but on this occasion he told his servant, Hannah Holmes, that it tasted disgusting and ordered her to throw it away. Wells spent an uncomfortable night vomiting and the following morning he allowed his son and daughter-in-law to send for a doctor, who prescribed medicine. Although Wells seemed to get better, several of the farm chickens died after eating his vomit, which was discarded outside.

The next evening, Hannah was again asked to make gruel but Wells didn't want it. To Hannah's obvious distress, his daughter-in-law Mary Jane decided that she would eat it and also fed some to her four-year-old child. Both ate only a spoonful but were seized with violent vomiting.

Sixteen-year-old Hannah was known to dislike Wells intensely and had often hinted that she would like to poison 'someone' and saying that she wished the old devil were dead. When Wells died, a post-mortem established that the cause of his death was arsenic poisoning and arsenic was also found in Mary Jane's vomit and in the corpses of the chickens.

Hannah was arrested and although she denied everything, while in police custody she wrote a letter to her parents. It was opened by Superintendent Hagne and found to contain a full confession.

Tried for wilful murder at the Leicestershire Assizes on 17 July, Hannah was found guilty and sentenced to death, although the jury recommended mercy on account of her youth. The death sentence was eventually commuted to one of penal servitude for life and on 16 August she was transported by train from Leicester to Millbank Prison in London.

5   MAY 1887   Ellen Kinsley appeared at the Derbyshire and Leicestershire Assizes charged with the manslaughter of her husband in Leicester.

During an argument on 17 February, twenty-two-year-old Ellen threw two cups at her husband, which cut his nose. Forty-two-year-old tailor John Kinsley was not a strong man and at the time of his death was suffering from sciatica and a heavy cold, which was inclined to make his nose bleed periodically. He died on 18 February and, according to surgeon William Charles Macalevey, the cause of his death was shock due to loss of blood, which had nothing to do with his constitutional weakness. Ellen told police that her husband had fallen over in the yard while tipsy but, when the broken cups were discovered, she changed her statement, claiming that he fell over the table and smashed them.

At Ellen's trial, her defence counsel contended that nobody had actually witnessed the events leading up to Mr Kinsley's death and asked the jury to give his client the benefit of the doubt by accepting her explanation that her husband fell and injured himself. When the jury found Ellen Kinsley guilty, Mr Justice Hawkins dealt with her leniently, sentencing her to just six weeks' imprisonment with hard labour.

6   MAY 1880   When farm labourer Henry Davis moved to Thurlaston from his native Shropshire, he took up lodgings with a widow, Mrs Woodward, and was soon engaged in a whirlwind courtship with her daughter, Elizabeth Annie. Although thirty-eight-year-old Elizabeth was ten years Henry's senior, they married on 8 March 1880.

After the wedding, Henry became jealous and suspicious about his wife's fidelity. Although his concern was completely unfounded, his workmates picked up on his insecurity and chaffed him mercilessly.

On 5 May, Henry walked home with a man named James Hancock and made a rambling complaint, voicing his fears that Elizabeth was having an affair. Hancock tried to reassure him but, when the two men parted, Henry seemed quite melancholy, telling Hancock, 'This will perhaps be the last time you see me alive.'

Early the next morning, Elizabeth went downstairs to light the fire and prepare her husband's breakfast. Minutes later, her mother heard a scream followed by a thud. She rushed downstairs and found her daughter lying on the floor, with blood streaming from her throat. Henry was kneeling by her side and while Mrs Woodward remained frozen through shock, he stood up and calmly cut his own throat with a razor. Both he and his wife bled to death before medical help could reach them.

An inquest found that Davis killed his wife then committed suicide while of unsound mind.

7 MAY 1895 At Bridge Street School, North Evington, seven-year-old Alfred Isaac Shipley was made to stand on a bench as a punishment for talking but fell off, hitting his head on the iron support at the bottom of the bench. He arrived home from school complaining of a headache but was well enough to go back to school the next morning. By the afternoon, he was feeling unwell, so his mother kept him at home and summoned a doctor, who informed her that Alfred was developing an abscess on his head.

This was not an uncommon occurrence for Alfred, who had suffered from small sores on his scalp for three or four years. On the doctor's instructions, Mrs Shipley poulticed her son's head, but instead of getting better Alfred's condition deteriorated rapidly and he died on 16 May. The cause of death was given as convulsions, due to an abscess on the brain, although the doctor who treated him didn't believe that the abscess had anything to do with Alfred's fall from the bench and could find no external signs to suggest that he banged his head.

The inquest jury eventually agreed on a verdict of 'death from natural causes', exonerating the school from blame. Strangely enough, although Alfred's classmates could remember him falling, the two teachers who were jointly in charge of the class couldn't recall making him stand on the bench and certainly didn't remember him falling off.

8 MAY 1944 The bodies of two six-year-old boys were found in a locker in a disused railway parcels van, which stood in a siding at Leicester Station.

Paul Reilly and Peter Wilcox went missing on 30 April, their disappearance prompting a week-long search. The bodies were discovered by chance when a lorry driver casually lifted the lid of the locker while waiting on the platform. The locker measured just 29½ inches x 13 inches x 20 inches and, tragically, hundreds of railway and post office staff had passed within touching distance since the boys disappeared.

It was thought that the boys climbed into the locker while playing and either closed the lid, or it accidentally closed, proving impossible to open from the inside.

9 MAY 1854 Carpenter and pump installer Thomas Oram went with his son William and son-in-law John Halam to a farm just outside Lutterworth, where he was to install a pump in a well.

The well was dug just before Christmas and, since then, had been covered with planks of wood. When the planks were removed, there was a lot of straw floating on the surface of the water 40 feet below. John volunteered to remove it and climbed into the bucket, which was lowered using a windlass. Almost as soon as he reached the water, he suddenly toppled in and, since he was known to suffer occasional fits,

Lutterworth. (Author's collection)

Thomas immediately went down to help him. He too fell into the water and, although William called out to him several times, there was no response.

William ran to fetch the farmer, who rushed to the well with some of the farm labourers. A lighted candle was lowered into the depths, revealing the presence of noxious gases and preventing anyone from rescuing Oram and Halam. When their bodies were eventually recovered, a post-mortem examination revealed that they died almost instantly from the inhalation of 'foul air'.

10 MAY 1895 As Amos Quemby stepped over a conveyor belt at the Charnwood Granite Works near Shepshed, he accidentally caught his toe on the edge and was swept off his feet and carried along, ending up wedged between the belt and the pulley that turned it. By the time the engine was stopped, eighteen-year-old Quemby was dead from a broken neck and a fractured skull, through which his brain protruded.

The inquest before coroner Henry Deane heard that the engine was stopped for a few moments while blasting took place at the quarry, during which time Quemby left his position on the conveyor belt, where he was sorting stones. When the signal to restart the machines was given, Quemby was back in his place by the conveyor belt but as the engines started, he was seen on the opposite side of the belt, trying to get over it. Nobody saw how he got to the 'wrong' side of the belt but all of the witnesses at the inquest were in agreement that he had no business being there since, as Quemby was well aware, crossing the belt was a sacking offence.

The inquest jury found that Quemby's death was due to his own negligence and, in returning a verdict of 'accidental death', determined that he was the only person at fault.

11 MAY 1829 William Petty and Joseph Thompson were awarded a free pardon, having been sentenced to death at the Leicestershire Assizes for breaking down part of a wall to gain access to a bakery at Witherley, with intent to commit a felony therein. Each lost a boot during the break-in and, when they were arrested, Thompson and Petty were both wearing only one boot, which matched those left behind at the scene of the crime.

The bricks in the wall they dismantled were loose, although according to the baker, not so loose that they would have fallen with the force of the wind. In sentencing the prisoners to death, the judge remarked that, had there been a hole in the wall, it would not have been burglary hence there would have been no felony.

Petty and Thompson were aged just fourteen and thirteen respectively and the judge told them that if any person came forward who was willing to take them into their care and employment, he would willingly intercede with His Majesty to obtain their discharge but, in the meantime, he had no other option but to record sentence of death against them.

12 MAY 1868 After Thomas William Sturges Frisby was discharged from the Navy at Christmas 1867, he returned to live at his father's house in Leicester. Father and son had disagreed in the past and by April 1868, Thomas Frisby senior was tired of his son staying out all night and associating with disreputable people, and told him to look for a place of his own.

On 19 April, Thomas left home but on 12 May, he visited a gun shop and asked for bullets, caps and powder, then returned to his lodgings and announced that he was going to kill his father. His landlord immediately locked him in his room until he calmed down.

At 10.30 p.m., Thomas knocked on his parents' door and when his mother answered, he asked to see his father. Elizabeth Frisby suggested that he came back another time but Thomas barged past her and into the kitchen, where his father was sitting by the fire, drawing his pistol and firing it at his father's head. Fortunately, the gunpowder was of poor quality and the shot merely penetrated Frisby's skin.

When Thomas Frisby junior was tried at the Leicestershire Assizes, the issue for the jury was whether or not he intended to kill his father. After due consideration, the jury found him guilty of unlawfully wounding, with intent to do grievous bodily harm rather than with intent to murder and he was sentenced to ten years' penal servitude.

13 MAY **1896**   There was a fair at Leicester's Humberstone
Gate and William Henry Smith was trying to sneak a look
at one of the sideshows through a tear in the canvas when
he was thumped from inside the tent. A bystander noticed
the boy's face bleeding and took him to hospital, where he was
found to have two small but deep puncture wounds between his nose
and forehead, made by a sharp instrument such as a pitchfork.

A complaint was made to the police and Detective Sergeant
Beamish went to speak to the owner of the attraction, twenty-
one-year-old Samuel Wood, who freely admitted to hitting some
boys for trying to view the show without paying. However, Wood
insisted that he had hit the boys with a hammer and had not
struck anybody with a pitchfork.

Brought before magistrates at the Borough Police Court, Wood
was adamant that if Smith's wounds were caused by a pitchfork,
he was not responsible. Yet the medical assistant from the
Infirmary was equally insistent that Smith's injuries could not
have been caused by a hammer.

Magistrates eventually found Wood guilty of assault, fining him
three guineas or one month's hard labour in default.

Leicester fair. (Author's collection)

14 MAY 1896 Three-year-old Reuben Bourne Moore died from scalds received two days earlier, when he fell into a copper of boiling water.

The cottages at Moira, where Reuben lived, had outhouses with coppers used for washing. On 12 May, Matilda Curtis lit a fire in her outhouse and, as she sat in her home waiting for the water to heat up, she saw Reuben and his five-year-old brother climbing on the copper. She shouted at the boys to get off, warning them that the hot water would burn them, and both children climbed down. Three minutes later, Matilda heard fearful screams and found Reuben in the copper, the near boiling water reaching almost to his waist.

It seemed as though Reuben stood on the lid, which buckled under his weight, plunging him into the water and severely scalding his legs and lower body. At the inquest into his death, coroner Henry Deane questioned how the child could have climbed onto the copper and was told that they were very low and could be reached by stepping onto the sinks, which were only 18 inches off the floor. In spite of the danger, the village children persistently played in the outhouses and the coroner told the jury that he thought it was necessary to obtain a recreation ground for the village, suggesting that they approached the Parish Council to see what could be done. The jury returned a verdict of 'accidental death'.

15 MAY 1896 John William Saunderson of Leicester appeared at the Borough Police Court charged with assaulting his wife on 7 May.

The couple had been married for less than three months when Mrs Saunderson complained that her husband got drunk at lunchtime and, after an argument about some furniture, seized her by the throat while holding a knife in his hand and put her out of the house, saying that he didn't want her anymore.

Mr Saunderson had a different view of the incident and categorically denied the assault, claiming that his wife hit *him*, knocked his head against the wall, smashed some of his pictures and threw a bowl of cocoa at him, before storming out, taking with her what she believed was her share of the furniture. He called a witness, who confirmed that he was not holding a knife and had not threatened or harmed his wife in any way.

Nevertheless, magistrates bound him over to keep the peace for six months.

16 MAY 1882 While Selina Brewin of Leicester was busy lighting the fire, her twenty-three-month-old son, Edward Harper Percival Brewin, toddled out into the street.

As soon as the fire was lit, Selina went to look for Edward, finding him lying on his back in the middle of the road, vomiting blood. Another toddler, Alfred Burdett, who was two years and nine months old, was walking away from Edward, the lower part of his smock heavily bloodstained. Alfred, who was a particularly rough and aggressive child, was carrying a small tin lid.

Selina scooped up her unconscious son and took him indoors, sending for a surgeon. Yet in spite of Mr F.K. Bell's care, Edward died on 20 May. A post-mortem examination revealed a fracture at the base of his skull, either from falling or being thrown onto a hard surface. However, the primary cause of Edward's death was injury to his stomach and intestines, consistent with his having been knelt or fallen upon when his gut was full of food.

Nobody saw how Edward got injured and Alfred was too young to talk. At the inquest into Edward's death, coroner Mr Harrison pointed out to the jury that no child under the age of seven could be guilty of a felony or punished for a capital offence. The jury returned a verdict in accordance with the medical testimony, adding that their supposition was that the injuries were caused by Alfred Burdett, who was not accountable in law for his actions.

17 MAY **1893** Plumber Edgar Lorndon Armson was engaged to repair a pump in a well at Swannington Manor. His father, who accompanied him, watched as Edgar descended a ladder onto a platform in the wall of the well, at a depth of 12 feet. Suddenly, Edgar began to climb back up the ladder as quickly as he possibly could. He got almost to the top when he loosed his hold and fell backwards into the well.

A collier who lived nearby tested the air in the well by lowering a lighted candle into the depths, confirming the presence of foul air as high as a yard below ground level. Having tested the air, Joseph Morley sensibly refused to allow anyone to go down into the well, thus it was some time before Edgar's body was retrieved using drags. Apart from a few abrasions, he had no external injuries and the cause of his death was determined to be asphyxia from the inhalation of foul air.

Coroner Henry Deane subsequently recorded a verdict of 'accidental death'.

18 MAY **1897** Farmer Joseph King was in a field at Osgathorpe with his children and two farm labourers, picking up sticks and small branches from a recently felled tree and loading them onto a cart.

The trunk of the tree was on top of a steep hedge bank and King's youngest son, also named Joseph, was amusing himself playing on it. Suddenly, the tree began to roll down the bank with Joseph junior lying on it, rolling over the boy and crushing him. The labourers managed to lift the heavy tree trunk off three-year-old Joseph but his head had been completely squashed and a surgeon later confirmed that all the bones in the boy's skull were fractured and death would have been instantaneous.

Coroner Henry Deane recorded a verdict of 'accidental death' at the later inquest.

19 MAY 1846 A horse belonging to Messrs Wing, grocers and druggists of Leicester, died from glanders, caused by infection by the bacteria *Burkholderia mallei*. The disease was zoonotic – it could be passed to humans via skin lesions – but knacker man Thomas Whittaker of Melton Mowbray, who bought the carcase for 3s, was not aware of that. As he skinned the horse, he continually wiped sweat from his bald head with his hand, inoculating himself with the disease through a scratch on his scalp. Whittaker endured twenty-one days of coughing, fever and nasal discharge, followed by septicaemia and death.

The disease also claimed another human victim, Robert Pick, who acted as a groom and handyman to Messrs Wing. It was impossible to determine how Pick contracted the disease but it was suspected that it was by inhaling the foetid breath of the horse as he tended it.

A man who helped skin the horse is also reported to have caught the disease, as did some pigs who came into contact with the straw it slept on, although the contemporary newspapers do not record whether or not they survived. Surgeons ultimately claimed to have contained the disease by burning everything that the two deceased came into contact with, including their beds, clothes and bedding.

20 MAY 1877 Thomas Dakin of Leicester borrowed a gun, intending to shoot some small birds, which he planned to stuff. Sitting with his wife, mother and fifteen-year-old sister, Sarah, he fetched the gun out of a cupboard, saying, 'See me frighten Sarah.'

He put a cap on the nipple and pulled the trigger, expecting a loud bang. Unfortunately the gun was loaded and the shot blew off part of Sarah's face and head, causing her instantaneous death.

When the police arrived, Thomas denied that there was a gun in the house and, when it was later found stuffed up the chimney, he swore he didn't know who put it there. When charged with shooting his sister, he gave two conflicting stories, saying that Sarah picked the gun up off the table and it went off, or that he was not even in the house at the time of the accident and opened the door just in time to see his sister fall.

He was tried for manslaughter at the Leicester Assizes on 14 July and it was established that the man who lent the gun to Dakin failed to tell him that it was loaded. The jury found Dakin guilty but recommended mercy and, knowing that he had been incarcerated while awaiting his trial, the judge sentenced him to a token one day's imprisonment.

21 MAY 1868 John Gillham was one of a group of men illegally fishing in a mill dam near Great Wigston when somebody came towards them in the darkness and shouted, 'If any man moves I'll blow his bloody brains out!'

Gillham stood up. 'Who will?' he asked. The answer was a gun shot.

As soon as the gun was fired, the shooter fled. One of the poachers pursued him to his garden gate, where he stopped and threatened to fire again before going indoors.

The gun shot broke Gillham's left arm, before entering his face just below his left eye, the pellets causing catastrophic damage to his brain. Although admitted to hospital, he died later that day, when miller George Keene was charged with his wilful murder.

There was little doubt that Keene shot Gillham, although at his trial at the Leicestershire Assizes, Keene's defence counsel insisted that his client had only acted in self-defence and to protect his property.

The poachers who were with Gillham all stated that he offered no violence towards Keene but, although they testified to that effect in court, it was pointed out that all had convictions for offences ranging from poaching to wife beating. William Walker, who was with Keene at the time of the shooting, told a different story, saying that three of the poachers were approaching Keene menacingly and he was in fear for his life when he fired at them. The jury chose to believe the defence and found Keene not guilty.

Note: The date of the murder is variously given as 21 and 31 May.

22 MAY 1869 Coroner John Gregory held an inquest at Mountsorrel into the death of a five-year-old boy.

On 10 May, William Lovett of Mountsorrel was playing with his friends when he accidentally stepped in some mud that went over the top of his boots. He removed the boots and went to the banks of a stream to wash his feet but the sandy bank gave way beneath his weight, throwing him into the water.

The water was high and fast-flowing and the little boy was quickly washed out of sight before anyone could even think about trying to rescue him. The stream was dragged several times over the next few days but William's body was not recovered until 19 May. The inquest jury returned a verdict of 'accidental death'.

23 MAY 1900 Seventy-year-old woodman Henry Mayes was felling trees at Gaulby with William Burgess. The men sawed through the trunk of a massive oak tree at the base and tied a rope around it, in order to pull it to the ground.

As it began to fall, both men ran in different directions, but Mayes didn't run fast enough and was dashed to the ground by a branch, which hit him on the head and cut open his scalp. He was taken to hospital, where he was diagnosed with concussion of the brain and, although he was fully expected to recover, he developed meningitis and died in the Infirmary on 4 June. Coroner Robert Harvey held an inquest two days later, at which the jury returned a verdict of 'accidental death'.

24 MAY 1877 Twelve-year-old Mary Ann Emma Jalland lived next door to twenty-six-year-old William Gibson and his wife in Harby, and was also a pupil at the Sunday school at which Gibson taught. She often visited Mrs Gibson to help with the housework and on 24 May, was at the Gibsons' house when William shouted for her to bring his shaving soap. He was in his bedroom and, almost as soon as Mary walked in with the soap, Mrs Gibson came upstairs. Gibson immediately told Mary to get under the bed but Mrs Gibson found her there and called her a bad girl. She also let rip at her husband, who told her that, if she didn't stop nagging, he would run away and leave her.

Three days later, Gibson went next door and asked if Mary could do some housework while his wife went to fetch butter. Alone with Mary, Gibson told her that, as a consequence of what happened in the bedroom, everyone would think she was a bad girl and she would be beaten at home.

Gibson convinced Mary that they should run away together and they travelled to Nottingham, Ratcliffe, Grantham, Boston, Grimsby and Cleethorpes, all the while living as man and wife. Mary's uncle pursued the couple as far as Nottingham and, although Mary wanted to return home with him, Gibson wouldn't allow it and managed to give him the slip.

Gibson was eventually apprehended at Cleethorpes and Mary was sent back to her family. When he was charged with abduction, Gibson told police that Mary had threatened to commit suicide if he didn't go away with her and he allowed himself to be persuaded, in order to save her from herself.

The jury at the Leicestershire Assizes didn't believe a single word and Gibson was found guilty of abduction and sentenced to eighteen months' imprisonment with hard labour.

25 MAY 1903 After a successful night's poaching, the last person Thomas Porter and Thomas Preston wanted to see as they walked home was PC William Ariel Wilkinson. As Wilkinson stood chatting to a man outside the churchyard at Sileby, there was a sudden volley of shots and the policeman fell dead.

Porter and Preston were seen running into Porter's house, where they barricaded themselves inside, threatening to shoot anyone who approached. At 1 a.m. on 26 May, the police surrounded the house but were kept at bay until 7 a.m., when the two poachers realised the hopelessness of their situation and gave themselves up.

They appeared together before Mr Justice Ridley at the Leicestershire Assizes on 29-30 June 1903, charged with wilful murder. Both said that they were drunk at the time of the shooting and, while Porter admitted to having fired the fatal shot, he claimed to have intended only to frighten Wilkinson. Preston believed that he bore no personal responsibility for the murder whatsoever, saying that he had become separated from Porter and had no idea that his companion was going to fire at the policeman. Even so, the jury found both men guilty and they were sentenced to death.

The two men died in a double hanging at Leicester Prison on 21 July. As they stood on the scaffold before hangman William Billington and his son John, who acted as his assistant, Porter and Preston both proclaimed, 'I am innocent.'

Mr Justice Ridley. (Author's collection)

26 MAY 1900 John Robert Jesson married his wife Elizabeth Mary in 1899 and took the tenancy of a small farm with her brother. However, the three argued constantly and the farm failed.

At Christmas 1899, Elizabeth returned to live with her parents at Illston-on-the-Hill and John joined her in mid-January. He had lost all of his savings on the farm and eventually returned to his first job as a carpenter, moving to lodgings in Leicester. The couple wrote and visited one another and Elizabeth expressed a strong desire for them to live together as a married couple, although John's feelings towards his wife seemed to be cooling.

On 26 May, John visited his wife at her parents' house and ate tea and supper with her family. John and Elizabeth went to bed together at about 9.30 p.m. and by 10 p.m., John was dead from strychnine poisoning, having apparently ingested a packet of Battle's Vermin Killer. Ominously, on his last visit to his wife, John was stricken with the symptoms of arsenic poisoning, the day after his father-in-law bought a tin of weed killer.

John's letters to his wife had all been destroyed but her letters to him were found in his belongings after his death. Elizabeth had specifically asked her husband to buy a packet of Battle's poison, since she had a mouse in her bedroom, although John didn't appear to have actually done so.

At the inquest into John's death, the presence of strychnine in his stomach contents was confirmed but the analyst also found currants, and none of the family had eaten anything containing currants that day. Elizabeth told the coroner that John was unwell when he came to bed and that she fetched him a cup of whisky.

Either John had taken the poison himself or Elizabeth had poisoned him and the inquest jury favoured the latter option, returning a verdict of wilful murder against her. She appeared before Mr Justice Channell at the Leicestershire Assizes in November 1900 on the coroner's warrant.

It was intimated at the trial that John was suffering from 'a certain disease' and was in the habit of dosing himself. (This was refuted by the prosecution.) It was also noted that Elizabeth's letters to her husband seemed genuinely affectionate but their tone suggested that his to her were somewhat cold. However, one of the key points for the jury was the presence of currants in John's stomach contents, which they felt gave weight to the theory that he had poisoned himself and led them to acquit Elizabeth Jesson.

Mr Justice Channell, 1897. (Author's collection)

27 MAY **1893** Twelve-year-old William Glover died at the Desford Industrial School.

On the evening of 25 May, around 150 pupils were playing cricket and rounders in the yard, using rubber balls. Glover was running, focusing intently on the ball he was trying to catch, when he strayed too close to a neighbouring game of cricket. Batsman Harry Stafford tried to hit a ball and instead, hit Glover on the throat with his cricket bat.

Glover was taken indoors, where a master rubbed his throat with 'white oils', after which he felt better. However, the following day, Glover began to struggle for breath and, in spite of the attentions of a surgeon, he died within twenty-four hours. A post-mortem examination revealed that the cause of his death was suffocation due to inflammation and swelling of the windpipe.

Coroner George Bouskell held an inquest on 29 May, at which the jury returned a verdict of 'accidental death'.

28 MAY **1899** Clara Ada Tansley of Leicester, who was just under two years old, had been suffering from measles, which left her with a cough and breathing difficulties. Her mother decided that she would benefit from a poultice and placed hot pancakes on Clara's back and chest.

Although Mrs Tansley tested the temperature of the pancakes before applying them, one was obviously far too hot. A doctor found a nine-inch diameter burn on the toddler's back and she developed complications and died on 17 June.

An inquest held on 19 June returned a verdict of 'death by misadventure', the coroner remarking that Mrs Tansley was clearly negligent.

29 MAY 1899 William and Mary Ann Evans of Hugglescote had been married for fourteen years and had five children. William was a good husband and father but in 1898, his own father was killed in a pit accident (*see* 19 April) and the body wasn't recovered for ten months. The tragedy deeply affected William and his melancholy state of mind wasn't improved when he had an accident and hurt his head and back. He began drinking and even the smallest amount of alcohol affected him very badly.

After drinking heavily on 26 and 27 May, he was behaving very strangely, telling his sister that four men were pursuing him and trying to kill him. Although William didn't drink on 28 May, he was morose and refused to eat anything.

Mary Ann eventually went to see her husband's brother, hoping that William would calm down if left alone. She stayed the night there and, on 29 May, William arrived and asked her if she was coming home. When she said that she wouldn't unless he changed, he sat down on the sofa next to her and the next thing she knew, her neck was bleeding heavily. Realising that William had tried to cut her throat with a razor, she called to his brother and between them they managed to disarm William, who was now cutting his own throat. While waiting for the doctor, William tried twice more to cut his throat with a penknife and a table knife, but his brother took them away from him.

For three weeks, William seemed dazed and was delusional, claiming that he had no idea what he was doing when he attacked his wife. He was charged with feloniously wounding Mary Ann with intent to kill and murder her, but at his trial at the Leicestershire Assizes in November 1899, both the judge and jury recognised that he was not of sound mind at the time of the offence. The judge proposed reducing the offence to unlawful wounding on the grounds that William was incapable of forming an intention of murdering his wife. The jury found him guilty but temporarily insane due to *delirium tremens* and he was ordered to be detained during Her Majesty's pleasure.

30 MAY 1922 Edith Mary Roberts was freed from Walton Gaol in Liverpool by order of the Home Secretary. Edith, of Hinckley, had become nationally known as 'the girl mother' and her case was to bring about a change in the judicial system.

Walton Gaol, Liverpool, 1913. (Author's collection)

In 1920, twenty-year-old Edith became pregnant. She was too ashamed to tell her family and kept her condition a secret until 17 April 1921, when she gave birth to a daughter in a bedroom she shared with her sister. Edith wrapped the baby in her chemise and hid her in a box, where she was later found by Edith's mother. Edith swore that the baby was stillborn but when later tests revealed that the cause of death was suffocation, she was charged with wilful murder.

Nobody could determine what actually happened to the baby. It was questionable whether Edith killed her daughter deliberately, whether she was out of her mind with pain and worry, or if the child accidentally suffocated during birth. However, at her trial at the Leicestershire Assizes, the jury found Edith guilty of wilful murder and, although they recommended mercy, she was sentenced to death.

The sentence was commuted to one of life imprisonment but a strenuous campaign to get Edith released was already underway. Petitions totalling more than 30,000 signatures were raised and letters were written to Queen Mary, the Prime Minister, the Home Secretary and the first female MP, Lady Astor, while General Bramwell Booth of the Salvation Army made a personal appeal to the Home Secretary on Edith's behalf.

After the Home Secretary authorised Edith's release, the death sentence was abolished for women found guilty of infanticide.

General Bramwell Booth.
(Author's collection)

31 MAY 1866 At about 4.30 p.m., a tremendous explosion occurred at the elastic webbing factory in Leicester owned by John Wolstenholme, which reduced the two-storey building to rubble. Fortunately, there were only three people in the premises at the time – Wolstenholme, his young son Arthur and his father-in-law, William Ralphs. Arthur escaped with minor injuries, John was badly injured but survived, while Ralphs was picked up in a factory yard almost 100 yards away, and died thirty minutes after his admission to the Leicester Infirmary.

At the inquest, Arthur stated that he had seen a lot of steam escaping from the boiler and told his grandfather [Ralphs], who went to check it. The boiler was nearly new and was said to be in good condition, although for a few days prior to the explosion, it was used without a water gauge, after the one fitted was broken. The boiler was blown to smithereens and there was no trace of parts such as the steam gauge or the safety valve lever, so the inquest was adjourned to allow further enquiries to be made.

When it concluded on 27 June, the jury returned a verdict that the death of sixty-year-old Ralphs was caused by an explosion attributed to 'shortness of water generating gas and exerting too great pressure' and asked the coroner to reprimand Wolstenholme for permitting the boiler to be run without a water gauge (some reports state that the boiler was also running without a steam pressure gauge).

It was a miracle that there was only one fatality. Children playing in the yard of an adjoining factory escaped unscathed, as did workers at nearby factories, where boiler parts and masonry rained through the roofs. Debris was scattered far and wide and the windows were blown out of houses within a 100-yard radius of the explosion.

JUNE

Mount St Bernard Abbey. (Author's collection)

1   JUNE 1892   Coroner Robert Harvey held an inquest into the death of one-month-old Norah Shread of Leicester.

Norah was a healthy baby but, since her birth, her mother had slept with her children to avoid disturbing her husband when Norah needed feeding at night. As well as Maud Shread and the baby, the bed was shared by two other children, one eight years old and the other aged sixteen-months.

Maud breastfed her daughter when she went to bed and again at 2 a.m. She woke at 5 a.m. to find Norah lying face down on the pillow, with her sixteen-month old brother, John Joseph, sitting on her head. Maud's screams as she picked up the lifeless baby alerted her husband, who ran for a doctor. However, surgeon Mr Hindle was able to do nothing apart from pronounce life extinct and was later to state at the inquest that the extreme discolouration of the baby's body indicated that she must have been rapidly suffocated by a great pressure. The inquest jury returned a verdict of 'accidental death' and coroner Harvey remarked that the practice of sleeping three or four people in one bed could not be too strongly reprehended.

2   JUNE 1832   An inquest into the death of John Paas opened with an inspection of the body by the jury. Since all that was left of Paas was a few fragments of charred flesh and bone, and those bones that remained had obviously been cut with a saw, it seemed evident that the London businessman had met with foul play.

The remains were found in the Leicester workshop of a bookbinder named James Cook, after neighbours broke into the premises when the chimney caught fire during the night. They found a large piece of meat cooking on an open fire and, when Cook was called to the workshop, he explained that it was dog meat that had spoiled.

As soon as Cook could get away from his shop, he fled, walking to Loughborough and then catching a coach to Manchester. Meanwhile, an examination of the 'dog meat' showed it to be a human pelvis and thigh and, when Cook's premises were searched, bloodstained clothes and a pencil case belonging to Paas were found. Police immediately set out to track Cook and he was arrested in Liverpool, as he was being rowed out to a ship bound for America.

Cook confessed to having killed Paas by beating him with an iron bar, after Paas visited him to seek repayment of an outstanding debt of twelve shillings. Tried at the Leicester Assizes on 8 August, Cook was found guilty and hanged at Leicester Prison two days later. After death, his body was hung on the Aylestone Road in an iron cage. However, such was the riotous behaviour of the estimated 20,000 people who came to gawk at Cook's body that it was cut down after only three days.

3 JUNE 1896 Five-year-old Agnes Annie Hancock died from a minor injury received while playing almost a month earlier.

On 12 May, she and her brother Arthur were among a group of children playing at Walton-by-Kimcote. The children had been busy filling an old salmon tin with dust when Arthur picked it up and threw it, but he didn't notice his sister standing nearby and the tin hit her below her left eyelid, drawing blood.

Arthur took Agnes home and their parents bandaged the wound. However, within three days it appeared angry and inflamed and Mrs Hancock took Agnes to the doctor, who cleaned and dressed the cut. Initially, it seemed to be healing but by 29 May, it was swollen and oozing pus. Soon the left-hand side of Agnes's face became paralysed as blood poisoning set in and she died on 3 June.

An inquest held by coroner George Bouskell recorded a verdict of 'accidental death' but only after the coroner had censured a juryman for gross contempt of court, after Mr Beeby Hubbard managed to avoid viewing the body. Bouskell made him go and look at it alone, sending a policeman to escort him so that he couldn't escape the onerous task. Although Hubbard told the coroner that he hadn't realised that inspecting the body was either compulsory or necessary, he did as the coroner asked and also apologised to the court when ordered to do so by Bouskell.

Walton. (Author's collection)

4 JUNE 1898 Sidney Shipman of Leicester went out to play with his friends just before noon. Within fifteen minutes, the eight-year-old returned, sobbing, 'Teddy Phipps has killed me.'

Sidney told his parents that he had thrown at tin at Edward 'Teddy' Phipps, who retaliated by throwing a half-brick at Sidney, hitting him on his back. Sidney's mother took off his shirt, finding an insignificant mark just below his left shoulder blade. She bathed it with cold water and Sidney went back out to play with Teddy, their argument completely forgotten.

Four days later, Sidney complained of backache and a pain in his leg. His mother took him to the doctor, who advised bed rest and rubbing his back with diluted methylated spirits. The following day, Sidney's condition had deteriorated and he was removed to the Leicester Infirmary, where he died on 13 June. The cause of death was pneumonia and blood poisoning, resulting from an abscess on Sidney's back, where a small piece of his spine had broken off.

Coroner Robert Harvey held an inquest on 16 June. Teddy confirmed that he had thrown a stone at Sidney, after an argument blew up about a butterfly belonging to Teddy's brother. Sidney threw a tin can at Teddy and, although the can didn't hit him, Teddy threw the first thing that came to hand – a half-brick – back at Sidney.

The coroner told the jury that there could be no doubt that Sidney's death was caused by Phipps. However, Phipps was only ten years old and, although he was legally accountable for his actions, it seemed obvious that there was no deliberate malice and the throwing was done in retaliation, with no time for aforethought. Thus there would be no benefit in committing him to the assizes.

The coroner led the jury to return a verdict that death was due to an abscess caused by a fractured bone, without specifying whether it was an accident or a criminal offence committed by Teddy Phipps. The jury complied, although they asked the coroner to have a private word with Teddy about the dangers of stone throwing.

5 JUNE 1884 Arthur Cockerill died from *delirium tremens* in Leicester Infirmary, where he was undergoing treatment for a broken leg. The fracture occurred during a fight and, after Cockerill's death, Alfred Chapman was charged with his manslaughter.

On 2 June, Chapman was playing bagatelle in The Free School Tavern in Leicester with a man named Alfred Hopkins, when a dispute arose between them over a penny. Hopkins and Chapman went outside to settle the matter and, after knocking down Hopkins, Chapman apparently hit an innocent bystander, Mr Godson. The latter then turned on Cockerill and knocked him over twice.

Cockerill's wife was among several people who witnessed the fracas and, when Chapman appeared at the Leicestershire Assizes, she told the court that, having been knocked down, her husband was unable to get up and was taken to the hospital. Yet when asked by surgeons how he sustained his fracture, Cockerill clearly stated that he fell off the kerb.

Doctors were adamant that the cause of death was *delirium tremens*, accelerated by the broken leg, but the defence maintained that the true cause of the DTs was the sudden cessation of Cockerill's intake of alcohol, when he was admitted to hospital. The doctors argued that this wasn't possible but the judge interjected that he believed that there was some evidence to support the defence's theories. When the judge summarised the case for the jury, he emphasised that, in his opinion, the evidence against Chapman was inconclusive and the jury found him 'not guilty'.

6   JUNE   1868   Coroner John Gregory held an inquest into the death of William Jones.

On 3 June, as Jones and his sweetheart Maria Webster were walking home, after a day at Burbage Wakes, they were overtaken by two men, one of whom began insulting the couple. Jones and Maria took no notice, which seemed to anger the man, who suddenly kicked out at Jones, then pushed Maria into a hedge. Forced to defend his girlfriend, Jones punched William Dilley's face. Dilley retaliated by punching Jones on the thigh, at which point Maria stepped between the two men to try and break up the fight. Dilley sidestepped her and punched Jones in the side but as he moved his hand away, Maria saw that he was holding a knife and had stabbed, rather than punched, her boyfriend.

Dilley's companion, William Caloe, ran for a doctor and Dilley walked away, while Jones climbed over a stile and lay down, saying that he was going to die. As he did, Dilley returned and pressed a handkerchief onto the bleeding wound in Jones's side, but ran off when he heard two men approaching. Jones died the following day, having given a deposition accusing Dilley of stabbing him and Dilley was charged with wilful murder.

At the inquest, Caloe admitted that he saw Dilley hit Jones but insisted that Jones started the fight after Dilley accidentally bumped into him. According to Caloe, Dilley did not knock Maria into the hedge, nor did he speak to the couple, other than to apologise for bumping into Jones.

The inquest found a verdict of 'wilful murder' against Dilley, who was committed for trial at the Leicestershire Assizes. The judge pointed out that Jones, Dilley, Caloe and Maria Webster all gave differing accounts of the stabbing and suggested to the jury that the main point for their consideration was whether the blow given by Jones was sufficiently violent to rouse Dilley's passions, so that he lost self-possession and committed the stabbing in hot blood. If they thought that this was the case, then a verdict of guilty of manslaughter was appropriate.

This was indeed the jury's verdict and forty-year-old Dilley was sentenced to fifteen years' penal servitude.

7 JUNE 1935 Brother John Holland went to the pumping house in a field near to Mount St Bernard Abbey to start the pumps. Nothing more was heard of him for three hours, when a passer-by found him lying on his back on the pumping house steps. He was breathing but unable to speak.

Holland was taken back to the monastery, where he died an hour later. He had a bad cut on the back of his head and the cause of his death was a fractured skull combined with shock, consistent with him having fallen backwards on the slippery steps to the pump house and banged his head.

Brother John's family had travelled from Ireland to attend his ordination, which should have taken place on 10 June. Instead they attended his inquest, at which the jury returned a verdict of 'accidental death'.

Monks from Mount St Bernard Abbey. (Author's collection)

8 JUNE 1874 William Hill Bates and his brother Alfred were walking home in Leicester, when a man attempted to pick Alfred's pocket. As soon as he realised what was happening, Alfred shouted and struck the pickpocket, Charles Biddle, on the arm with his stick. Biddle immediately challenged Alfred to a fight and, although Alfred declined, William drunkenly stepped forward, saying, 'I'll have a go at him.'

Alfred told William to stand back and hit Biddle twice more, this time with the thick end of his stick, knocking him down. Somebody came to see what was happening and, while Alfred was explaining, Biddle stood up and William rushed towards him, putting up his fists.

Biddle landed one blow on William's jaw, which knocked him out cold. Alfred needed the assistance of another man to carry his brother home, where he died the following afternoon without fully regaining consciousness. When Dr Blunt carried out a post-mortem examination, he found no external marks of violence on thirty-four-year-old William but noted a blood clot the size of a walnut in his brain. The brain tissue surrounding the clot was softened and Dr Blunt was of the opinion that William died from apoplexy and that his brain was already diseased. The blow from Biddle might or might not have caused the softened brain tissue to give way but, in the doctor's opinion, William died from natural causes.

Coroner George F. Harrison held an inquest on 9 June, at which Biddle's companion, Solomon Wykes, claimed that Biddle had merely brushed against Alfred in passing, at which Alfred immediately began shouting and belabouring Biddle with his stick, accusing him of picking his pocket. Biddle was furious at the accusation and offered to fight but only hit William in self-defence, after he rushed at him in a fighting attitude.

The coroner told the jury that, had this blow actually killed William Bates, Biddle would have committed justifiable homicide, since the blow was given by a man who was about to be attacked. The deceased was the aggressor and, according to the doctor, although it was possible that Biddle's blow caused William's death, it was more probable that William died from a pre-existing brain disease, which could have killed him at any time. The jury returned a verdict of 'death from natural causes', exonerating Biddle from all blame.

9 JUNE 1906 Miss Mary Jane Eckersley of Oldham and her friends Miss Brierley and Miss Marsden went on a day trip to London. On the return journey their train stopped at Leicester, where a porter obtained some tea for them.

When the train set off again, Miss Marsden was concerned that the porter hadn't shut the door properly. She was so perturbed that after ten minutes Miss Eckersley got up from her seat to check. She shook the door handle from the inside and reassured her friend, 'We are fast in.' Yet even as the words left her mouth, the door suddenly swung open and fifty-two-year-old Miss Eckersley fell out. The train was halted and she was picked up unconscious and taken to the Leicester Infirmary, where she died later that night. At the inquest into her death, porter Mr Hutt insisted that he had secured the door and both the chief porter and the guard stated that they saw him turning the handle to shut it.

The inquest jury returned a verdict of 'accidental death' without passing an opinion on whether Hutt shut the door properly or whether Miss Eckersley opened it from the inside, while trying to allay her friend's concerns.

10 **JUNE 1897** Sixty-year-old drover William Scott was a regular customer at The Old Cheese Inn on Abbey Street, Leicester, and often did odd jobs for the landlord, John Bushell.

On 10 June, Bushell asked Scott to tidy up the yard, after which Scott went to help in the brew house. At one stage, Scott was standing on a step between two coppers, the smallest of which was being used to wash the brewing utensils. It had about 2½ inches of water in the bottom and a small fire underneath.

With the brewing work complete, Bushell left the brew house. Scott was putting on his coat and Bushell believed that he too was on the point of leaving but as Bushell walked towards the pub, he heard a crash and a scream. He ran back to the brew house to find Scott sitting in the small copper. Bushell pulled him out and applied linseed and limewater to his bottom, before sending for a doctor, who recommended taking Scott to the Infirmary. There he was found to be suffering from severe scalding on the lower part of his body.

Scott died on 15 June from bronchitis and exhaustion resulting from his scalds. Coroner Robert Harvey held an inquest the following day at which the jury heard that Scott was not drunk, 'having had no more than his usual allowance of beer.' The jury was also told that Scott was not at all unsteady in his movements, given that the step between the two coppers was 'usually more or less wet and slippery.'

A verdict of 'accidental death' was returned.

11 **JUNE 1887** Five boys aged between five and eight years old went to play in Abbey Park, Leicester. They were throwing grass into the river when eight-year-old Ernest Ross stumbled. He grabbed his cousin, George Moore, to try and stop himself from falling into the water, but instead pulled five-year-old George in too.

Their friends alerted PC Archer, who fetched some drags and ran to the scene but by the time he arrived, Ernest and George had sunk without trace. Their bodies were removed from the water more than an hour later, but life was long extinct.

Only five-year-old Charles Ernest Spencer actually saw the boys fall into the river and his evidence at the inquest, held by coroner George F. Harrison, was not clear. However, the jury concluded that 'boys will be boys', arriving at two verdicts of 'accidental death'.

12 **JUNE 1900** Coroner George F. Harrison held an inquest into the death of fifty-three-year-old John Cooper from Derby.

The chief witness was Charles Austin, who said that he was walking between Rothley and Birstall on 10 June when he caught up with Cooper and the two walked on together for some distance.

At around 3 p.m. there was a sudden thunderstorm and Cooper complained that his face had been struck by lightning. Austin could see nothing unusual about Cooper's face but about a mile later, Cooper suddenly collapsed. Unable to rouse him, Austin went for a policeman. PC Gotheridge tried to give Cooper some brandy but he was unable to take it and, although a carriage was sent for, Cooper died on the roadside before it arrived.

Cooper was carrying no money and appeared destitute. However, his wife appeared at the inquest and informed the coroner that her husband had been rather strange in his manner recently, although he had said nothing to anyone about leaving their home in Derby and taking to the road.

The inquest returned a verdict in accordance with the medical evidence, which suggested that Cooper died from heatstroke. Why he was in Leicestershire proved impossible to fathom.

13 **JUNE** **1911** The trial of William Henry Palmer for wilful murder concluded at the Leicestershire Assizes with a controversial guilty verdict.

Palmer was an itinerant fish hawker and, on 24 January 1911, a man matching his description was seen loitering in the village of Walcote, trying doors and generally acting suspiciously. The following morning, concerned neighbours found seventy-two-year-old Ann Harris dead in her cottage. She had been beaten and strangled and her home ransacked.

Among the missing items were a collection of silver 3d coins, a watch and some gold jewellery. The police checked at Lutterworth Station and found that a man resembling Palmer had purchased a ticket to London, paying the fare with 3d coins.

Palmer, who had been turned out of a Lutterworth lodging house on the night of the murder, was eventually arrested at Folkestone on 28 January and, when questioned, denied all knowledge of the murder, claiming to have found a large number of 3d coins tied up in a handkerchief on the side of the road. He admitted to using them to pay his rail fare to London but then stopped off at Rugby, where he visited two pubs and sent a telegram. He then continued to London and onwards to Folkestone.

Although the only evidence against him was the 3d coins, Palmer was charged with wilful murder and committed for trial. On 3 June, a publican in Rugby was cleaning out a lavatory cistern and found some jewellery, glasses, a purse and a watch. They belonged to Ann Harris and, since Palmer had admitted to being in Rugby, the discovery was thought to strengthen the case against him. However, while the prosecution at his trial called a jeweller to testify that the condition of the watch was consistent with it having been immersed in the cistern since January, the defence called a watchmaker, who attested that it could not have been in the water for more than two or three days.

The jury deliberated for an hour before pronouncing Palmer guilty, a verdict the judge claimed was appropriate. Palmer's defence counsel appealed his death sentence and the appeal judges admitted that there was no direct evidence to connect Palmer with the murder but declined to interfere with the original verdict. Palmer was hanged by John Ellis on 19 July and fought all the way to the scaffold, shouting, 'Are you going to let these fellows murder me?'

14 JUNE 1878 Thomas Warner, who was employed by Frederick Hawkes of Leicester, was ordered to clean out the cellar. While he was down there, he found a bottle that appeared to contain brandy and took a large swig.

Unfortunately, it was carbolic acid and sixty-three-year-old Warner's screams of pain echoed through the house as the corrosive liquid burned his mouth, throat and gullet. A doctor was called and he was transported to the Leicester Infirmary, where he died in agony soon after arrival.

An inquest held by coroner Mr Harrison returned a verdict of 'death from misadventure.'

15 JUNE 1868 An inquest was held at Mountsorrel on the death of twenty-year-old mill worker George Webster.

Two days earlier, Webster was at work at Mountsorrel Mill and decided to oil the waterwheel. The wheel was in motion and, as it revolved, a protrusion snagged Webster's smock and dragged him several times around the shaft. By the time the wheel was halted, Webster was so severely injured that he died within twenty-four hours.

Hearing that Webster had been told never to work on the wheel while it was moving, the inquest jury returned a verdict of 'accidental death'.

16 JUNE 1934 While competing in a showjumping class at the Leicestershire County Show, the horse ridden by Roger Toye of Etwall, near Derby, bolted. The spectators lining the ring were nine deep and it seemed inevitable that the out-of-control horse would plough into the crowd causing serious injuries, if not death.

Unable to stop, Toye took a bold decision – he deliberately set the horse to jump over the heads of the crowd. Women and children screamed as the horse soared upward, clearing the people by at least a yard, before landing safely on the other side of the crowd. Three people received minor bruises from the horse's hoofs but the spectators were otherwise unharmed and were full of praise for Toye, who was described as 'magnificent'.

17 **JUNE** **1866** When Mrs Griffin of Sibson walked into her kitchen she was horrified to find her fourteen-year-old son Robert completely unresponsive, his head stuck in the roller towel. Robert's father lifted the boy and found that he was dead.

Robert was known to suffer from dizzy spells and, at the inquest held by coroner John Gregory, it was theorised that, after washing his hands, he suffered a bout of giddiness and fell face first into the towel, either hanging himself or suffocating. The medical evidence supported this theory and the inquest jury returned a verdict of 'accidental suffocation'.

18 **JUNE** **1854** Two men walking to Coventry Fair at 3 a.m., found a dead body near Braunstone. They informed the landlord of The Red Cow Inn, who asked the driver of the mail coach to notify the police.

The deceased – Kirby Muxloe farmer Samuel Adcock – had been shot behind the right ear and his pockets were turned out. The position of the body suggested that it had been moved from the road onto the footpath.

The inquest returned a verdict of 'wilful murder against some person or persons unknown' but the police already had a suspect. George Frederick Ashton had been lodging in the area for several months, giving lectures on phrenology, and showed a keen interest in details of the murder, visiting the site and then leaving the area very suddenly. He was rumoured to have been an admirer of Adcock's sister, Dorothy, and it was said that Samuel believed him an unsuitable suitor.

Braunstone. (Author's collection)

Ashton was arrested in Northampton and brought back to Leicester, where he was released after his claims to have been in Nottingham at the time of the murder were substantiated. However, he was charged with 'unlawfully pretending to tell fortunes by the planets and thereby deceiving and imposing on Her Majesty's liege suspects.' The prosecution expected Miss Adcock to appear as a witness against Ashton but when she was unwilling to do so, they were forced to withdraw the charge. On 6 July, Dorothy Adcock wrote a letter to the local newspaper denying any relationship between herself and Ashton, although she admitted that she had consulted him professionally.

According to Ashton, the police wasted so much time focusing on him that the real murderer escaped justice – be that as it may, the murder remains unsolved.

19 JUNE 1879 At least three people walked past the young woman lying in a ditch at Evington, assuming that she was drunk. It wasn't until two men who had passed by earlier realised that the girl hadn't moved a muscle in the intervening period that she was found to be dead, her throat cut. She had been dead between five and six hours and the irregularity of the wound precluded suicide as the cause of death.

The deceased was Mary Ann Bromwich, whose boyfriend, eighteen-year-old John Biggs, seemed to have disappeared. Handbills were printed with details of the murder and Biggs was arrested when he was seen intently studying one posted at Wigston Station.

'I am the man. I did it,' he told police, claiming that he was intending to commit suicide by putting his head on the railway line. When Biggs was searched, two suicide notes were found in his pocket, one to his mother and the second giving the location of Mary Ann's body and asking to be 'berried' with her.

While imprisoned awaiting his trial for murder, Biggs spent much of his time composing poems to be printed on Mary Ann's funeral card. (His letter to his mother contained one such verse.) The prison chaplain believed that Biggs was delusional and labouring under some kind of mania, as he gave several different explanations for Mary Ann's death and seemed preoccupied with meeting her again in heaven.

At his trial for wilful murder at the Leicestershire Assizes on 18 July, it was revealed that Biggs suffered from epileptic fits and had several close relatives in lunatic asylums, including his mother, father and a maternal uncle. The prosecuting counsel took the unusual step of telling the judge that, if doctors testified in court that Biggs was insane, he would not press the case any further.

Doctors did indeed confirm that they believed that Biggs was insane, but the judge wasn't happy about the prosecution's withdrawal from the case and asked the jury to give a verdict anyway. Unbelievably, they found Biggs guilty, with no reference to his mental state, although they did recommend mercy on account of his youth, leaving the judge no option but to pass sentence of death. The sentence was later repealed and Biggs was sent to Broadmoor Criminal Lunatic Asylum.

Entrance gate to Broadmoor Criminal Lunatic Asylum. (Author's collection)

20   JUNE 1856   Baker Alfred Routen was travelling from Asfordby to Grantham and, on reaching the toll gate at Thorpe Arnold, he called out to the gatekeeper several times but received no reply. Routen opened the door of the gatehouse and was shocked to find Edward Woodcock dead on the floor, his throat cut and a gunshot injury and several stab wounds on his torso. Woodcock's ten-year-old grandson lay close by, his head almost severed from his body.

Nothing had been stolen from the gatehouse but a pistol had apparently been left by the killer(s). Police quickly established that a man had been seen loitering near the gatehouse, asking questions about Woodcock and his routine. They issued a description of the man, who was

> 35 years old, 5ft 9in high and has a peculiar leer or squint with his right eye, the lid of which is let down so as to cause him to have a sidling upward look; his dress consisted of a rather long brown coat, a whitish waistcoat, corduroy trousers and light boots with a black hat.

Bloodhounds were brought in to search the area and a £20 reward was offered for information leading to the apprehension of the culprit(s).

William Brown (aka
Peppermint Billy or
Blinking Billy).

The description matched a man named William Brown, also known as 'Peppermint Billy' and 'Blinking Billy', who had long held a grudge against Woodcock, whom he blamed for having him transported for stealing in 1843. Eventually, Brown was arrested near Wetherby, after a pub landlord recognised him from a description in a newspaper.

Tried at the Leicestershire Assizes on 11 July, Brown was found guilty of wilful murder and hanged before an estimated crowd of 25,000 at Leicester Prison. It was the last public execution to be held there.

21 JUNE 1900 Thomas Ryan appeared at the Leicester Borough Police Court charged with assaulting a fellow Irishman, Alfred Freere. Ryan admitted fighting Freere but vehemently denied having assaulted him.

Freere told the magistrates that, on 16 June, he was sitting quietly on his own doorstep when Ryan walked up and struck him on the head, before taking a running kick at Freere's ribs. Freere asked Ryan why he was attacking him, at which Ryan hit him on the head with a glass bottle.

PC Wallis stated that, at about 11.30 p.m. on the night in question, he found Freere unconscious in the street, bleeding heavily from a

Sackville Street, Dublin. (Author's collection)

head wound. Ryan was nearby and told the policeman that he had done it and would have done the same to anyone who had done what Freere did.

Ryan's explanation of the incident was that an argument between the two men over whether Sackville Street was the best street in Dublin got out of hand. Ryan insisted that Freere attacked him first and said that, for several hours after being released from hospital after treatment for his head injury, Freere continued to demand that he come out of his house and fight.

Magistrates remarked on Ryan's long string of previous convictions for various offences, dating back to 1875.

'I haven't been convicted for assault before,' Ryan protested, although before sentencing him to two months' imprisonment with hard labour, the magistrates reminded him that he once served thirty-two days in prison for assaulting a policeman.

22   JUNE   1889   It was a very hot day and the sight of a number of people bathing at Coleorton Reservoir proved tempting to colliers Sykes Pickering and Fred Curtis, even though neither could swim.

The two men walked to the other side of the reservoir and undressed. Curtis was first to get into the water, wading in up to his neck. Pickering became worried and called to him to come out but Curtis had found a piece of wood in the water. Holding it with his hands, he pretended to swim, not realising that he was drifting out of his depth. When he tried to stand up again and couldn't, Curtis panicked. Pickering bravely went into the water to try and save him but soon got into difficulties himself and had to be rescued by a passer-by.

By the time Curtis was pulled from the water he was dead and, at an inquest on 25 June, coroner Henry Deane recorded that he had accidentally drowned.

23   JUNE   1900   Coroner George Bouskell held an inquest at Huncote on the death of fifty-seven-year-old carpenter William Wilson.

On 23 May, Wilson was sent to repair a chute at the Enderby Granite Quarries. In order to do the job, he had to stand on a plank about 3 feet from the ground, one end of which rested on a heap of gravel and the other on an upright supporting the chute. Wilson fell from the plank and landed on the gravel, sliding down it head first and colliding with a pile of timber.

He sustained a cut on his forehead and slight concussion but what nobody realised was that he had also fractured his skull and a tiny splinter of bone had penetrated a blood vessel, allowing blood to seep very slowly into his brain. Initially, Wilson was expected to recover but his condition gradually worsened until he died early on 23 June.

Nobody witnessed Wilson's fall but he did not suffer from dizziness or fits and the plank was sturdy and wide and was not wet or slippery. Coroner Bouskell told the jury that, in his opinion, nobody was to blame in the matter and they agreed, returning a verdict of 'accidental death'.

24 JUNE 1898 Coroner Robert Harvey held an inquest at the Municipal Buildings into the death of an unnamed male child, who was born on 21 May and died on 17 June. The baby was premature but his death was remarkable since his mother, Mary Ann Carter, was exhibiting all of the symptoms of lead poisoning.

A post-mortem examination was conducted on the baby, whose organs tested negative for the presence of lead or any other poison. However, although the baby had only one symptom of possible poisoning – a muscular paralysis known as 'drop-wrist' – doctors gave the cause of death as marasmus, a form of malnutrition deriving from lead poisoning.

The baby's mother was unmarried and had purchased some pills from Sarah Hands, in order to bring about a miscarriage. Both Mary Ann Carter and another woman, Rose Burgess, had been seriously ill and, when Mrs Hands was visited by the police, 320 tablets were found at her home. Mrs Hands gave the police four tablets, telling them, 'These are the kind she [Carter] has been taking,' and, on analysis, one of the pills proved to be a diachylon tablet, frequently used by women who wanted to 'bring on a period'.

Mrs Hands was arrested and appeared at the Leicestershire Assizes in October 1898, charged with wilfully supplying certain pills to Mary Ann Carter with intent

Municipal Buildings, Leicester, where the inquest was held. (Author's collection)

to procure miscarriage, with a second identical charge in respect of Rose Burgess. However, the prosecution's entire case depended on the analysis of one tablet and Mrs Hands claimed to have no knowledge of how it came to be in her possession, although she admitted to running a legitimate business, selling harmless 'female pills'.

Whereas there was little doubt that Mary Ann Carter and her baby were suffering from the effects of ingesting lead, there was some doubt as to whether Mrs Hands supplied that lead and the jury gave her the benefit of that doubt and acquitted her.

It was decided to hold the indictment concerning Rose Burgess over to the next Quarter Sessions in January 1899, where, once again, Sarah Hands was given the benefit of the doubt and discharged from court.

25 JUNE 1918 As the Loughborough to Quorn bus neared its destination, people noticed it zigzagging wildly down a hill, before running off the side of the road into a tree. There were only two passengers on the bus at the time, who escaped with minor cuts and bruises and were able to walk home. However, the driver collided with the steering wheel, causing serious internal injuries, and died in hospital three days later from peritonitis.

Coroner Henry Deane held an inquest into the death of driver Thomas Sparks, at which it was noted the steering gear had failed, probably due to the bolts breaking or shearing off. The manager of the Loughborough Road Car Company assured the coroner that the bus was in good condition when it left the depot on the morning of the accident, blaming the appalling condition of the roads, which had numerous potholes.

Quorn War Memorial and Little Green. (Author's collection)

One of the inquest jury was able to confirm this, having been thrown from his bicycle by a pothole on the night of the accident, and the jury returned a verdict of accidental death. They added that they were satisfied that the bus was in good working order and exonerated the company from blame, attributing the cause of the accident to the state of the roads.

26 JUNE 1895 Coroner Henry Deane held an inquest in Sileby into the death of labourer Thomas Draycott, who was killed by a fall of clay while working at Messrs Wright and Co. Brickyard.

Fifty-two-year-old Draycott and John Newby were sent to fetch clay on 24 June and were 'holing under' – undermining the clay preparatory to its removal, leaving two columns or 'legs' intact at each side to support the overhang. Draycott called to Newby to say that he had finished, and waited for his colleague to get clear before knocking away the supporting leg of clay on his side. However, having done so, Draycott then unaccountably picked up his tools and walked down the incline in front of the area where he had just been working. Newby shouted, 'Look out, Tom!' but a small piece of clay bowled Draycott off his feet, before the bulk of the falling clay landed on him, causing multiple fractures and internal injuries, from which he died within a couple of minutes.

The foreman testified at the inquest that he had examined the clay before it was undermined and noticed no cracks. He was supervising the two labourers but had no time to caution Draycott for walking in the wrong direction and could only suggest that Draycott automatically and unthinkingly took the quickest route to the clay tubs, where he was heading. The inquest found a verdict of 'accidental death'.

27 JUNE 1899 On 25 June, fourteen-year-old Samuel White Clarke and his friends bumped into sixteen-year-old Albert Edward Stretton and his friends in Leicester. There was a bit of banter between the groups, which was not unfriendly until Stretton spat on Clarke's new coat and hat.

Clarke was furious and complained that his mother would give him a hiding for getting his clothes into such a state. Suddenly, without warning, he pulled off his coat and attacked Stretton. The boys scrapped for a couple of minutes before Clarke kneed Stretton in the stomach and winded him. Stretton said that he didn't want to fight any more but Clarke insisted that they fought again properly the next day.

On 26 June, the boys fought again briefly before Clarke claimed to have a headache and withdrew, saying that he would settle Stretton once and for all tomorrow. Clarke still had a headache the following day and didn't really want to fight. His friends urged him not to but he was afraid of appearing weak and the two boys wrestled for three rounds, at the end of which Stretton walked away. Clarke lay on the ground, unable to get up and when his friends went to help him, he began vomiting and had a fit.

After waiting for an hour for Clarke to recover, his friends carried him to a doctor's surgery, where he died. A post-mortem examination showed multiple cuts and bruises, consistent with recent fighting. There were some ruptures in the blood vessels in Clarke's brain but, according to the surgeon, the cause of death was a violent blow to the stomach, which arrested the heart's action.

An inquest held by coroner Robert Harvey found a verdict of wilful murder against Stretton, although the jury didn't believe that he had any intention of killing Clarke and, when Stretton was brought before magistrates, they committed him to the next assizes for manslaughter.

Everyone who witnessed the three fights affirmed that all were instigated by Clarke, who was a head taller than Stretton and much stronger. All the witnesses agreed that, on the last occasion, Stretton didn't even hit Clarke but simply ducked his head to avoid Clarke's blows and accidentally butted him in the stomach. Thus, when Stretton appeared at the Leicestershire Assizes, the Grand Jury found 'no bill' for either murder or manslaughter and he was discharged.

28 JUNE 1872 In Lutterworth, Mrs Hurley was preparing breakfast. Her children were sitting at the table waiting for their father to return from work when Mrs Hurley was momentarily distracted by her mother-in-law, who was going off for the day on a bus trip.

High Street, Lutterworth. (Author's collection)

As the two Mrs Hurleys talked, four-year-old Horace Coaton Hurley suddenly made a choking noise, pointing at the coffee pot and saying, 'Kettle'. To his mother's horror, she realised that Horace had drunk scalding hot coffee from the spout of the coffee pot. When Thomas Hurley arrived home minutes later, his son was wailing in pain. Thomas inspected Horace's mouth, noticing that his lips looked burned. He gave him some castor oil and moistened the child's lips with water but by eleven o'clock Horace was struggling to breathe, so his concerned parents sent for a doctor.

When the doctor arrived, he found Horace's mouth and throat badly blistered. He performed an emergency tracheotomy, which seemed to help the child's breathing but then Horace began to cough and shortly after four o'clock, he died. An inquest later recorded a verdict of 'accidental death'.

29 JUNE 1898 Elizabeth Hallam appeared at the Loughborough Petty Sessions charged with cruelly neglecting her four children, twins William and Elizabeth (13), Ernest (8) and Mary Ann (7).

Elizabeth's husband John worked as a needle maker in Kegworth. He sent his wife fifteen shillings every week, in addition to the six shillings she received weekly from an older child's wages, but Elizabeth spent all that and more on drink. Her children were so filthy and verminous that their teachers were forced to separate them from other pupils. Their hair was matted and they were dressed in shabby, ill-fitting clothing, with no underwear.

When an Inspector from the NSPCC visited the Hallams' home, he found a rabbit hutch containing two rabbits sitting on a heap of rotting cabbage in the living room. The only food in the house was a piece of margarine and three rotten herrings. John Hallam told magistrates that he had done his best for his children, buying new boots when he came home and found them without shoes, but his wife had pawned the boots to get money for drink.

The magistrates came to the conclusion that Elizabeth Hallam was a confirmed drunkard and was perhaps more to be pitied than blamed, since drunkenness was a disease. They believed that the kindest thing to do was to separate her from drink for a while, in the hope that it might break the habit – she would have to remain sober for at least three months, as that was the length of the prison sentence they were awarding.

30 JUNE 1897 Twenty-seven-year-old Herbert Wheatley was tried at the Leicestershire Assizes for a criminal assault on nine-year-old Agnes Holland.

As Agnes returned home to Stoney Stanton on 22 April, after walking to Croft to fetch milk, she met Wheatley, who pounced on her and sexually assaulted her.

Agnes arrived home in hysterics and, when her mother found out what had happened, she summoned her husband home from work, contacted the police and took her daughter to a doctor, who confirmed that an assault had taken place. Agnes's father then walked her back to Croft to see if she could spot the man who hurt her and she identified Wheatley as the culprit. Wheatley was taken to the police station at Stoney Stanton, where he denied ever having seen Agnes before, until her father brought her to the workmen's hut at the quarry where he was working.

In the course of their investigations, the police interviewed several people who had seen Wheatley on the lane where Agnes was assaulted and several who had seen Agnes walking in the opposite direction. However, the lane was the route to work for most of the quarrymen and nobody had seen Wheatley and Agnes together.

At Wheatley's trial, he swore, as he had from the outset, that he had never seen Agnes before her father brought her to the hut and that he was 'as innocent as a babe'. The jury didn't believe him and, having been found guilty, he was sentenced to three years' penal servitude. He left the court still trying to protest his innocence.

JULY

Hill Street, Ashby-de-la-Zouch. (Author's collection)

1   JULY 1896   Three-year-old Thomas Sansome was playing in the recreation ground opposite his home in Hinckley and at 7 p.m. was carried home by a man, who told his mother that he had been kicked in the face by a horse. A doctor was summoned immediately but Thomas died the following evening from 'inflammation of the brain'.

At an inquest held by coroner George Bouskell, the jury was told that the land belonged to Hinckley Urban District Council and that horses were grazed there to keep the grass down. According to surveyor William Thomas Howse, they were quiet animals and were rarely turned out before 7.30 p.m. However, numerous people living within sight of the park stated that the horses were often chased by the children, who sometimes threw stones at them. Others stated that the horses sometimes galloped about wildly and one member of the jury had personally escorted children across the park, as one of the horses would charge and kick at the children.

Two people witnessed Thomas being kicked and one stated that the child threw something at the horse, sending it trotting away then following behind it. The other witness only saw Thomas running behind the horse, which suddenly lashed out.

The inquest jury returned a verdict of 'accidental death' and, although surveyor Howse insisted that the horses posed no danger to playing children, the jury urged the council to reconsider allowing them to roam on a public recreation ground.

2   JULY 1883   John Rowbottom appeared at the Leicestershire Quarter Sessions charged with unlawfully and maliciously wounding his wife, Ann.

Rowbottom had served a prison sentence for assaulting Ann and on 25 June, two days after his release, he sought her out at her job as a washerwoman at Ashby-de-la-Zouch and asked her to shake hands with him and be friends.

Ann repulsed him several times and threatened to call the police if he didn't leave her alone, but Rowbottom stepped forward as if he were going to hit her. Ann instinctively put her hands up to protect her face but her husband had a knife and her hands were stabbed several times. One thrust of the knife went straight through her hand into her face, although luckily none of her wounds were life-threatening.

Two men witnessed the attack and when Rowbottom was later arrested, a bloody knife was found in his pocket. 'That is the knife I did it with,' he told the police.

At his appearance at the Quarter Sessions, fifty-year-old Rowbottom pleaded guilty to common assault but made an impassioned plea, blaming his wife for making him perpetrate the offence against her. He claimed to have twice caught her in the act of committing adultery, which caused him to stab her in a fit of jealousy. The jury found him guilty as charged and he was sentenced to nine months' imprisonment with hard labour.

3 **JULY 1893** John Francis Kettle appeared before Mr Justice Vaughan Williams at the Leicester Assizes on 3 July, charged with attempted murder.

Only six weeks after their marriage in April 1893, Kettle assaulted his wife, who promptly left him and went back into service. On 11 June, Kettle happened to meet her and asked her to come back to him, which she refused to do. Later that night, she went for a walk with a friend and, returning to her employer's home in Leicester, found her estranged husband waiting on the doorstep.

Kettle slashed at his wife's throat but she was wearing a high-necked dress and escaped with two large gashes on her lower jaw. Her screams brought people rushing to her assistance and as they pulled Kettle away from his wife, he told them he wished that he had 'finished her'. He was said to be a quiet, steady man, who loved his wife and had been driven to drink by her refusal to live with him.

At his trial, the jury found Kettle guilty of the lesser offence of wounding with intent to do grievous bodily harm. To everyone's surprise, Kettle's wife interceded on his behalf, asking for him to be treated mercifully, and the judge sentenced him to nine months' imprisonment with hard labour, telling Kettle that but for his wife, his sentence would have been much longer.

4 **JULY 1872** Coroner John Gregory held an inquest into the death of labourer John Merriman, who drowned in the River Soar at Loughborough.

He and three other men were mowing a field on 2 July and got very hot. When Merriman suggested a swim in the river to cool down, his colleagues warned him against it, saying that he was foolish to swim when he was overheated. Merriman took no notice and said he was going to swim whether his friends did or not. He undressed and got into the water at about 4 p.m., while the other men returned to mowing. Three hours later, they noticed that Merriman's clothes were still on the bank where he had left them and alerted the police, who dragged the river and retrieved his body.

In returning a verdict of 'accidental death', the inquest jury asked the coroner to reprimand Merriman's three workmates for not raising the alarm earlier.

5 **JULY 1919** Annie 'Bella' Wright went to post some letters and go for a bicycle ride. She ended up at her uncle's house at Gaulby and, after chatting for half an hour, decided to head home.

A man was hanging around outside Bella's uncle's house, as if waiting for her, and he and twenty-one-year-old Bella walked off together, pushing their cycles. Thirty minutes later, Bella was found dead on the road at Little Stretton, her bicycle nearby. Her body was moved to a small chapel, where a cursory examination by candlelight suggested that she had fallen off her bicycle. It wasn't until the following morning that the true cause of death was established – Bella had been shot in the face.

In spite of thorough investigations by the police, there was no breakthrough in the case until 23 February 1920, when a bargeman dragged a green bicycle out of the River Soar. Knowing that Bella's companion on the night of her death had a green bicycle, which numerous appeals in the press had failed to locate, the bargee contacted the police. The serial number had been filed off but the police found a second number on the forks, through which they traced the bicycle to Ronald Light, a former Army officer, who was now teaching maths at Dean Close School, Cheltenham.

Light was arrested on 4 March but insisted he knew nothing about Bella's murder. However, on 19 March, a pistol holster and bullets matching the one that killed Bella were dredged from the river, close to where the bicycle was found.

Ronald Light.

Dean Close College and chapel, Cheltenham. (Author's collection)

Charged with wilful murder, Light was tried at the assizes, where he calmly admitted being the person with Bella on the night of her death, saying that he had left her alive and well. He admitted that the bicycle, holster and bullets belonged to him, saying that he disposed of them so that his mother would not be worried.

His defence counsel, Sir Marshall Hall, pointed out that Light had no motive for murder and suggested that a shot at close range would have caused more damage to Bella's face. Hall advanced the theory that Bella was shot accidentally, by someone using a gun at a distance.

Light's calm demeanour in the dock helped to convince the jury that he was not guilty and he was acquitted. The case remains unsolved, with opinions divided on Light's guilt or innocence.

6 JULY 1892 Gertrude Alice Winter, who was almost fourteen years old, worked as a servant for the Hargreaves (or Hargrave) family in Pinwall. She was a pretty girl, who looked considerably older than her years and who actually believed herself to be a year older than she was.

Gertrude attracted the attention of Albert Ernest, the son of the household, and the two began a consensual sexual relationship. Gertrude made no complaint to anybody about Albert's actions, until she happened to mention to her mother that she felt unwell. Mrs Winter questioned her and, on hearing what had been going on, she had Albert charged with criminal assault.

Albert was tried at the Leicestershire Assizes on 21 November 1892. He maintained that Gertrude was always pursuing him and, since the charge against him made no mention of rape, it was widely accepted that Gertrude had given her consent to the activities, even though she now insisted that Albert had threatened to kill her if she told anybody.

After deliberating the case for ninety minutes, the jury found Albert guilty as charged but recommended mercy, on account of his youth, his previous unblemished character, the fact that Gertrude looked at least sixteen years old and temptation to which she allegedly exposed Albert.

In considering his sentence, the judge remarked that female servants should be able to rely on the men of the household for protection and that Albert had rendered himself liable to two years' imprisonment by his actions. Several spectators wrongly understood this to be the sentence and Albert promptly fainted. He was quickly revived to hear that he had actually been sentenced to two months' imprisonment, with hard labour.

7   JULY 1898   Coroner George Bouskell held an inquest into the death of twenty-three-year-old labourer John Pearson.

On 4 July, Harry Copson was sent with a horse and 'wagonette' to collect a party of people from Thornton Wakes and bring them back to Ratby. The wagonette normally carried ten or eleven people but when Copson arrived at Thornton, he found seven men, three women, four children and five dogs waiting.

Copson refused to allow two of the men on board but the person who had hired the wagonette insisted that all should ride and Copson eventually backed down, allowing one woman and two men to sit on the box seat with him, while the others travelled inside.

After about a mile, as the wagonette travelled downhill, the horse suddenly broke into a gallop. As Copson struggled to stop, passenger John Sutton snatched one of the reins from him and tugged it. The horse turned sharply to the left and the wagonette overturned, spilling its passengers onto the road. Seven were knocked unconscious and Pearson died the next day from 'compression of the brain.'

At the inquest, Sutton denied snatching the rein, saying that he jumped off long before the vehicle overturned. However, he had already told several people that he had grabbed the rein and, when pressed by the coroner, changed his mind several times before finally conceding that he may have caught the rein with his foot as he jumped. Copson was absolutely adamant that Sutton did not jump until the wagonette was actually overturning, having caused the horse to swerve by pulling the rein. Copson believed that the overloaded vehicle had 'over run' the horse as it travelled down the steep hill and was confident that he would have regained control if Sutton hadn't interfered.

The inquest jury eventually returned a verdict of 'accidental death', asking the coroner to severely admonish Sutton for the manner in which he gave his evidence.

8   JULY 1884   Labourer Thomas Grant appeared at the Leicestershire Assizes, charged with 'carnally knowing and abusing Harriet Grant aged ten years and seven months at Leicester on 18 June last.'

Harriet stated that her thirty-six-year-old father had used her sexually ever since the death of her mother four months earlier and surgeon Mr G.C. Franklin confirmed that she had been 'outraged'.

At his trial, Grant maintained an air of complete indifference, saying that if he had done it, he didn't remember, and refusing to cross-examine the witnesses or to address the jury in his own defence. When the jury found him guilty, Grant was immediately charged with a similar offence relating to another daughter, twelve-year-old Sarah Ann, but the prosecution declined to offer any evidence and the judge directed the jury to acquit him on that charge, before sentencing Grant to fifteen years' penal servitude for the offence against Harriet. He served his time at Parkhurst Prison on the Isle of Wight.

9 JULY 1872 Eighty-year-old James Wright appeared before Mr Justice Byles at the Leicestershire Assizes, charged with wilful murder.

On 12 May, Wright sat down to breakfast with his son-in-law Francis 'Frank' Welbourn (or Welbourne) at Plungar. Frank's wife and son were adamant that the two men seemed on good terms, yet immediately after they finished eating, Wright went into the parlour and returned with a gun, deliberately shooting Frank as he stood in the doorway.

The top of Frank's head was blown off and he died instantly. Wright then put the gun away and calmly sat down in an armchair, waiting for the police to arrive. As he was taken to the police station, Wright explained that he shot Frank because of his drinking habits, after his son-in-law came home intoxicated in the early hours of the morning and disturbed his sleep. 'I have broken the law. You have nothing to do but hang me,' Wright insisted phlegmatically, as coroner Mr E.H.M. Clarke committed him for trial for wilful murder.

At his trial, Wright could not be dissuaded from pleading guilty, leaving Mr Justice Byles no alternative other than to pronounce the mandatory death sentence. 'It is the sentence of the law of the land, not the judge,' stated Byles emotionally. Wright's defence counsel intimated that he would 'take steps in the matter' and the prosecution counsel announced that his team would gladly assist.

Because of his age, Wright was reprieved and his sentence commuted to one of life imprisonment. He is believed to have died in Pentonville Prison in 1874.

10 JULY 1890 Thirty-three-year-old Richard Nicklinson appeared before Mr Justice Hawkins at the Leicestershire Assizes charged with the murder of his brother-in-law, Samuel Haywood.

Nicklinson was an ill-tempered, morose man but, as he was married to his sister, Haywood felt obliged to give him a job in his tile manufacturing works at Moira. Nicklinson took advantage of his relationship with the boss and was frequently reprimanded for lateness, sloppy work, and for neglecting his work because of drinking. On 24 March, a reprimand deteriorated into fisticuffs, with Nicklinson getting the worst of the fight. Haywood then went towards the kilns with Nicklinson following and, moments later, there were cries of 'Murder!' Haywood was stabbed seven times, six of the wounds being in his back, and he died from loss of blood. In the ensuing chaos, Nicklinson walked off but was quickly apprehended and charged with wilful murder.

At his trial, Nicklinson's defence was that, although he started the fight, Haywood retaliated by striking him with a shovel he was holding in his hand at the time. The alleged provocation of a blow from a shovel, along with the fact that the killing was done in hot blood, without prior intent or malice aforethought, persuaded the jury to find Nicklinson guilty of the lesser offence of manslaughter and he was sentenced to twenty years' imprisonment.

11 JULY 1864 John Upton was tried at the Leicestershire Assizes for the wilful murder of his son, William, on or around 26 January.

William was described as 'not quite right' and 'of weak intellect' and was unable to get a job, leaving him dependent on his father and stepmother for his upkeep, which Mr and Mrs Upton resented bitterly.

Eventually, Leicester chemist Mr Edwards took pity on William and offered him employment. However, some goods went missing from the chemist's shop on High Street and it was noted that William suddenly seemed to have extra spending money. When Edwards spoke to William on 26 January about his unprecedented wealth, the boy gave a convoluted explanation about where the money came from, claiming it was given to him by a strange woman from Nottingham.

Edwards told William that the story would have to be investigated, at which the boy flushed bright red and ran out of the shop, leaving behind his coat and cap. Meanwhile, John Upton heard that his son was suspected of stealing and came to try

High Street, Leicester, 1923. (Author's collection)

and persuade Edwards to charge the boy with theft, claiming that William had always been a great trouble to him. Edwards found his attitude disgusting and refused to be pressured, so Upton left, returning a couple of hours later with some of William's things and asking Edwards if they had been stolen from him.

When William's body was pulled from a canal nearly three weeks later, a post-mortem examination showed that he had been beaten to death with a blunt instrument. There were four wounds on his head and, as well as a fractured skull, through which a portion of his brain protruded, William had ten broken ribs and a chipped pubic bone.

More than one person claimed to have seen John Upton, with a woman, carrying a heavy bundle to the canal on 26 January, but at his trial, the evidence they gave in court was confused. One witness didn't come forward until after the inquest and another gave such contradictory testimony that the judge called her as a 'disreputable old woman' and eventually went on to dismiss the case against Upton altogether due to a lack of evidence.

William's murder went unsolved, although many people remained convinced of his father's guilt.

12 JULY 1896 Coroner Robert Harvey held an inquest into the death of fifteen-month-old Kate Pick.

Kate's half-sister, Clara, asked if she might take her to her grandmother's house in her pram. On the return journey, Clara saw a horse and dray coming towards her and, as the horse passed, something on the dray caught the pram and it tipped over, spilling Kate onto the pavement. Her head hit the kerb and although a doctor was called, he could do nothing to save Kate, who had several skull fractures. The nature of her injuries suggested that her head was crushed between the dray wheel and the kerbstone.

At the inquest, drayman John Ballard stated that he was leading the horse, which was walking at a sedate pace. As he passed the children, he heard a scream and, looking back, saw Kate lying in the gutter. The jury were told that the pavement where the accident occurred was very rough and the pram was 'rickety'. They decided that the tragedy was a pure accident, attaching no blame to anybody for Kate's death.

13 JULY 1841 A sheep belonging to farmer William Jordan of Kibworth Beauchamp was grazing in a field near the Harborough turnpike road when it was mutilated. At some time during the night of 13/14 July one of the animal's legs was carefully

Kibworth Beauchamp. (Author's collection)

amputated and the skin removed and left lying by the side of the injured animal, which was still alive when found by the shepherd the following morning.

People in the neighbourhood were so incensed by the barbarity of the unknown butcher that they opened a collection for the purpose of offering a reward on conviction of the offender(s).

14   JULY **1896**   Coroner Robert Harvey held an inquest at the Leicester Infirmary into the death of four-year-old Violet Muriel 'Madge' Ramsden, who was killed while attending a Sunday school treat on 11 July.

Almost 500 children were assembled in a large field on Mowacre Hill, where games and sideshows had been arranged. By the evening, the children had tired themselves out and most were sitting on the grass listening to the brass band.

Thomas (or James) Pole was picking up empty tea urns and left his horse and cart in the charge of his seventeen-year-old son, James. The horse was grazing quietly but, as it moved forwards, it accidentally stepped on a trailing rein, throwing its head up and breaking the throat lash of the bridle, which came off. James managed to grab the horse by the nostrils but was unable to hang on to it and it bolted, dragging the cart behind it.

The band scattered as the horse dashed into a group of screaming children, among which were Madge and her sister Gertrude. Both girls were knocked flying and Madge suffered a fractured skull, dying that evening in hospital. (Several children were injured in the accident, including Gertrude, but apart from Madge, all are believed to have survived.)

The coroner told the inquest that they must establish whether or not there was any criminal negligence, either by the organisers of the treat or by Pole, or his son. The horse was considered to be a very quiet animal and some witnesses stated that it was hit by a cricket ball before bolting, so the jury eventually ruled that Madge's death was accidental.

15 JULY 1880 Much of Leicestershire experienced hours of torrential rain, leading to devastating floods throughout the county. Several houses in Syston, Langton, Kegworth, Melton Mowbray and Leicester were inundated and people were forced to take refuge upstairs. Crops, railway lines and bridges were washed away and a tramcar was swept off its rails and almost carried away in Belgrave, while a viaduct in Thurmaston was completely destroyed.

At Ratcliffe Weir, the River Soar was 7 feet higher than normal, at the highest level recorded since 1817, and in Market Harborough alone, the floods caused an estimated £15,000 worth of damage.

There were several fatalities, among them a boy who fell into a swollen stream at Loughborough and was carried off by the current and a labourer at Hoby, who tried to cross a flooded field on a pony. At Melton Mowbray, Midland Railway employee Joseph White was warned not to walk home but disregarded the warnings. He was swept into a deep hole and drowned.

16 JULY 1895 A sudden thunderstorm hit Leicester Forest West, sending those working outdoors scurrying for cover. Sixty-five-year-old farmer, Michael Barrs, took shelter under a tree, while his son and a young labourer scrambled under a hedge at the other end of the field.

When the storm passed, Barrs was found sitting beneath the tree, quite dead. There was a distinct smell of charred flesh and the farmer's beard was badly singed. When he was later examined by a doctor, there were scorch marks on his chest, face, neck and clothing and his death was attributed to shock, resulting from being struck by lightning. An inquest held by coroner Mr Bouskell recorded a verdict in accordance with the medical evidence.

17 JULY 1921 At Aylestone, more than a hundred people took advantage of the hot weather to bathe at the open-air baths.

When bathing finished for the day, the attendants found a man's clothes in the changing area, which went unclaimed as night fell. Eventually, the police were contacted and, when the pool was dragged, the body of twenty-four-year-old Edwin Hewitt was recovered from the bottom.

Aylestone, 1956. (Author's collection)

Remarkably, Edwin had drowned in the busy swimming pool amongst a crowd of people without anybody noticing his plight or even realising that anything was wrong. An inquest later returned a verdict of 'accidental death'.

18 JULY 1893 A livestock auction was taking place in Leicester cattle market when a bullock suddenly went berserk, escaping from the selling pen and plunging into the crowd.

Butcher Edward Riley was talking and had his back towards the rampaging bullock when it hit him, tossing him several feet into the air. He landed very heavily on his back, his head hitting the ground with a terrible thud. He immediately began bleeding from his ears and although a policeman rendered first aid, Riley was found to have a fracture at the base of his skull and died that afternoon in the Infirmary.

An inquest returned a verdict of 'accidental death' and the bullock was slaughtered.

19 JULY 1896 Thirty-three-year-old David Adcock died at his home in Syston from the effects of a paraffin lamp explosion two weeks earlier.

On 5 July, Adcock went out with his wife and children. When the family got home, the children were put to bed and their parents followed shortly afterwards, Mr Adcock walking upstairs first, then his wife, who was carrying a lighted paraffin lamp. Unfortunately, Adcock slipped on the stairs and fell onto his wife, knocking her down. The lamp smashed and his clothing caught fire. Adcock ran out into the yard, where he met a neighbour and asked her to throw her jacket over him. She was too frightened to do anything, so Adcock stood under the communal pump, where another neighbour pumped water on him until the flames were extinguished.

Two doctors treated Adcock, who was very badly burned. At first, he seemed to be recovering but, on 16 July, he began to suffer from diarrhoea and died three days later. An inquest held by coroner Henry Deane on 20 July returned a verdict of 'accidental death'.

20 JULY 1877 Edward Web Handcock and William Fletcher supplemented their income as railway labourers by poaching and at 9 p.m., were walking the lanes around Plungar in search of game.

They were spotted by Matthew Grass, gamekeeper to the Duke of Rutland, who suspected that they were up to no good. Grass hid for a while until he caught sight of the gun that Handcock was carrying, at which point the gamekeeper challenged him. When Handcock ran away, Grass set his dog on him. The dog cornered him by a gate and, as Grass caught up with it, he saw Handcock point the gun at the dog and pull the trigger, although luckily, it failed to fire. Grass told him to surrender his weapon but he refused to do so and meanwhile the dog continued to nip at Handcock, who finally took a swipe at it with the gun. It broke in two and, when Handcock tried to aim a second blow at the worrisome dog with the butt, the gun went off, shooting Handcock in the chest.

Handcock was taken to The Anchor Inn, Plungar, where a doctor pronounced life extinct. An inquest held by coroner Mr F.J. Oldham the next day returned a verdict of 'accidental death'.

21 JULY 1852 John Stone (or Stones) and Stephen Hunt appeared at the Leicestershire Assizes charged with a brutal rape in Abbey Meadow, Leicester.

The prosecutrix, nineteen-year-old Ann Curtis, showed the court her skirt, which still bore men's footprints. She explained that, on 12 July, she was feeling unwell and was making her way home with her sweetheart, John Bent, when a gang of men suddenly attacked them, knocking Bent unconscious. She offered them 6d to stop but they called her a 'silly bitch' and told her to put it back in her pocket. They later took the money before fleeing, after committing a prolonged sexual assault on Ann lasting more than an hour.

Bent recalled very little of the night's events, other than regaining consciousness and finding his girlfriend being raped.

Of the men, only Stone and Hunt were apprehended, blaming the rape on a man named William Clough. Hunt claimed to have been just passing by and Stone said he knew nothing of any assault.

At the trial, four men said that they walked home with Stone and Hunt but insisted that they parted company before the offence took place, although one admitted that Hunt ran after him and told him 'some of the chaps' were asking a young woman for her money.

The judge expressed surprise that only Stone and Hunt were in the dock, considering that the four so-called witnesses had done nothing to help Ann. Their reprehensible conduct was not that of honest, right-feeling men, said the judge, adding that, if it was proved that they were present at the time of the offence, they too could have been convicted. When the jury found the two defendants guilty, the judge expressed disappointment that he could no longer order them to be executed. However, he told them that he intended to pass the next best sentence, ordering twenty-year-old Stone and eighteen-year-old Hunt to be transported for the rest of their natural lives. Both men collapsed on hearing the sentence.

22 JULY 1898 Eighteen-year-old servant Harriet Storer finished cleaning the fireplace at her employer's home on Market Street, Ashby-de-la-Zouch, at 6 a.m. She lit the fire but it didn't take, so, in a hurry to start breakfast, she threw some benzoline onto it.

The fire immediately exploded, setting Harriet's clothes alight. She ran out into the street towards The George Inn, where workmen threw buckets of water at her to try and extinguish the flames. However, Harriet's underclothing continued to burn until plumber Fred Smith wrapped her in sacks. She was taken to Ashby Cottage Hospital, having first told Smith to go and see about the kitchen, which was well alight. Smith put out the fire, before going upstairs to wake Harriet's employer Mr Hutchins, who slept through the entire incident.

Harriet died in hospital from the effects of burns on her legs, back and arms, and an inquest later returned a verdict of 'accidental death'.

23 JULY 1895 Forty-three-year-old Major Richard Louis Milne resigned from the Army, after a long and distinguished career. It was suggested that his resignation, following allegations that he had committed a series of 'unnatural offences' with drummer boy Verdi Attfield, was deliberately timed to avoid an embarrassing court-martial.

Even so, Milne was charged by the civil authorities with gross indecency, committed at Glen Parva between 6 and 20 December 1894 and between 21 January and 4 June 1895. His alleged offences came to light when Attfield, who was then seventeen, was sentenced to three months' imprisonment with hard labour at the Leicestershire Assizes in July 1895, for committing an act of gross indecency with another soldier in Milne's quarters, while Milne was away on leave.

Milne appeared at the Leicestershire Assizes in November 1895, where Attfield claimed that, after questioning him about whether or not he liked girls, Milne engaged him as his private servant. A series of homosexual acts took place between the two men over a period of approximately seven months and, after each one, Milne allegedly gave Attfield a florin or half-a-crown, or presented him with a gift, such as tickets for the Opera House, warning him to say nothing about what had just occurred between them.

Although no 'overt act' had ever been witnessed, Attfield was often in the Major's quarters, during which time the window blinds were invariably drawn closed, although it would have been impossible for anyone outside to see into the room. Other officers tactfully mentioned that Milne seemed 'partial' to Attfield and that he seemed to give the boy preferential treatment, while some of Attfield's contemporaries testified to having seen coins and gifts, supposedly given to him by the Major.

Glen Parva Barracks, 1914. (Author's collection)

After a brief discussion, the jury at Milne's trial decided that they were not satisfied with the evidence and that the prosecution had not proved the case against him. They found Milne 'not guilty' and he was discharged from court.

24 JULY 1899 Hawker James Duggan (or Dugan) quarrelled with his wife at their home in Ashby-de-la-Zouch and gave her a thorough beating. Mrs Duggan was pregnant and immediately complained of excruciating pain. Later, lodger Louisa Poyser was woken by the resumption of the argument and, when she went downstairs to complain about the noise, she found Mrs Duggan on the floor, her husband standing over her. Mrs Duggan clambered to her feet with difficulty, clutching her bulging belly, but assured Louisa that she wasn't seriously hurt.

Nevertheless, she continued to complain of pain until her daughter was born on 12 August. Midwife Annie Taylor, who delivered the baby, was shocked to find her covered in bruises and on 15 August, she took the child to Drs Highett and Williams. Both doctors noted heavy bruising on the baby's head, arms, shoulders, ribs and back, which had apparently been inflicted some time ago. The little girl failed to thrive and died on 20 August, when a post-mortem examination indicated that the cause of death was severe injuries occasioned by external violence inflicted on the child's mother, while she was carrying the baby in her womb.

Mr Justice Lawrence. (Author's collection)

The police took the unusual step of charging Duggan with the manslaughter of the un-named baby. He was tried at the Leicestershire Assizes on 24 November and, although he pleaded not guilty, he admitted striking his wife but insisted that he had only done so after she threatened him with a poker. Duggan told the court that he was very sorry for what had happened and begged the judge to be lenient with him, pointing out that if he were imprisoned, his wife and family would be left destitute.

Mr Justice Lawrence commented tartly that Duggan hadn't shown much mercy towards his wife in assaulting her while she was heavily pregnant and sentenced him to eighteen months' imprisonment, with hard labour.

25 JULY 1853 Coroner John Gregory held an inquest at Countesthorpe into the death of William Palmer.

The previous day, carrier Job Herbert found Palmer's body lying in a gateway. The police and a doctor were summoned and found that Palmer had been shot, the bullet passing through his upper jaw, teeth and the roof of his mouth, before lodging in his brain.

Earlier that evening, seventeen-year-old Palmer was seen with Charles Goude and Joseph Needham of Whetstone. At the time, Palmer was carrying a gun but when police spoke to Goude, he initially told the constable that he was not with Palmer, suggesting that Palmer had taken his gun without his knowledge. However, before long, both Goude and Needham told the truth.

All three of them were out with Goude's gun, which Goude kept hidden in a field so that his father wouldn't know of its existence. Palmer badgered Goude to let him have a go and was finally allowed to shoot at some crows. However, as he approached them, they flew away, so Palmer walked through the hedge and across the next field, out of sight of his companions. Hearing a shot, Goude and Needham ran towards the sound. Needham got there first and, when Goude called out to ask what Palmer had shot, Needham replied, 'Himself.'

It seemed obvious that Palmer had accidentally shot himself while climbing over a gate. Mindful of Goude's father's disapproval of firearms, the two youths threw the gun as far as they could into a field of oats then went home.

Goude and Needham took police to where the gun lay and the fact that both it and the gate were heavily bloodstained supported their account of Palmer's demise. The inquest jury accepted their explanation and returned a verdict of 'accidental death'.

26 JULY 1900 Coroner George Bouskell held an inquest into the death of two-year-old Laurence Henry Enoch Best. The child's mother related that Laurence was playing in the yard of their home in Hinckley when he suddenly turned pale and was very sick. Emma Best gave the toddler a little soda water, then a little whisky and water, and took him into her own bed to sleep.

He woke twice during the night and, on the second occasion, was again very sick. Emma went downstairs at 4.30 a.m. and lit the fire to warm the room, before fetching her son down. Laurence was given a few sips of tea and some more whisky and water, but his condition worsened and at 5.20 a.m. Emma sent for a doctor, but Laurence died before he arrived.

Bouskell questioned Emma about her family and she told him that she had given birth to four children, two of whom had died. Emma then revealed that the father of

The Borough, Hinckley. (Author's collection)

her children, with whom she lived as man and wife, was her own brother. Alfred Best was questioned about his 'wife's' startling admission and confirmed that he and Emma had lived together since 1893, after his return from service in India with the Army.

A doctor testified that Laurence and the other children in the family were well fed and well cared for and that Laurence appeared to have died from convulsions. The inquest jury returned a verdict in accordance with the medical evidence, but asked the coroner to severely reprimand the parents of the child for their 'simply vile' conduct. The coroner did so in the strongest terms.

27 JULY 1896 As hawker George Foster was walking between Hinckley and Earl Shilton, he met Frank Crossley with two companions.

Without warning, Crossley suddenly grabbed Foster and tipped him upside down over his shoulder, shaking him so that the coins fell out of his pocket. He then dropped Foster head first onto the ground, picked up the coins and walked off, although one of his friends handed Foster 3d back, asking him not to press charges.

Two people witnessed the attack and, when the police were informed, they quickly apprehended the three men. Crossley immediately confessed, telling PC Taylor and Sergeant Oakley that he was the guilty party and they needn't bother to arrest the others.

Frank Crossley appeared at the Leicestershire Assizes on 20 November charged with robbery with violence, and, although he insisted that the robbery had been 'done in

Flogging with the cat-o-nine-tails.
(Author's collection)

fun', the jury were not amused and found him guilty. Mr Justice Day sentenced him to one month's imprisonment, with twenty lashes from the cat-o-nine-tails.

28 JULY 1890 Caroline Jones of Leicester appeared before magistrates at the Town Hall charged with wilfully neglecting her four children, aged between two and five years old, between 1 May and 23 July, in a manner likely to cause injury to their health.

Forty-one-year-old Mrs Jones did not beat or starve her children but the two rooms that she shared with her seventy-five-year-old husband and the children were so disgusting that they were judged unfit for human habitation. The children were described as 'loathsomely filthy' and were infested with fleas.

Inspector Walker and Mr Simpson of the NSPCC told magistrates that they had visited the house and warned Mrs Jones several times, but nothing could induce her to clean. Simpson recalled scraping a covering of dirt off the table but Mrs Jones was unrepentant, telling Simpson, 'It's clean muck.'

With the house getting progressively filthier with every visit and Mrs Jones unwilling to mend her ways, the NSPCC saw no alternative other than to prosecute. Magistrates sent Mrs Jones to prison for one month and ordered her children to be removed to the Workhouse.

29   JULY 1865   A person drawing water at Pegg's Green, Ashby-de-la-Zouch, drew up the dead body of a baby, who had evidently been forced through a gap in the woodwork covering the well. The baby was identified by Mrs Castledine of Whitwick as the child of a widow named Eliza Adkins. According to Mrs Castledine, Eliza called at her house on 28 July and asked if she might sit down and rest, so that she could get her child to sleep as they had a long way to walk.

The police tracked Eliza through Griffydam, Beedon and Wilson, where she was arrested and taken back to Ashby-de-la-Zouch police station. Initially, Eliza denied all knowledge of any baby and remained obstinately silent when questioned, but she developed a relationship with the wife of Inspector Ward and, after being transferred to Leicester Prison, Eliza asked to see her and made a full confession.

Eliza told Martha Ward that she was homeless and impoverished after the death of her husband six months earlier. Her sister was keeping her baby, Zadok, while she worked but needed payment for the baby's keep. Eliza applied to the Loughborough Union and asked for two shillings a week to keep her child. She asked for nothing for herself, being happy to continue working, but the Union refused to help, saying she and Zadok must go into the Workhouse.

Reluctantly Eliza agreed but was immediately separated from Zadok and was tortured to hear him crying for her. Eventually, she went to talk to her son through the bars that separated them but when the authorities saw her, they snatched the child away from her and beat it, refusing to allow Eliza any food as a punishment. Unable to bear her son's misery, Eliza left the Workhouse on 28 July but had no money or food for her baby. 'The poor thing is in heaven now, out of all of its sufferings,' she concluded.

Eliza was tried at the Leicestershire Assizes for wilful murder on 7 December and, having been found guilty, she was sentenced to death. The sentence was later commuted to one of life imprisonment and she was sent to Woking Female Prison in Surrey.

Note: Although the child's name is given as Zadok in the contemporary newspapers, official records suggest that his name may have been Joseph.

30   JULY 1896   Coroner Robert Harvey concluded an inquest into the death of thirty-three-year-old James Wardle, who died three days after an incident at Enderby Hill Quarry on 21 July.

Wardle was employed as an engine driver at the quarry and was just about to leave work when manager Mr Hewitt called him back. As the two men stood talking, Wardle suddenly fell over. 'Something hit me,' he told Hewitt, who could see that Wardle's leg was bleeding and that his trousers were torn. He was transported to hospital, where he was found to have a compound fracture of one thigh and, when doctors examined the wound, they found small fragments of Wardle's trousers embedded in his leg, along with several pea-sized pebbles.

After Wardle's death from shock, coroner Harvey opened an inquest and adjourned it so that the government mines inspector could attend. When the inquest resumed on 30 July, the coroner was told that 'springing' was taking place at the time of Wardle's injury.

'Springing' involved using small charges of gunpowder to enlarge the bottom end of a drilled hole, which could then accommodate a larger charge for blasting purposes. All springing took part during meal breaks or after working hours and the two men in charge of the operation shouted 'Fire!' as a warning, long before detonating the charges. In addition, men were sent to walk around the quarry and warn anyone who might be in danger. On this occasion, the drilled hole was 514 feet from where Wardle and Hewitt were standing, the opening at the top pointing directly at Wardle.

Once the gunpowder was placed in the hole, it was packed with sand and fine gravel. This was either riddled or filtered through the labourer's fingers to ensure that it contained no large stones.

Powder man Joseph Young and his assistant Frederick Seer told the coroner that they were aware of Wardle and Hewitt but believed that they were too far away to be in any danger. Both men swore that the sand and gravel were carefully checked and contained no pebbles.

In summary, the coroner told the jury that any stone in the hole would be driven out by the blast at great velocity, similar to a bullet from a gun. It was obvious that the stones that injured Wardle came from inside the hole but it was possible that they were just dislodged from the walls by the process of ramming. The inquest jury returned a verdict of 'accidental death', adding that they believed that there had been some carelessness by Young and Seer.

31 JULY 1818 Michael Shipman of Hinckley was tried at the Leicestershire Assizes on a charge of 'having assaulted Miss Emma Dalton and administered laudanum or some other exciting drug for the purpose of producing unconsciousness, insensibility or appetite in that young lady, with the view of rendering her subservient to his passions.'

Twenty-one-year-old Emma, who worked as a governess for the Shipman family, retired to bed on 19 December 1817, complaining of chest pain. Just before midnight, another servant, Clara Johnson, was sent to see if she was any better. Emma said that she wasn't and when Clara reported this to her employers, Michael Shipman went to

Emma's room. He sent Clara for brandy and water and, as soon as he and Emma were alone, he put his hand on her.

Emma was too weak to remove Shipman's hand but he took it away himself when Clara returned. After drinking some of the brandy Emma went to sleep but woke again at about 5 a.m. Her cries of pain woke the Shipman's oldest daughter, who in turn woke her father, who ordered Emma to be dressed and taken downstairs, where there was a fire. He made Emma drink two cups of tea then poured out another but Emma noticed that he went to the cupboard where the laudanum was kept and refused to drink the third cup of tea because it smelled horrible. Shipman forced her to drink it by holding her nose and then ordered Clara to take the bones out of Emma's stays, after which Shipman 'gave his hand more unrestrained liberties than hitherto upon her person.'

For the next three days, Shipman kept Emma drugged with either brandy or laudanum and repeatedly groped and indecently assaulted her. The drugs drained her of the strength to resist and, in spite of her repeated requests to see a doctor, it wasn't until 23 December that Mrs Shipman contacted a surgeon while her husband was out. When Shipman returned and heard that a doctor was coming, he flung down his hat in a rage and said, 'I am undone.'

At the trial, the judge told the jury that there was 'abundant proof' of Shipman's guilt and, when the jury agreed, the judge fined him £100 and sentenced him to twelve months' imprisonment.

AUGUST

Market Place, Loughborough. (Author's collection)

1 **AUGUST 1877** Henry Ward was a pork butcher in Quorn, who was known as 'Sausage Ward' because he made such fine sausages. Henry's wife, Ann, took his wares to market in Loughborough and the neighbouring villages but the couple were both addicted to drink and, consequently, their behaviour could be a little strange.

On 1 August, their shop remained closed and, wanting some meat for her husband's tea, Mrs Perry called at the Wards' house to see when they would be opening for business. Having knocked, she waited on the doorstep until the front door swung open, revealing Ann Ward, who was bleeding heavily. Ann grabbed Mrs Perry by the skirts and dragged her into the house, all the while sawing determinedly at her own throat with a razor.

Mrs Perry wrested it from her and threw it into a corner. Meanwhile, Henry Ward wandered drunkenly downstairs to see what all the commotion was about. Ann Ward bled to death and, although she was unable to speak, she indicated more than once that she had cut her own throat.

When the time came for her funeral on 3 August, Henry was still blind drunk. He insisted that Ann was not dead, tipping her out of the coffin and urging her to speak to him. He was so inebriated that he was unable to attend the funeral, although he got up early the next morning and went to sit by his wife's grave. He told everyone he met that day that Ann wasn't dead, claiming to have held a conversation with her at the graveside, and that afternoon he was found hanging in a storeroom behind his house.

An inquest had already recorded a verdict of 'suicide while of unsound mind' in respect of Ann's demise and when coroner Henry Deane held an inquest into Henry's death, the jury's verdict was that 'the deceased hanged himself whilst of unsound mind, induced by excessive drinking.'

2 **AUGUST 1892** Samuel Hunt had been courting Bridget Gray of Loughborough for some time, much to the disapproval of her friends and family, who considered the fifteen-year-old too young to have a boyfriend. Bridget lived with her aunt and, on 2 August, Margaret Gray gave her niece a thrashing for associating with Hunt. The following morning, Bridget ran away and, when she was later traced to Hunt's lodgings, he was charged with her abduction.

By the time the case came to the Leicestershire Assizes in November 1892, Bridget was over the age of sixteen and had married Hunt. The prosecution counsel asked the judge if he believed that it was worth pursuing the case under the circumstances, pointing out that when Bridget arrived at Hunt's lodgings, he had very properly arranged for her to sleep with his landlady's daughter.

The judge expressed concern that, since Bridget was now legally married to the defendant, she could not now be called to testify. He was keen to satisfy himself that

Hunt had married Bridget for the right reasons, rather than to prevent her from appearing as a witness against him. The case was adjourned until the following day when, having read all the depositions, the judge agreed to the case being dropped. Records show that the couple went on to have at least six children.

3 AUGUST 1882 The bodies of Millicent Jackson and her four-year-old illegitimate son John Bingley Jackson were found in a reservoir at Braunstone.

Millicent had complained of pains in her head for some weeks before she finally left her mother's house, saying that she was going for a walk. At the reservoir, she tied her child tightly to her waist using a long handkerchief, before throwing herself into the water.

An inquest held by coroner Mr Oldham returned verdicts of 'wilful murder' against thirty-six-year-old Millicent in respect of the death of her son and 'suicide while temporarily insane' in regard to her own death.

4 AUGUST 1869 Six-year-old John Anthony Astill was playing with other children on his father's farm at Glenfield. The children were amusing themselves by climbing a ladder that was propped against a straw stack then sliding down.

John had picked up a short piece of wood, used in thatching, which was sharpened at one end. As he slid, the stick hit the ground point upwards and, as John's full weight hit the stick, the point was driven 3 inches into his abdomen. In spite of the efforts of a surgeon, he died within hours and an inquest later returned a verdict of 'accidental death'.

5 AUGUST 1825 Thirty-six-year-old Hannah Read was hanged in Leicester, having been found guilty of the wilful murder of her husband, James.

Hannah and James had been married for eight years but separated for two, during which time Hannah lived with another man and even had a child by him. James found out about Hannah's new relationship and insisted that she returned to live as his wife. The couple were reconciled on 6 March 1825 but, on 21 April, Hannah sent for her husband's brother and told him that James had gone completely mad. She described him dancing, swearing and jumping around, before falling to the ground and tearing up handfuls of grass, then finally running off towards the canal at Foxton.

Thomas Read immediately accused Hannah of drowning his brother in the canal, which Hannah vehemently denied. Nevertheless, Thomas communicated his suspicions to the police, who dragged the canal and recovered James's body.

At Hannah's trial, the prosecution suggested that she was far from happy about leaving her lover and living with her husband again, contending that she pushed James into the canal and walked away, leaving him to drown. However, Hannah

Canal and Foxton Locks, where James Read drowned in 1825. (Author's collection)

insisted that James went suddenly and inexplicably mad and ran away from her, presumably dashing into the water.

When the jury found her guilty, Hannah fainted. Having been brought round, she sobbed as the death sentence was pronounced, begging the judge, 'For God's sake forgive me. Spare me, my Lord, for the sake of my six poor children.'

Her pleas fell on deaf ears and before her execution, Hannah made a full confession, saying that she wanted to go back to her lover and, after taking her husband's money, she pushed him into the water and watched him drown.

6 AUGUST 1896 Samuel Williams was drinking in a Leicester pub with his wife, Annie, and his father Edward, when factory worker Thomas Tow accidentally knocked over his drink. Tow apologised and offered to buy Williams another, explaining that he would have to go and fetch the money first but, on leaving the pub, he was followed by the Williams family, who set upon him and knocked him down. While Tow was on the ground, Samuel held him still as Edward and Annie kicked and jumped on him.

Mr Justice Day. (Author's collection)

Tow was taken home unconscious and died two days later from a ruptured bladder. However, in the opinion of a surgeon at Leicester Infirmary, Tow's injuries were more likely to have been caused by a fall rather than a blow.

Samuel, Edward and Annie appeared before Mr Justice Day at the Leicestershire Assizes in November, charged with manslaughter. Although the jury found all three defendants guilty, they recommended them to mercy. Day sentenced Edward to eighteen months' imprisonment, Samuel to fifteen months and Annie to nine, each with hard labour.

7 AUGUST 1906 The South Leicestershire coroner held an inquest at Blaby on the death of one-year-old Phineas Donald Edward Ayton.

The child's family were camping close to the village of Blaby when another child accidentally dropped an empty glass ginger beer bottle onto a full one. The full bottle exploded, sending shards of glass flying in all directions and, unfortunately, one happened to strike Phineas in the neck, severing his jugular vein.

The little boy bled to death before a doctor could reach him, and the inquest returned a verdict of 'death by misadventure'.

8 AUGUST 1944 Having been found guilty of wilful murder at the Nottingham Assizes, William Alfred Cowle was hanged by Albert Pierrepoint at Leicester Prison. He shared the scaffold with William George Frederick Meffen, who murdered his stepdaughter in Derbyshire.

On 18 May, Cowle walked up to a policeman in Leicester and told him, 'I have just stabbed someone. It was a girl. I did it in a fit of temper.' Thirty-one-year-old Cowle was taken into custody and, when Nora Emily Payne died later that day in the Leicester Infirmary from a stab wound to the neck, he was charged with her murder.

Cowle was a married man, although separated from his wife, and, since 1941, he and Nora had been conducting a relationship. However, Nora had recently broken off their association and, when Cowle was unable to persuade her to reconsider, he lost his temper and stabbed her in an alleyway as she walked back to her job after her lunch break.

9 AUGUST 1869 In Market Bosworth, three-year-old Harry Barsby was playing in the garden with his mother. When she left him alone for a few minutes, Harry tried to pick some fruit off a tree. Unable to reach, he stood on the handle of a wheelbarrow but it tipped over, throwing him into a nearby ditch.

Although there was barely any water in the ditch, Harry was unable to get out. He was still alive when his mother returned but died later that day, the surgeon in attendance being of the opinion that death was caused by mud getting into his stomach.

An inquest later returned a verdict of 'accidental death'.

10 AUGUST 1878 Collier William Edwards fancied himself as an acrobat and performed a few tricks for the amusement of the crowd, while watching a cricket match at Heather. One of his favourite stunts was turning a backward somersault from the shoulders of another man and he sought out a volunteer to help him. However, since thirty-year-old Edwards had been drinking heavily, nobody was prepared to step forward.

Edwards eventually dragged an unwilling and protesting man from among the spectators and climbed onto his shoulders but was so drunk that he fell, landing on his head. He was picked up unconscious and taken to his home in Ibstock, where he lingered until 13 August before dying from concussion of the brain.

The inquest at Ibstock on 15 August returned a verdict of 'accidental death'.

Station Road, Heather, 1927. (Author's collection)

11 AUGUST 1933 A lorry driven by Reginald Daniel Jesse Rushton from Boston, Lincolnshire, crashed into a tram standard in Leicester. Rushton was seriously injured and was taken to hospital. His wife was rushed to his bedside, where he was able to talk to her before his death, explaining that he must have 'dozed off'. At the subsequent inquest, Mrs Rushton stated that, in the four days before his accident, her husband slept for just ninety minutes.

At the time of his accident in the early hours of Friday 11 August, he was delivering potatoes to Coventry. In the previous four days, he had delivered to Leeds, Rochdale and Scarborough, returning to Boston between deliveries, and had told his wife that he was 'dead beat'.

The coroner called Rushton's employer to the inquest and asked him when the driver was supposed to get any rest. 'After he delivered his loads, between journeys,' replied haulage contractor Joseph Hare.

The inquest jury returned a verdict of 'accidental death' but informed the coroner that they felt that much of the blame lay with Mr Hare, who they believed was morally responsible for the accident.

'I should call it slave driving,' agreed the coroner.

12 AUGUST 1895 Nine-year-olds Alfred Holmes and Thomas Taylor were waiting to cross the railway line at a level crossing near Braunstone. They watched as a goods train went past then immediately ran around the back of the train, not realising that there was a passenger train approaching from the opposite direction. The driver had no chance to stop and hit both boys, who were mutilated almost beyond recognition and died instantly.

There were two witnesses to the tragic accident, who stated that the boys' view of the passenger train was blocked by the goods train and, although one person shouted a warning to the boys, the train was upon them before they could react, even assuming that they heard the shout above the noise of the two trains. A child who saw the accident suggested that Alfred and Thomas might have run round the back of the goods train specifically to watch the passenger train, without realising that it was so close.

An inquest held by coroner Mr W.A. Clarke was told that it was a favourite pastime for boys to place things on the line for the train to flatten and both victims were playing on the line shortly before their deaths. The inquest jury returned two verdicts of 'accidental death', adding that they were of the opinion that no blame could be attached to anyone.

13 AUGUST 1870 A boiler exploded at a brickyard in Coalville, leaving, in the words of the local newspaper, 'a heap of dead and dying.' When the dust settled it was discovered that three people had been killed and several more injured, one of whom later died.

The deceased were Frank (or Frederick) Underwood (5), who was delivering his brother's dinner, William Davis (10), Joseph Thomas Armstead (13) and Alfred Orton (11), who were all employed at the yard doing odd jobs.

A lengthy inquiry into the cause of the explosion found that the safety valve on the boiler was defective and far too small, as a result of which the readings it gave were incorrect. Thus, the cause of the explosion was attributed to 'the over pressure of steam'. The jury at the subsequent inquest returned verdicts of 'accidental death' on all four victims but recommended that more experienced hands were employed at the yard, since the person in charge of the boiler on the day of the explosion was only fifteen years old.

14 AUGUST 1893 John Richardson from Hinckley was conducting a relationship with his eighteen-year-old niece, Elizabeth, which was anything but avuncular. He impressed on her the need for secrecy, telling her that he would kill her if she ever told anyone, but Elizabeth, who was not a willing participant, told her aunt – John's sister – after which her grandmother threw thirty-four-year-old John out of her house.

Banned from ever setting foot in the house again, John waited until the middle of the night to take his revenge. He broke into the building and, believing that it was her husband coming upstairs, Elizabeth's aunt sent her to the top of the stairs with a lamp to light his way. When Elizabeth met John on the stairs, he hit her on the head with a coal pick then tried to strangle her. Fortunately, he was disturbed by other members of the household and, although he fled the scene, he was arrested in Nuneaton on 19 August and later stood trial at the Leicestershire Assizes for attempted murder. He was found guilty and sentenced to fifteen years' penal servitude.

Note: Some sources state that the murder happened early in the morning of 13 August, others in the early hours of 14 August.

Castle Street, Hinckley, 1916. (Author's collection)

15   AUGUST   1870   Coroner John Gregory held an inquest into the death of seven-year-old Sam Cattle, which occurred at Quorndon on 13 August.

Drayman John Cross was returning from Leicester to Kegworth with a load of empty barrels, his dray pulled by three horses. As he passed through Quorndon, he saw a number of small boys playing and, unnoticed by Cross, one tried to climb on the back of the dray by placing his foot on the wheel spokes. His foot slipped, trapping his leg between the wheel and the body of the cart and crushing him between the two as the wheel revolved. Sam was picked up with a compound fracture of the left leg, three broken ribs and head injuries, and, although he was rushed to the Loughborough Dispensary, he died within two hours.

Cross was sober at the time of the accident and was driving very slowly, so the inquest jury returned a verdict of 'accidental death', absolving him of any blame.

16   AUGUST   1886   At Breedon-on-the-Hill, a farm labourer walking to work at 4.30 a.m. found the body of thirty-five-year-old PC Thomas Barratt lying in a brook. Barratt's face was terribly battered and doctors surmised that he had been beaten and kicked to death.

Suspicion quickly fell on local men James Banton and Joseph Gadsby, who spent all of 15 August drinking and were then seen arguing with the policeman about an outstanding fine.

Throughout 16 August, Banton bragged to all and sundry that he had killed Barratt and when nobody came to arrest him, he announced that he was going to Derby to visit his brother. He was apprehended there and brought back to Leicester to appear before magistrates. Gadsby was arrested in a local public house and, although he admitted having spent the day with Banton, he denied any involvement in the murder.

Both men appeared at the Leicestershire Assizes in November 1886, charged with wilful murder. There was insufficient evidence against Gadsby, who was discharged, but Banton was found guilty and sentenced to death. He was executed by James Berry at Leicester on 30 November.

17   AUGUST   1871   At just before 6 p.m., Ada Harvey heard shouts coming from the wool-spinning factory adjacent to her Leicester home and discovered that the factory was on fire. The conflagration went on to claim two lives and many more workers were badly injured.

The blaze started in a room on the second floor of the building known as the 'willeying room', where fibres were fed into a machine to separate, comb and blend them. Willeyer Peter Lay was in charge, but briefly left his assistant Joseph Fletcher

Fatal fire at Leicester, 1871.

supervising the machine while he visited the lavatory. As he returned, Lay met Fletcher coming downstairs, saying that the machine had caught fire.

The blaze spread rapidly through the factory, leaving those workers on the third and fourth storeys trapped. Fourteen-year-old Alice Timson stood on a fourth-floor window ledge and announced that she was going to jump, begging the crowd below to catch her. She was persuaded to go back inside but, as she tried to climb through the window, she was suddenly overcome by smoke and fell backwards, fracturing her skull.

Meanwhile, overlooker Joseph Lee was helping people out of another top floor window onto a ladder. He lifted thirteen-year-old Anna (or Anne) Scott onto a window sill but, having injured his left hand, was unable to hold her in place and was eventually forced to abandon her to her fate and save himself.

An inquest held by coroner John Gregory heard that willeying machines were notoriously dangerous and prone to catching fire. A small piece of stone in a fleece could cause sparks, which could ignite the greasy wool, and any wool lodged in the rapidly revolving fan in the neck of the machine could cause friction, with the same result.

The inquest jury found two verdicts of 'accidental death', although they asked the coroner to censure Lay for leaving the machine in the hands of an inexperienced operative. They recommended that willeying machines should be located in separate buildings and suggested that when the factory was rebuilt it should incorporate two staircases.

18 AUGUST 1868 Coroner John Gregory opened an inquest at Coalville into the death of nine-year-old Sarah Bretnall, who died in an accident on the Leicester and Burton Railway.

Sarah and another little girl were sheltering under an umbrella, waiting to cross the line to get to the Snibston Colliery. The Burton train passed on the up line and the two girls immediately began to cross the tracks, failing to notice the train coming in the opposite direction. A points man approximately 90 yards away saw what was about to happen and shouted, 'Get back!', but the girls didn't hear him. He also signalled to the engine driver, who tried his best to stop the train, but was unable to avoid hitting the girls. Sarah's companion was seriously injured but is believed to have survived, while Sarah suffered catastrophic head injuries and was killed instantly.

The inquest was adjourned while inquiries were made about whose responsibility it was to man the crossing and when the proceedings resumed, the jury returned a verdict of 'accidental death', having been assured that people going to the colliery now had to use a different crossing, where a policeman was stationed.

19 AUGUST 1876 Nine-year-old William Henry Vann and six-year-old Ernest Deacon went out to play at about 6 p.m. A short while later, Charles Davis was passing through Abbey Meadow when he saw Vann's cap fall into the canal and, as Vann tried to retrieve it, he tumbled into the water.

Ernest stretched out his hand to try and pull William out of the water but William was bigger and heavier than his playmate and, rather than pulling his friend to safety, Ernest ended up in the water with him. Both boys sank almost immediately. Charles ran for help and within minutes, the canal was being dragged for the boys. They were retrieved from the water lifeless and, although their bodies were still warm, it proved impossible to resuscitate them.

Deputy-coroner Mr F.J. Kirby held an inquest on 21 August, at which the jury returned two verdicts of 'accidentally drowned'.

20 AUGUST 1876 John Thomas Green was well known in Leicester as a violent thug but had apparently been happily married to Emma for twenty years, until he started an affair with a woman from Loughborough. The Greens began to row constantly and more than once John was heard threatening to kill his wife.

In mid-August, John purchased a pistol, telling the man he bought it from that he wanted it for his son to shoot sparrows. John and Emma quarrelled all day on 20 August and at around 5 p.m., he sent his daughter for some beer. 'This is the last beer I shall ever have,' he told her after drinking it and, moments later, he walked into the kitchen and shot Emma twice in the neck.

Hearing the shots, neighbours rushed into the house and found Emma slumped over the table and her husband with a gun in his hand. Emma was taken to the Leicester Infirmary, where it was found that the bullets had penetrated her spine. When she died the following day, her husband was charged with her murder. At first, he admitted shooting his wife but changed his statement to say that she dared him to do it, and finally claiming that the gun went off accidentally while he was handling it, after having drunk at least fourteen pints of beer.

Green appeared at the Leicestershire and Derbyshire Assizes on 1 December, where he remained seemingly unmoved as he was found guilty and sentenced to death. He was hanged on 20 December 1876.

21 AUGUST 1894 Forty-two-year-old William Newell of Loughborough was formerly in the Marine Light Infantry, with medals for service in Egypt. He left the army in 1890 with a pension and went to join his wife Isabella, who ran a grocer's shop at Loughborough.

Newell took to drink and became suspicious about his wife's fidelity. Although his fears were groundless, jealousy drove him to behave violently towards Isabella and she eventually had him bound over to keep the peace towards her. However, on the evening of 20 August, the couple had yet another violent argument and Isabella threatened to leave. Rather than sleep with her husband, she retired to bed that night with her children.

The following morning, after the couple's two eldest daughters and the family lodger had gone to work, Newell confronted his wife in their eight-year-old son's room.

'Now then, what did you say you would do last night?' he asked her menacingly, and, when she saw that her husband had a coal pick in his hand, Isabella fainted. Newell immediately began to belabour his wife's head with the pick and when their son ran for his ten-year-old sister, both children watched in terror as he murdered their mother before their eyes.

Newell was arrested close to his home and told the police that he had killed his wife because of jealousy, vowing, 'I'll go to the gallows with a good heart if she is dead.'

Newell appeared at the Leicestershire Assizes on 20 November. His defence counsel tried to convince the jury that he was insane, revealing that several of Newell's relatives had been patients in asylums and that a second cousin was found insane, after shooting his wife. However, several doctors testified that they believed Newell to be perfectly sane and he was found guilty. Sentenced to death, he was hanged on 10 December 1894.

Note: Isabella Newell is alternatively named Clarabella in some newspapers.

22 AUGUST 1896 Mrs Pearson of Ellistown heard a child screaming and found three-year-old Harry Ball standing in a ditch, the water over his knees.

Every Friday evening, the boilers at the local colliery were emptied of water for cleaning. The water ran down a 92-yard pipe, before discharging into the ditch, so the water in which Harry was standing would be extremely hot. A doctor called to attend the child found him in a state of collapse, suffering from severe scalds to his legs and lower torso.

Harry died from shock the following afternoon and an inquest held by coroner George Bouskell heard that the ditch had been used for the same purpose for the past twenty years. This was the first ever accident, although until four years ago, the boiling water was mixed with cold, before being discharged into the ditch.

When the jury returned a verdict of 'accidental death', Bouskell stated that he considered the practice highly dangerous, telling the colliery that it should be stopped immediately. A representative of the pit owners expressed their regret at the fatality and undertook to remedy the matter forthwith.

23 AUGUST 1899 Carter William Hewins of Broughton Astley and his wife were returning home from Leicester with a heavily laden cart. When they reached Bryan's Hill in Narborough, fifty-seven-year-old Hewins found that the brake was not working properly and pulled the cart to the side of the road, intending to examine it. As he did so, the inside wheel passed over the end of a small drainage pipe running under the footpath and the cart tipped violently, precipitating Hewins onto the pavement.

When the cart tipped, several things fell onto the horse's rump and it immediately took off at a gallop. The rim of the cart wheel neatly sliced off the top of Hewins's skull, killing him instantly.

Fortunately for Mrs Hewins, passers-by in Narborough managed to stop the bolting horse before she came to any harm.

24 AUGUST 1867 Thomas Wormleighton of Leicester heard screaming and saw a child leaving his neighbour's house, clutching his bleeding throat. As Wormleighton went to assist, Mrs Hutchins ran out of the house screaming 'Murder!'

Wormleighton ran inside, closely followed by two other neighbours. They could hear movement upstairs and found another young boy in bed, also bleeding from his throat. Wormleighton passed the child downstairs then tackled the boy's father, Thomas Hutchins, who stood watching the excitement with a knife held to his own throat. Wormleighton took the knife from Hutchins, who then followed him downstairs and, picking up a knife and fork, renewed his attempt to commit suicide. His neighbours disarmed him and restrained him until the police arrived.

George and William Hutchins both survived, as did their father, who was tried for feloniously wounding George with intent to murder and with feloniously wounding him with intent to do grievous bodily harm.

It emerged that Hutchins was a kind, affectionate father who had become addicted to drink and had experienced an attack of *delirium tremens* shortly before the attempted murders. He had absolutely no recollection of stabbing his sons, claiming to have been getting ready to go to work when something came over him.

The jury found Hutchins guilty of the lesser offence of unlawful wounding and the judge deferred sentencing so that he could make some enquiries about the prisoner. When Hutchins was recalled for sentencing, the judge said that he had obviously committed the offence through drink and advised him to keep away from it in the future. With that proviso, the judge discharged Hutchins, saying that if he ever committed a similar act again, he would receive a very severe punishment.

25 AUGUST 1933 An inquest was held in Derby into the death of twenty-year-old Colin Mackenzie Blair Gordon, who died following an accident at Donington Park motor racing track. The jury heard that Gordon was the passenger in a car that skidded at a hairpin bend during a practice run, hit a tree and overturned.

A letter from Gordon's mother was read out, begging officials to stop motor racing at the track, where there had been six deaths during the previous seven meetings. However, in his summary, the coroner pointed out that the previous deaths could be attributed to mechanical failures rather than to the condition of the track, which he personally regarded as safe. Besides which, motor racing was one of the most dangerous sports in which young men engaged and a bend was a normal hazard that might be expected on any track.

The outbreak of the Second World War put an end to motor sport at Donington Park, which was requisitioned for the storage of military vehicles. It wasn't until the 1970s that motor sport returned to the circuit, happily with a much better safety record.

26 AUGUST 1875 While in charge of a ward at the Leicester Borough Asylum, John Smith went into the scullery to make a cup of tea. Inmate George Fordham crept in after him and appropriated a carving knife, which he later used to stab Smith in the abdomen.

Hearing Smith's screams, the other staff rushed to his assistance, securing Fordham in a padded cell. However, even though the asylum doctor arrived on the ward quickly, he was unable to save Smith's life.

Fordham believed that Smith was persecuting him and told everyone, 'I have had my revenge; they can hang me as soon as they like.' An inquest found a verdict of wilful murder against him and he was committed for trial at the next Leicestershire Assizes, where he was found guilty and sentenced to death.

Fordham was an elderly man, who suffered from epileptic fits and had been confined in the asylum since February 1874. Prior to that, he was an inmate of the imbecile ward of the Workhouse, where he frequently displayed violent behaviour. His death sentence was commuted to one of life imprisonment, which he served at Woking Invalid Prison in Surrey.

Leicester Borough Asylum. (Author's collection)

27   **AUGUST** **1900**   Having been out of work for some time, bricklayer Abednego Sutton of Loughborough was feeling depressed and low spirited. On the afternoon of 27 August, he asked his stepmother, Mary Ann Pearson Sutton, to fetch him some tobacco, which she agreed to do 'in a minute'.

Abednego handed her the money, at the same time punching her in the face with his other hand and knocking her down. As she lay bleeding, he knelt over her and tried to cut her throat, although fortunately the razor was deflected by the stiff collar on her dress. Mary Ann struck out at her stepson and the open razor folded closed over his thumb, giving her the chance to escape.

Although Abednego later claimed that his stepmother had tried to hit him with a poker, there seemed no real motive for his attack and questions were asked about his sanity. However, while he was imprisoned waiting to appear before Mr Justice Channell at the Leicestershire Assizes, he was seen several times by the prison surgeon, who considered him to be completely normal. Found guilty of attempted murder, he was sentenced to six months' imprisonment.

28   **AUGUST** **1844**   An inquest was held on the death of Elizabeth Atkins, who was crushed or suffocated to death in a railway accident.

The twenty-three-year-old dressmaker had been to visit her mother and caught her train home at Desford. The train had thirteen coal waggons at the front and a further thirteen at the back, with two passenger carriages in between.

Desford. (Author's collection)

When the train stopped to pick up Elizabeth and another passenger, Mrs Daniells, the sudden jerk broke one of the axles. As the train continued its journey, one waggon was dragged along, rather than moving freely on its wheels, which caused the chains attaching the waggons to the engine to snap. The front thirteen waggons stopped instantly, while those behind continued moving and smashed into the passenger carriages, which were crushed between the coal waggons. Mrs Daniells survived to describe the terrifying sensation of intense pressure but Elizabeth was not so fortunate, and by the time her body was removed from the wreckage ten minutes after the crash, she was dead.

By a miracle, Elizabeth was the only fatality and few passengers sustained any serious injuries. The inquest jury returned a verdict of 'accidental death', condemning the railway for placing passenger carriages in the midst of a coal train.

29 AUGUST 1898 Arthur Parker and Thomas Taylor were sheeting waggons in the Falcon Works railway sidings at Loughborough when Taylor spotted a goods train on the main Midland Railway line and realised that it was about to shunt more waggons into the siding.

The siding foreman shouted and signalled to Taylor to be aware of the waggons and Taylor signalled back to say that he had understood. He and Parker waited until the new waggons were in the sidings, before continuing their work, not realising that one of the waggons was still moving until it rammed into the back of a stationery waggon, crushing Parker between the two.

Coroner Henry Deane later recorded a verdict of 'accidental death'.

30 AUGUST 1938 Coroner Edward Fowler held an inquest into the death of three-year-old Roy Greatorex, who drowned in the lake in Abbey Park, Leicester.

Roy was described as 'backward' and was unable to walk, although he was capable of shuffling along on his bottom. On 27 August, his father took him to the park to feed the ducks then fell asleep on the grass, until he was woken by a thirteen-year-old girl to say that there was a little boy in the lake. The child in the water was Roy.

A police officer who interviewed Mr Greatorex after the tragedy recalled that he smelled of alcohol and the girl who woke him stated that he didn't respond when she shook him and shouted and she had to slap his face before he stirred. Roy's father claimed to have felt drowsy because of the heat and said that he had drunk only three half pints of beer.

The inquest jury returned a verdict of 'accidental death' and the coroner commented that it was an accident that should never have happened.

The lake, Abbey Park, Leicester. (Author's collection)

31 AUGUST 1895 When twenty-year-old George Law appeared at the Leicester Police Court charged with indecent assault and attempted rape, his only concern was that it wasn't reported in the newspapers. On 30 August, Jane Agar was pushing her baby along Wigston Lane in its pram when Law suddenly approached her and threw her onto the ground. Jane struggled to her feet but Law knocked her over again, this time stuffing a handkerchief in her mouth to silence her terrified screams. Once more, Jane got up but was thrown down for a third time by Law, who began to tear at her clothes like a madman. Fortunately for Jane, he was disturbed by the approach of another person and fled.

Later that day, Maria Winstanley was picking blackberries at the side of Wigston Lane, when she was approached by a stranger. After remarking that it was a nice day, the man suddenly jumped on Maria and knocked her down. She struggled and screamed and was fortunate to escape with her virtue intact after her attacker was disturbed. Although Law ran away, this time he was pursued and captured.

At the Leicestershire Assizes, Law insisted that both women were consenting parties, but, having heard medical evidence that Jane Agar was subjected to great violence, the jury found Law guilty on two counts of unlawful assault and attempting to outrage.

He was sentenced to two years' imprisonment, with hard labour.

SEPTEMBER

St Mary's Church and Leicester castle (site of the assizes), 1950. (Author's collection)

1 **SEPTEMBER** 1927 A fire broke out in a Leicester factory which produced celluloid toys and, since there was a large amount of highly flammable material on the premises, an order was given to evacuate the building as quickly as possible. However, once the forty-strong workforce got outside, they realised that seventeen-year-old Alice Salt wasn't among them.

The fire brigade were hampered by the narrow streets, which prevented them from getting to the rear of the building. Alice was eventually found very badly burned near the stairs on the third floor, and had obviously been prevented from escaping by the intensity of the fire.

Uncannily, Alice had told several of her workmates that morning that, the previous night, she had dreamed of being in a burning building. In her dream, Alice was unable to move and eventually fainted as the spreading fire prevented her from breathing.

2 **SEPTEMBER** 1928 Villagers from Great Glen watched an aeroplane circling low over the village. Suddenly the engine backfired and the plane dropped from the sky and nosedived into a field, where it burst into flames. So fierce was the fire that nobody was able to get within 20 yards of the crashed plane and it was only when the flames finally died down that they saw the charred remains of the pilot still sitting in the cockpit. Twenty-six-year-old RAF Pilot Officer George Herbert Aldridge died instantly in the crash and, since the DH9A plane was too badly burned to establish the cause of the accident, the jury at the subsequent inquest returned a verdict of 'accidental death'.

3 **SEPTEMBER** 1872 Catherine Frances Musson was staying with her father-in-law, the Governor of Leicester County Gaol. When she awoke on the morning of 3 September, thirty-year-old Catherine found the atmosphere in her room very close and, thinking to clear the air, she lit a piece of paper and waved it around.

Unfortunately, the burning paper made contact with her nightgown and she found herself on fire. She rushed screaming onto the landing, where she was met by a nursemaid, who threw a bucket of water over her, but Catherine was very badly burned. She lingered in hospital in agony for ten days until her death, when an inquest returned a verdict of 'accidentally burned'.

4 **SEPTEMBER** 1884 Two men were employed by the management to inspect the stone quarry at Enderby every morning to ensure that it was safe. This was done as normal on 4 September but during the afternoon, a large stone weighing around 15cwt fell from the wall and bounced down into the quarry, knocking down two men, before landing on a third.

Once the stone was shifted, Robert Harrison was found dead beneath it, his skull fractured. Meanwhile, in the course of its descent, the boulder hit Thomas Street, amputating both of his legs and injuring his head. Although Street was taken to hospital, he died the next morning as a result of his injuries. (The third victim sustained a broken thigh and is believed to have survived.)

At inquests held by coroner George F. Harrison, the juries heard that numerous people had worked on, under or around the stone on the day of the tragedy and not one person had expressed any safety concerns. The two inquest juries each returned verdicts of 'accidental death'.

5 SEPTEMBER 1874 PC John Meadows was patrolling his beat at Waltham-on-the-Wolds when he heard a gunshot. Suspecting poachers, he hid in a ditch and, soon afterwards, two men walked past him. The policeman followed the men until he was close enough to recognise thirty-two-year-old John 'Jack' Harding, greeting him with, 'Oh, Jack, it's you is it?'

Harding immediately ran off, with Meadows in pursuit. They had not gone far when Harding stopped and aimed his gun at the policeman. 'Jack, don't shoot me,' Meadows pleaded and Harding slowly lowered the gun and ran on. After 200 yards, Meadows was gaining on him and shouted at him to stop but with less than 10 yards between them, Harding turned and shot Meadows in the arms and chest, before running off again.

The policeman survived and Harding was later charged with shooting at Meadows with intent to murder him and, when found guilty, was sentenced to seven years' penal servitude.

6 SEPTEMBER 1862 Coroner John Gregory concluded an inquest at Market Harborough Town Hall on Thomas Stinson, the sole victim of a train crash on 28 August.

To the surprise of the stationmaster, who had just closed up the station for the night, an excursion train returning to Burton-on-Trent from London unexpectedly stopped at Market Harborough Station to take on water. As it was moving off, another excursion train returning to Leicester ploughed into the back of it.

'The line all around the broken carriages was deluged with blood and presented a most sickening spectacle,' reported a contemporary newspaper. Initial reports suggested that three people had died and several hundred people were injured.

After a lengthy investigation, the inquest jury returned a verdict of manslaughter against Ezra Stubbs, the driver of the second train, who appeared at the Leicestershire Assizes in February 1863. The prosecution maintained that Stubbs was well aware of the position of the first train and should have proceeded with more caution.

Council offices, Market Harborough. (Author's collection)

However, on hearing conflicting evidence on whether the signal for the second train showed clear or danger ahead, Mr Justice Willes directed the jury to acquit him.

Note: Different newspaper accounts of the accident suggest that it took place either just before or just after midnight on 28 or 29 August.

7 SEPTEMBER 1895 Coroner Robert Harvey opened an inquest into the death of fourteen-year-old Herbert Payne, who died the previous day at Gimson's Iron Founders' Vulcan Works, Leicester.

It was part of Herbert's job to prepare a sandpaper band machine. He should have used a ladder but preferred to climb up some shelves fixed to the wall, which was considered by most of the workers to be a safer method of reaching the machine. When Herbert finished, another workman was horrified to see him grasp the belt with both hands in order to get down. His body weight caused the belt to engage with a revolving shaft and Herbert was whipped round at ninety revolutions a minute. Before anyone could stop the machine, Herbert had been carried round the shaft at least eight times, each time hitting his head on a ceiling beam. When he was extricated from the machinery, most of the back of Herbert's head was missing and his brain had literally been dashed out. He also had a broken arm and injuries to his left leg.

At the time of the accident, Herbert was working unsupervised, although the person who should have been supervising him was his brother, Albert.

The inquest was adjourned so that a factory inspector might be present and when it resumed on 13 September, the coroner told the jury that it was for them to say whether Herbert's death was accidental or if anyone at the factory was criminally to blame. The jury plumped for a verdict of 'accidental death'.

8 SEPTEMBER 1838

Blasting was taking place at Pegg's Green Colliery near Thringstone. Four holes had been drilled and packed with gunpowder and, as the fourth was fired, a piece of lighted paper floated down and landed on a bag of gunpowder.

The colliers around it scattered, with the exception of nineteen-year-old John Birch, to whom the gunpowder belonged. Birch tried to knock the burning paper off the bag but, as he did, it exploded, blowing him backwards.

He was picked up very badly burned on the front of his body, but lived for a week before succumbing to his dreadful burns. In recording the jury's verdict of 'accidental death', the coroner described Birch's actions as 'fatal rashness'.

9 SEPTEMBER 1926

Everyone who knew twenty-five-year-old Dorothy 'Dot' Evelyn Cain tried to persuade her not to make an exhibition parachute jump. One of her relatives even showed Dot a photograph of someone who died while jumping but she was undeterred and, eventually, her husband reluctantly gave her his blessing.

After some instruction on the ground, Dot was flown to a height of 1,000 feet before climbing onto the wing of the aeroplane. To everyone's horror, Dot and her parachute had somehow become separated and as she jumped, the parachute remained inside the plane. Dot plummeted to her death, landing among the crowds of spectators at the Royal Showground, Leicester, in full view of her husband.

Dot was in the charge of experienced parachutist and instructor Captain Arthur Frederick Muir of the Surrey Flying Services. At the inquest, Muir declared himself baffled by the accident, adding that he personally attached the parachute cable before Dot got out of the plane and was confident that it was secure. An inspection of the parachute, harness, cable and quick-release lifeline by a Government Inspector showed that all were intact and in excellent working order.

The inquest jury eventually returned a verdict of accidental death, saying that they could not attach any blame to anyone, but, as a direct result of the accident, the Air Ministry brought in a ruling that future descents could only be made by permit.

Dot was buried in Welford Road Cemetery, her gravestone bearing the poignant inscription 'Someday we'll understand.'

10 SEPTEMBER 1892 An inquest was held by coroner George Bouskell into the death of thirty-two-year-old collier Moses Heward.

When Heward finished his shift at Ellistown Colliery on 8 September, he and another four colliers got into the cage and the signal was given to 'draw up'. The cage was about 60 yards from the top of the shaft when Heward suddenly said, 'Oh dear.' Daniel Gimson turned round to see Heward falling out of the cage and tried to grab him, just touching the heel of his boot.

The colliers waiting for the cage at the bottom of the shaft heard something falling and quickly moved out of the way. Heward landed with a terrible thud and died instantly, his head split almost in two.

Heward had worked at the pit for more than twelve years and was laughing and joking with his colleagues only seconds before he fell. Although there were no safety rails at the ends of the cages, they were fitted with handrails and Heward was holding on with one hand as the cage ascended. The ascent was perfectly smooth, with no bumps or jerks that could have unbalanced Heward. He was not unwell and was not known to suffer from fits.

The inquest jury found that Heward's death was caused by injuries sustained by accidentally falling out of the cage to the bottom of the shaft, although they could offer no explanation for the fall. They added a rider recommending that gates or bars should be fitted at both ends of the cage to prevent future accidents.

11 SEPTEMBER 1925 An inquest was held in Leicester into the death of seventeen-year-old Walter Taylor, who suddenly dropped dead while being chased by a policeman.

PC Day testified that Taylor was one of a group of youths behaving in a disorderly fashion, who ran away when he challenged them. Day gave chase and insisted that he was never any closer than 20 yards to the group, when Taylor suddenly collapsed.

A doctor explained that the cause of death was cardiac failure, following nervous excitement, but Taylor's relatives were far from satisfied and heckled the coroner, asking why there was a mark on the back of Taylor's neck. The coroner's officer told them to ask civilly if they wanted an answer and the doctor explained that the mark was 'a common post-mortem stain'.

Eventually, to the obvious displeasure of Taylor's relatives, the coroner recorded a verdict of 'accidental death', saying that no blame for the tragedy could be attached to PC Day.

12 SEPTEMBER 1870 At 2 p.m., farmer's wife Mary Ann Harrison of Shawell took her ten-month-old daughter for a walk.

A little later, a thirteen-year-old boy working on a neighbouring farm heard groans from a pit in the next field and noticed somebody lying very still in the water. He raced to find his father, who pulled Mary Ann out, unconscious but still breathing. As soon as she was on the bank, her rescuers could see a baby in the muddy water, although Mary Ann junior was already dead.

Mary Ann Harrison was known as an excellent mother, who suffered from melancholia – what would be known today as post-natal depression. By December 1870, she was an in-patient at the Leicestershire and Rutland Asylum and, although committed to the Assizes on a coroner's warrant for wilful murder, she was judged unfit to plead. It took until the assizes of December 1871 before the medical superintendent at the asylum considered her fit to face her trial. However, there was very little to indicate how her daughter got into the water and, feeling that they had insufficient evidence to prove a charge of wilful murder, the prosecution asked the judge's permission to withdraw. The judge agreed and directed the jury to acquit the prisoner.

Note: Some publications give the date of the murder as 11 September.

13 **SEPTEMBER 1892** Annie Elizabeth Hearne was making a killing by telling fortunes from her home in Leicester and on the evening of 13 September, at least eleven girls called at the house to learn their future, paying 2d each for the privilege. She was summoned for 'unlawfully pretending to tell fortunes, to deceive and impose upon Sarah Birchall and others.' Annie had already served fourteen days' imprisonment on a similar charge in 1891 and had been cautioned by police only three months earlier.

Sarah Birchall told magistrates at Leicester Borough Police Court that Annie had incorrectly told her that she had a son, who treated her very unkindly. In court, Annie appeared 'feeble-minded' and witnesses were asked, 'Did she seem as feeble as she does now?'

When it became obvious that her feeble-mindedness was an act, sixty-three-year-old Annie suddenly got better and told magistrates that she didn't charge for fortune-telling and if people wanted to give her a donation she could hardly help that. She was fined 40s, or sentenced to one month's imprisonment in default.

14 **SEPTEMBER 1899** Coroner Robert Harvey held an inquest into the death of farm labourer Jonathan Richardson.

On 12 September, thirty-seven-year-old Richardson was thatching a straw rick at Desford with Joseph Plant. Richardson was standing on a ladder, while Plant handed straw to him but there was a rung missing from the ladder and Richardson fell.

He was holding a two-pronged pitchfork in his right hand and, after the handle embedded itself in the ground, Richardson fell onto one of the prongs, which penetrated his brain behind his right ear to a depth of almost 6 inches. Plant pulled out the pitchfork with considerable difficulty. 'Joe, it will kill me,' Richardson told him and those were the last words he ever spoke, dying from his injuries in the Leicester Infirmary that evening.

The inquest jury returned a verdict of 'accidental death'.

15 **SEPTEMBER** 1928 After attending a dance at Sapcote, twenty-year-old Albert Baker walked back to Sharnford and was about a mile from home when he was hit from behind by a motorcycle and knocked unconscious.

After hitting Albert, the motorbike travelled on for several yards, before its rider fell off. Witnesses rushed to pick him up but he collapsed as soon as he was raised from the ground and died the following night without regaining consciousness.

At the time of the inquest on the motorcyclist, Albert was said to be making satisfactory progress in hospital. The inquest jury returned a verdict of 'accidental death' on the man who knocked him down – his twenty-three-year-old brother, David.

16 **SEPTEMBER** 1874 John (or William) Cooke of Leicester was a violent drunk and on 16 September, after a day spent drinking, he quarrelled with his wife, Ann.

At just before 6 p.m., her terrified screams brought a neighbour running into the house. Cooke was just about to strike her with a hobnailed boot and the neighbour got between him and Ann, taking the blow on her own arm. Ann, who had recently been in hospital, remarked that her husband had given her 'a death blow' and when she died later that evening, he was charged with her manslaughter.

A post-mortem examination revealed that Ann had severe heart disease and although her husband's blows had not proved fatal, the excitement of the fight had hastened her death. Consequently, at the Leicester Assizes in December, John Cooke was found guilty of manslaughter and sentenced to five years' penal servitude.

17 **SEPTEMBER** 1867 Coroner John Gregory held an inquest in Leicester into the death of fifteen-year-old Robert Arthur Robins.

The key witness was twelve-year-old John Eayrs, who told the coroner that on Saturday 14 September, he met the deceased near North Bridge on the River Soar, where Robert hired a rowing boat and John a canoe. The boys went downriver but John struggled to keep up and ended up quarrelling with Robert. As they turned for home, John challenged Robert to a race and managed to pull the canoe in front of the boat but Robert quickly overtook him.

Realising that John was being left behind again, Robert grabbed the string at the front of the canoe and tried to fasten it to his boat to give John a tow. When he was unable to tie the string, Robert was returning to the seat in the boat when it tipped sideways and Robert fell out. John caught a brief glimpse of the top of his friend's head before the water closed over it, leaving just his hat floating on the surface.

John paddled his canoed back to the boathouse and raised the alarm but it was three hours before Robert's body was recovered with drags. The inquest jury returned a verdict of 'accidental death'.

18 SEPTEMBER 1925 Seventy-five-year-old Margaret Bottrill of Oadby died after being stung by a wasp.

An inquest heard that Mrs Bottrill was stung on the underside of her tongue while eating her dinner, leaving a small puncture wound that penetrated a vein. Mrs Bottrill collapsed and, according to the doctor called to treat her, the venom from the sting went directly to the part of her brain that controlled respiration. Although the doctor arrived within minutes, he found Mrs Bottrill in 'a state of extreme collapse'.

He administered strychnine and tried artificial respiration, but Mrs Bottrill's condition was hopeless and she died from a combination of shock and suffocation by her swollen tongue. The doctor told the inquest that it wasn't possible to save her, even had he been present when she was actually stung.

The inquest jury returned a verdict of 'accidental death'.

19 SEPTEMBER 1870 Thomas Knight of Barrow-upon-Soar wanted a quiet drink but unfortunately George Perkins was already at the pub when Knight arrived.

Perkins had a long-standing, petty grudge against Knight and told landlord Joseph Smith that he intended to settle it once and for all. Smith warned him that he would have no fighting and made sure that the two men were in separate rooms but forty-five minutes later, Perkins sought out Knight and the two men began scuffling.

Smith stepped in to break up the fight, grasping Perkins round his waist and holding him for sufficient time to allow Knight to leave. When Perkins was finally released he threatened, 'I'll kill him if I can catch him.' He then chased after Knight and gave him a good kicking when he caught up with him.

Knight was carried home, where he was found to be covered in cuts and bruises and, although a doctor was called, Knight died before he arrived. A post-mortem examination showed that death was due to an effusion of blood to the brain, caused by kicks or blows to the head.

Perkins was arrested on 19 September. 'I've done it. I can't help it and I shall have to suffer for it,' he said philosophically, adding that he was sorry that Knight was dead and that he hadn't meant to kill him.

He was charged with killing and murdering Thomas Knight and, when the jury at the Leicestershire Assizes found him guilty, the judge sentenced him to twenty years' penal servitude.

20 SEPTEMBER 1838

An inquest was held in Leicester into the death of twenty-one-year-old Elizabeth Billiard, who worked at a worsted factory.

It was Elizabeth's job to supervise a machine called a drawing frame – a machine that twisted and wound yarn by moving it through pairs of rollers. It was powered by steam engine, a leather strap looping from the machine to a revolving cylinder near the ceiling.

Elizabeth should have finished work at 8 p.m. but the overlooker informed her that she would have to work overtime until 10 p.m. Seconds later, one of the girls nudged the overseer to draw his attention to Elizabeth, who was spinning around the revolving cylinder, having caught one of her arms in the leather strap and been dragged into the machinery.

By the time the engine was stopped, Elizabeth's head and feet had struck the ceiling an estimated thirty times and she had two large wounds on the back of her head and serious injuries to her feet. A surgeon was sent for but Elizabeth was already drawing her last breaths and died fifteen minutes after being disentangled from the cylinder.

The inquest jury heard that the factory had an excellent safety record and that Elizabeth had worked there for between four and five years. They returned a verdict of 'accidental death'.

21 SEPTEMBER 1929

Professional dirt-track rider Roy Sims-Reeves was killed at Melton Road Speedway in Leicester.

Twenty-two-year-old Reeves crashed on a bend on the second lap. The rider immediately behind him managed to swerve to avoid him but the following rider struck Reeves just as he was getting to his feet.

Reeves, who was said to be a skilful and daring rider, was on a borrowed machine since his own was broken. At the inquest held on 23 September, his wife, who was in the crowd and witnessed her husband's death, informed the coroner that her husband had ridden on tracks all over the country.

Records show that in June 1928, Reeves was arrested at Torquay after he was observed riding with his arms folded and his feet on the handlebars, with one leg around his neck, standing on the saddle and jumping off then remounting the moving bike.

When he appeared before magistrates, it was noted that he had already been fined three times for not having a silencer fitted to his motorbike.

In reporting Reeves's appearance before magistrates, which resulted in a £1 fine and a suspension of his license for six months, the *Torquay Times* stated that he 'possessed remarkable talents, developed unfortunately in the wrong direction.'

The inquest jury returned a verdict of 'accidental death'.

22 SEPTEMBER 1893 The death of three-year-old Gertrude Thacker in Leicester was deemed suspicious, given that it closely followed a dose of medicine for a sore throat. Coroner Robert Harvey opened an inquest and adjourned it so that the child's stomach contents and the remaining medicine could be analysed.

When the inquest resumed, public analyst Dr Priestley outlined the results of his tests. In the stomach contents, he found traces of meconic acid, a marker for the presence of opium, as well as milk, blood and mucus. Analysis of Gertrude's medicine revealed the presence of meconic acid, along with traces of morphine, camphor and alcohol.

Priestley had calculated that Gertrude had ingested the equivalent of three or four drops of opium. He told the inquest that there were cases on record of children of Gertrude's age having been killed by six drops but, in Priestley's opinion, four drops would be unlikely to kill a healthy three-year-old. However, Gertrude was far from healthy, having contracted scarlet fever on 13 September, which was thought to have damaged her kidneys.

Priestley told the inquest that Gertrude's death was ultimately due to scarlet fever but had probably been accelerated by the effects of a dose of opium on her feeble constitution. Coroner Harvey told the jury that they must first decide whether they believed that the child's death was due to opium poisoning and, if it was, whether there was any culpable negligence on the part of chemist and druggist Mrs Staines.

The jury were told that Gertrude's grandmother requested ipecacuanha wine for Gertrude's sore throat but Mrs Staines had almost run out and instead supplied a mixture of ipecacuanha wine, syrup of squills and a small quantity of laudanum. Gertrude died shortly after her first dose and the timing of her death was consistent with her having been poisoned by something in the medicine.

The jury eventually returned a verdict of 'death through misadventure', explaining that they believed that, although the poison accelerated the child's demise, Gertrude would have died anyway, even without the medicine. Mrs Staines apparently faced no criminal charges.

23 SEPTEMBER 1896 After lengthy consideration, an inquest returned a verdict of 'accidental death' on forty-two-year-old painter Edward Crooks, who died after a fall from scaffolding, while lime washing walls at the Wigston Locomotive Works.

The problem for the inquest was that nobody could work out what caused Crooks to fall. He was sober, was not subject to giddiness or vertigo, and the scaffolding on which he was working at the time seemed perfectly safe.

Crooks was seen falling legs first but turned as he neared the ground, eventually landing heavily on his head and dying on impact. Labourer Conyers Boulter recalled Crooks telling him to make himself safe while he moved a scaffold plank but then turned his back on Crooks and didn't see what caused him to fall. Although one scaffold plank fell, nobody in the vicinity could recall whether it hit the ground before or after Crooks and Boulter could only guess that Crooks simply overbalanced. With little evidence to the contrary, the jury accepted Boulter's theory.

24 SEPTEMBER 1882 An inquest was held into the death of John Brookes (aka Ward) at Markfield Quarry.

Henry Pickard was quiet and inoffensive, whereas Brookes was a fighting man, with a reputation as a skilled boxer. On 23 September, both men were working at Markfield Quarry, where Brookes was annoying Pickard by continually hiding his tools. Eventually, Pickard remarked that Brookes had been 'messing him about all day', an observation to which Brookes took objection. He punched Pickard twice in the face before turning away and, as he bent to carry on working, Pickard hit him on the head with the side of his pick.

Brookes slumped to the ground but, within a couple of minutes, was able to resume work and, at the end of the day, climbed eighty-two rungs up a ladder to get out of the quarry. However, on reaching home he complained of a headache and went straight to bed. He quickly fell unconscious and died within a couple of hours from a fractured skull and bleeding on the brain.

At the inquest into Brookes's death, most of the jury and witnesses had known Pickard since he was a boy and were devastated by the necessity of returning a verdict of 'wilful murder' against him. However, when Pickard appeared before magistrates, they viewed the offence as manslaughter, hence Pickard appeared at the assizes in November charged with both offences.

The prosecution declined to offer any evidence on the indictment for murder and, on the advice of his counsel, Pickard pleaded guilty to manslaughter. In sentencing him, the judge recognised his previous good character, the great provocation that led to the offence and the fact that Pickard had used the side of his pick rather than the point, but said that he couldn't ignore the fact that Brookes was stooping to his work when Pickard hit him. Noting that Pickard had already spent one month in prison awaiting his trial, the judge sentenced him to a further five months' imprisonment.

25 SEPTEMBER 1850 Labourer James Bennett of Desford had suffered from rheumatism since the hay harvest but Mr Evans of Moira kindly allowed him to use his bathroom for a hot bath on occasions and on 25 September, Bennett walked to Moira with the intention of bathing.

Mr Evans's fifteen-year-old son ran the bath for him and helped him to take off his coat in the dressing room. The boy carefully tested the temperature of the water and found it to be 96°C but Bennett asked for the water to be hotter, so the hot tap was turned on and the temperature increased to 98°C.

Bennett was then left to take his bath but when he didn't reappear, Mr Evans went to check on him. He found Bennett lying dead in the bath with the hot tap turned on and the temperature of the water at 130°C. He was scalded almost all over his body and at the inquest, it was suggested that he turned the hot water on and fainted from the heat before he could turn off the tap. A verdict of 'accidental death' was recorded.

26 SEPTEMBER 1880 As it was a Sunday, brothers Arthur and Elijah Statham of Newbold Verdon and their lodger, William Arnold, retired to an outhouse for some surreptitious drinking. At about 4 p.m., William went home, where he began an argument with Mrs Statham, his landlady and the mother of Arthur and Elijah.

Arthur came in at the height of the argument, and took exception to William's attitude. Blows were exchanged and William was knocked down, at which point Elijah entered the fray. William snatched up a coal hammer and used it to defend himself, hitting Elijah on the left temple. Elijah dropped to the ground but quickly got up and re-joined the fight and it wasn't until sometime later that he began to feel unwell and was diagnosed with a fractured skull.

Elijah died in hospital on 1 October and surgeons found that a portion of his skull had been driven into his brain. There was absolutely no doubt that his death was due to a blow on the head and an inquest found a verdict of 'wilful murder' against William Arnold.

He was tried at the Leicester Assizes on 30 October, where the jury found themselves sifting through a great deal of conflicting and contradictory evidence. None of the witnesses could agree on how the fight started and two swore that Arthur struck the first blow, while William was actually sitting in a chair. They also stated that William picked up the hammer to defend himself, grabbing the first thing that came to hand after being set upon by both brothers at once. The jury found William Arnold guilty of the lesser offence of manslaughter and he was sentenced to seven years' penal servitude.

27 SEPTEMBER 1900 Coroner Robert Harvey held an inquest in Leicester into the death of one-year-old Frederick Moore.

Frederick's grandmother was seriously ill and the boy's mother nursed her and took care of her house. On 26 September, Mrs Moore left Frederick playing in the back yard while she did some housework. She kept an eye on him through the kitchen window but suddenly looked up at midday to find that Frederick had vanished.

He was found minutes later by neighbour Mrs Clark, in a bucket of water, his head and hands underwater in the bucket and his feet off the floor. A doctor was called but there was nothing that he could do, since Frederick had already been dead for at least fifteen minutes.

The cause of Frederick's death was suffocation by drowning and the inquest jury determined that it was accidental.

28 SEPTEMBER 1898 Kate Danvers appeared at the Loughborough Petty Sessions, charged with cruelly neglecting her children. It was the second such prosecution for Mrs Danvers (*see* 7 February), who spent one month in prison earlier in the year.

While she was incarcerated, the children were properly cared for and were clean and healthy when they were returned to their mother on her release from prison on 9 March. However, Inspector Barnes of the NSPCC kept a close eye on the family and quickly realised that Mrs Danvers had learned nothing from her sentence. She refused to clean her house and the children grew gradually filthier until Barnes visited the house on 9 September and observed maggots crawling under their skin.

In her defence, Kate Danvers insisted that the children's matted, louse-infested hair was hereditary rather than the result of dirt or neglect. She denied visiting public houses and getting drunk, saying that there was no woman in Shepshed who did more for her home and family than she did. Magistrates sent her back to prison for a further month, remarking that they hoped that it would prove more effective this time.

29 SEPTEMBER 1899 An inquest was held at the Leicester Infirmary into the death of forty-seven-year-old carpenter, Joseph Bent Bright.

Bright left home at 6.15 a.m. on 26 September to go shooting. Nine hours later, farm labourer Alfred Duffin was working in a field at Humberstone when he heard a gunshot and more than an hour afterwards, saw Joseph sitting in the corner of a field. When he went to speak to him, Duffin noticed a gun at his side.

'Go and fetch your father. The gun has gone off and shot me,' Joseph told Duffin, who ran for help. 'Do take me away, or I shall die,' Joseph begged George Duffin, who procured a cart and drove him to hospital, where doctors found his right arm peppered with lead shot.

Joseph was conscious and said that he had been shot hours before Duffin found him and had been trying to make his way home, although bloodstains showed that he had moved only 200 yards. The injuries to his arm were so severe that surgeons amputated it shortly after his admission to hospital, but Joseph died from shock and blood loss eight hours later.

Although it was impossible to show how Joseph was shot, the coroner believed that what little evidence there was pointed to an accident. The jury were in agreement and a verdict of 'accidental death' was recorded.

30 SEPTEMBER 1899 At Stanford Hall, thirty-three-year-old Percy Sinclair Pilcher had intended to demonstrate his latest development – a powered tri-plane – in an effort to gain sponsors. However, the weather was somewhat stormy and the tri-plane had a broken crankshaft. So as not to disappoint his invited guests, who included Mr Henniker Heaton MP, Percy decided to fly his Hawk glider instead, with which he had already broken the world distance flying record.

He took off at about 4 p.m., but had travelled only 150 yards when a sharp gust of wind caught the glider and it overturned, dropping 60 feet to the ground. Percy was badly injured and died on 2 October.

At the inquest into his death, it was demonstrated that the crash was due to a snapped crossbar, which caused the wings to fold and collapse. The jury found that proper safety precautions were taken and returned a verdict of 'accidental death'.

OCTOBER

St George's Church, Leicester, with Revd C.L. Robinson, who was conducting a service when a fire destroyed the church (see pages 182-183). (Author's collection)

1 OCTOBER 1894 Coroner Henry Deane held an inquest into the deaths of two people.

The previous day, Henry Hind, Gertrude Ellen Robinson and Percy Wagstaffe were rowing from Beeston to Loughborough. When they arrived at Kegworth Lock, Percy got out of the boat to open the gates but the sudden inrush of water swept the boat up against the lock and its rudder caught on the gates.

The boat rapidly began to fill with water and overturned, sending Henry and Gertrude into the water. Percy jumped in after them but was unable to find them and so climbed out and began undressing, in order to be able to dive in search of them.

Two mill workers heard the commotion and assumed that it was people larking about. When they saw Percy undressing, they realised that something was very wrong and went to help. Percy was clinging to the lock and was pulled out of the water exhausted, but it was some time before the bodies of his companions were recovered, Henry having been washed through the sluices at the bottom of the lock gates.

A post-mortem showed that both Henry and Gertrude had drowned and the inquest jury returned two verdicts of 'accidental death'. After the inquest, the coroner was informed that Henry Hind was an assumed name – the dead man was actually Thomas Henry Matthews, a married man from Birmingham, who had adopted the name Hind for 'private reasons'.

2 OCTOBER 1873 When Ann Armston married Thomas Orton, he was aware that she had an illegitimate daughter, Ada, but did not realise that six-year-old Nelly, who lived with an aunt in Ashby-de-la-Zouch, was also his wife's child.

In September 1873, the aunt's home broke up and Ann was told to make alternative arrangements for Nelly's care. She tried to get the little girl into the Workhouse but failed, so took Nelly to her marital home in Appleby Magna but Thomas told Ann that he could not afford to keep other people's children. On 2 October, Ann called in at her cousin's house in Measham with Nelly and told her that a woman from Measham had agreed to take the child.

Later that evening, two women crossing a bridge over the River Mease heard a child screaming, followed by a woman's voice saying, 'Hold your noise. I've got you.' Three weeks later, a child's body was found in the river and when it was identified as Nelly, Ann told the police, 'What else could I do? My husband did not know it was my child – I dare not tell him. Nobody would have it.'

Ann appeared at the Derbyshire Assizes in March 1874 charged with wilful murder. After hearing the evidence, the jury returned a verdict that Ann was 'guilty

Mr Justice Baron Pollock.
(Author's collection)

of drowning the child whilst her mind was in a proper state.' Judge Mr Baron Pollock advised them that they must return a verdict of either guilty or not guilty and, after a further twenty minutes deliberation, the jury chose the latter option. Pollock asked if they had arrived at this verdict because they believed that the defendant was insane and, when the jury answered in the affirmative, he sentenced Ann to be detained during Her Majesty's pleasure. She was sent to Broadmoor Criminal Lunatic Asylum.

3 OCTOBER 1896 PC John Ireland was called to Bosworth Street, Leicester, by the wife of Edwin Gallaway. When Ireland arrived, he found Gallaway in the street, very drunk and 'acting like a madman'. Mrs Gallaway's face was bleeding and she complained that her husband had assaulted her.

Ireland persuaded the couple to calm down and they went back indoors. However, minutes later, Mrs Gallaway came rushing out, pursued by her husband, who was brandishing a knife.

Ireland got between the couple, allowing Mrs Gallaway to escape. Meanwhile, her husband punched PC Ireland on the nose before fleeing back into his house. He emerged carrying a fender and, expecting him to use it as a weapon against him, Ireland focused his attention on it. Instead Gallaway kicked the policeman, catching him on the hand. Gallaway fought PC Ireland's attempts to arrest him and they wrestled on the ground until a member of the public came to Ireland's assistance and Gallaway was securely handcuffed.

At the Borough Police Court, Gallaway maintained that PC Ireland struck the first blow. Gallaway stated that Ireland called him 'a little monkey', to which he retaliated that the policeman was 'a gorilla'. According to Gallaway, Ireland then flew at him, striking him several times on the chest, before knocking him over.

Gallaway's mother-in-law was called as a witness and corroborated his story. She denied that Gallaway had picked up a knife or the fender and even denied that her daughter's face was bleeding. (Asked to explain the fresh cuts on Mrs Gallaway's face, her mother backpedalled and told magistrates that she thought their questions referred to another of her daughters.)

Magistrates found Gallaway guilty of 'a most brutal assault' and sentenced him to one month's imprisonment, with hard labour.

4 OCTOBER 1894 Coroner Henry Deane held an inquest at Rothley into the death of forty-six-year-old farm labourer Henry Godwin.

Two days earlier, Charles Clements was harvesting potatoes in a field in Cossington when Godwin arrived with a cartload of manure. Once the cart was emptied, Godwin led the horse out of the field, leaving it momentarily unattended while he closed the gate. The horse moved off then stopped and when Clements walked to the gate to see why, he saw Godwin lying on the ground about 20 yards away, bleeding from his ears, nose and mouth and unable to speak. Marks on the grass indicated that the cartwheel had passed over Godwin's head and he died within minutes from a fractured skull.

The horse was said to be a quiet animal and, as far as Clements was aware, nothing untoward had occurred which may have startled it. With no obvious explanation for Godwin's demise, the inquest jury returned a verdict of 'accidental death'.

5 OCTOBER 1911 As the congregation of St George's Church in Leicester enjoyed a Harvest Festival service, a fire broke out in a nearby factory. With the church in jeopardy from the flames, vicar Reverend Robinson made a decision to cut short the service.

The fire and subsequent damage at St George's Church, October 1911. (Author's collection)

Before long, the fire spread to the church, which was completely gutted, as were two neighbouring factories. The fire started in the premises of hosiery manufacturers R. Rowley and Co. Ltd and by the time it was under control, had caused around £150,000 worth of damage, making it arguably the worst fire Leicester had ever witnessed to that date.

6 OCTOBER 1907 Collier Archibald Ernest Page and domestic servant Annie Elizabeth Haines had been courting for a year but Page was exceedingly jealous. During Annie's annual leave, she visited relatives at Attleborough, near Nuneaton. Page was working at a colliery in the area and, on 6 October, he followed Annie and her relatives to chapel and saw her talking to a young man.

The next day, Annie had arranged to visit her parents at Broughton Astley and took the train from Nuneaton to Croft. Less than three hours after leaving Nuneaton, she was found strangled in a ditch on the road between Croft and Broughton Astley and, when her body was moved, a bundle of love letters that she had written to Page during their relationship fell out of her blouse.

The victim, Annie Elizabeth Haines, from *The Penny Illustrated Paper*, 19 October 1907. (Author's collection)

An ambulance medal, some broken braces and a shirt front and collar were found near to the body, which were later traced to Page, who had been seen loitering near Croft station and on the lane where Annie was found. At 5 a.m. on the morning after the murder, he called at a labourer's cottage pretending to be a detective working on the case and, later that day, he was

The murderer, Archibald Ernest Page, from *The Penny Illustrated Paper*, 19 October 1907. (Author's collection)

arrested at Rugby. He immediately confessed, 'I killed the young girl,' going on to explain that he had strangled her with one hand because she refused to tell him the name of the man she was speaking to at chapel. When Archibald was searched after his arrest, a written account of the murder entitled 'A Lover's Crime' was found in his possession, along with an unused razor, with which he said he intended to kill himself.

Tried for wilful murder at the Leicester Assizes less than three weeks after the murder, Page's defence tried to show that he was of weak intellect. They also suggested that, rather than strangling his girlfriend, Page merely shook her hard, causing her accidental death from syncope.

The spot where Annie's body was discovered. (Author's collection)

The jury found Page guilty of wilful murder, with no concession to his mental state, and he was sentenced to death. His sentence was later commuted to one of life imprisonment, part of which was served at Dartmoor Prison. He appears to have been freed to fight in the First World War and to have married in 1918. Page is believed to have died in 1949 a free man.

7 OCTOBER 1863 Men working underground at the Califat Pit in Coleorton observed a trickle of water coming through a wall and although carpenter Jeremiah Rose tried to plug the holes, the trickle rapidly became a flood, as water rushed from the abandoned workings of an adjacent pit.

At first it was feared that at least six men and twenty-nine horses had perished but, while the number of equine victims was accurate, three of the assumed human fatalities were rescued alive. Rose died, as did Thomas Bird, leaving fifteen fatherless children between them, while the third victim, Harry Clements, was little more than a child himself.

In January 1864, mine manager Julius C. Ibbotson Bailey was charged with wilful neglect in respect of the disaster and appeared before magistrates at Ashby-de-la-Zouch. He was found guilty and fined £15, with an additional £6 10s costs. The fine was divided between the families of the three deceased.

8 OCTOBER 1900 As Dr J. St T. Clarke was crossing London Road, Leicester, several shots were fired at him. Although Clarke was not killed by the hail of bullets, one penetrated his spine and doctors were unable to remove it for fear of causing paralysis.

London Road, Leicester. (Author's collection)

The gunman was forty-five-year-old dairyman Sidney James Kirby, who had long held a grudge against the doctor. In 1896, Clarke was one of two doctors who signed papers to have Kirby committed to an asylum, and Kirby was under the impression that Clarke had placed a 'blister poultice' on the back of his neck and 'drawn his brains away.'

Kirby's current doctor was of the opinion that he was not responsible for his actions due to insanity and, when he was tried at the Leicestershire Assizes on an indictment of shooting with intent to murder, the jury agreed, finding him guilty but insane. He was ordered to be detained during Her Majesty's pleasure.

9   OCTOBER 1863   Seventy-one-year-old Charles Gregory kept cows and behind his house in Leicester was a large cistern used for storing cattle feed, which was accessed by a trapdoor and ladder. Such was the stench from the silo that even the cows refused to go anywhere near it.

On 9 October, Gregory ordered one of his labourers to fetch some grain but he refused. Gregory ridiculed him for his reluctance and said that he would go himself, but no sooner had he descended the ladder than he collapsed. The labourer raised the alarm and Gregory's daughter, Charlotte, sent him to fetch help. He ran to the nearby pub but, in the meantime, seeing her father unconscious at the bottom of the cistern, Charlotte went down to help him.

She too collapsed and Charles Freeman (or Truman) and Joseph Tacey, who arrived from the pub, had no hesitation in going down to get her. Not surprisingly, they too were overcome by fumes and eventually all four were pulled from the cistern using drags. Doctors were unable to revive them and, at the inquest, the coroner remarked that all four of the deceased were 'within an arm's reach' of assistance, adding that he hoped that anyone who stored grain would take warning. The inquest jury found 'that the deceased persons met with their death through having inhaled carbonic acid gas accidentally.'

10 OCTOBER 1867 Work continued for the Midland Railway on widening the railway lines and constructing new sidings next to the passenger station at Leicester. At about 10.30 a.m. on 10 October, a group of three labourers were 'holing' – undermining a section of earth prior to removing it – when, suddenly, the 40-foot high embankment above them gave way.

A large lump of falling earth hit Benjamin Chappell on the head and he was knocked to the ground, the upper part of his body completely buried by soil. His workmates immediately extricated him but he was already dead, his head crushed.

Chappell's was the third fatal accident at the site since the construction work began.

Midland Railway Station, Leicester, 1904. (Author's collection)

11 OCTOBER 1882 Coroner George F. Harrison held an inquest at The George Hotel, Hinckley into the death of forty-five-year-old John Bailey.

Although originally from Yorkshire, Bailey had lived in Leicester for the past year and, on 10 October, he and James Bradshaw were invited to go shooting at a farm near Hinckley. They were given lunch, after which they continued with the day's sport. Walking across a field, they came to a brook and as Bradshaw went to cross it, Bailey stopped him, warning him that the ground he was about to step on was unsafe. Bradshaw thanked him and moved along the bank a little way, then watched in astonishment as Bailey proceeded to cross at the precise place he had just warned his companion against. The bank collapsed as he was about to leap over the brook and he fell, landing heavily on another man who was in the process of unloading his own gun in order to cross the stream safely. The gun went off, hitting a halfpenny in the pocket of Bailey's breeches and forcing it into his groin, and, although a doctor was sent for, Bailey had died by the time he arrived.

A verdict of 'accidental death' was returned.

12 OCTOBER 1868 Coroner Mr J. Gregory held an inquest into the death of five-year-old Laura Scattergood of Shepshed.

On 9 October, Laura went out to play and didn't return. Initially, her family weren't concerned, as the little girl often went to her aunt's house, but when she hadn't arrived home by 6 p.m. and they discovered that she hadn't visited her aunt, almost the entire village began searching for her. Eventually, somebody thought to check the well in the yard of the Scattergoods' house. There was no sign of anything untoward but when a woman remembered having used the well that morning, the searchers fetched drag lines and Laura's body was recovered.

At the inquest, neighbour Mrs Colton recalled taking a bucket of water out of the well and leaving the cover off for a few minutes, intending to fetch another. The hinges had been broken for some time, as had the pump, and thus the only way to get water was to remove the cover completely. It was surmised that Laura must have fallen into the well when the cover was off and had probably already drowned when it was replaced.

In returning a verdict of 'accidental death', the jury asked the coroner to write to the landlord, ordering him to repair the cover before there were any further tragedies.

13 OCTOBER 1899 Friday 13th was certainly an unlucky day for fifty-year-old Stephen Main, who met his death at Mr T.A.W. Clarke's Iron Foundry in Leicester.

It was Main's job to stamp metal tongs using a steam hammer, the head of which weighed 4cwt. The hammer was raised by depressing a foot lever then, on the operator's signal, the hammer head was dropped by an assistant operating a hand lever. Frank Hardman, who was operating the lever for Main, saw him put the tongs in place and, when he clearly heard Main say, 'Right,' which was their usual signal, he released the hammer, which dropped onto the top of Main's skull, smashing it like an eggshell.

The inquest could find no possible explanation for Main's death other than suggesting that he might have slipped and lost his balance. Coroner Robert Harvey told the jury that, although there was no direct evidence to show how Main met his death, the likelihood was that it was accidental and the jury concurred.

14 OCTOBER 1930 An inquest was held into the death of seventy-five-year-old May Ann Smallbone.

Two days earlier, some of the occupants of a house in Leicester were awakened by the smell of smoke. Nathan Riley Smith went to investigate but couldn't determine where it was coming from and so opened the back door for a few minutes to allow the smoke to dissipate, before going back to bed.

Samuel Thomas Turton was woken by his daughter and he too wandered around the house looking for the source of the smell. Arriving on the top floor, he found the corridor thick with smoke, emanating from a bedsit occupied by Mrs Smallbone. Turton tried the door, which was locked and, when knocking produced no response, he went back to his own room and got ready for work. It was more than an hour before someone thought to call the fire brigade, by which time Mrs Smallbone had burned to death.

The coroner couldn't believe that in a house occupied by ten people – six of whom were adults – nobody had thought to either break down Mrs Smallbone's door or to summon the fire brigade. In fact, not one person took the slightest notice of the smoke, even though it was a sure sign of fire. The coroner recorded a verdict of 'accidental death', suggesting that the conduct of the residents of the house was both astounding and amazing, adding that he didn't think they had an ounce of common sense between them.

15 OCTOBER 1900 Twenty-one-year-old Alfred Lakin from Derby operated the roundabout in a travelling fair, collecting money and maintaining the ride. When the fair arrived at Leicester, he had been drinking steadily for three weeks and by midday on 15 October, he was so drunk that proprietor Frederick Hodder sacked him on the spot.

Hodder saw no more of Lakin until 9.30 p.m., when there was a sudden scream from the roundabout. Lakin was lying face down on the tracks on which the roundabout's cars ran and died soon afterwards from 'collapse and shock, consequent on internal injuries'. Although he had no broken bones, he had a contusion running from his waist, across his chest and round his neck, as though one of the car wheels had passed over his body.

At the time, the roundabout was being operated by Laurie Lount, who told coroner Robert Harvey that he saw Lakin on the machine immediately before the accident. A woman riding the roundabout stated that Lakin took her money, while standing on the back of the car she was sitting in. Mrs Jakins recalled remonstrating with Lakin, who was obviously very drunk and said that he fell between her car and the next.

Having been sacked, Lakin had no business anywhere near the ride and the inquest returned a verdict of 'accidental death', adding that there was nobody but Lakin to blame.

16 OCTOBER 1835 Farmers George Turner junior and Henry Wells met by chance in a pub at Great Dalby. Turner grew pugnacious as he drank and kept challenging Wells to fight but Wells refused, telling him that neighbours shouldn't fight each other.

When Wells left, Turner tried to buy more beer and was told that he could have one pint and no more. He flew into a rage, telling the landlady that he would be back later that day to pay off his 'slate', after which he would never set foot in her establishment again. Shortly afterwards, Turner caught up with Wells on the road and was seen by a witness seizing him by the collar and renewing the challenge to fight. The witness heard Wells say that he would gladly go a few rounds with him when he was sober.

Soon afterwards, a farmer driving cattle along the road came across an abandoned horse and cart and a little further on, found Wells lying dead in the road. He had two black eyes, a broken nose and a wound on each side of his head. His neckerchief was torn and lay some yards away, as did his handkerchief and whip, and twelve large pools of blood on the road extended back several yards towards the cart. Wells was black and blue all over and was later found to have eleven broken ribs on one side, ten on the other.

Suspicion immediately fell on Turner and a crowd of about forty villagers, including the constable and the surgeon, surrounded his farmhouse. Turner surrendered an hour later, when his boots and stockings were seen to be covered in blood.

Turner initially stated that Wells threatened to horsewhip him and he fought in self-defence, but at his trial at the Leicestershire Assizes his defence was that Wells was run over by his own cart. The presiding judge told the jury that if they believed Wells was run over, his death was accidental. If they thought that Turner had deprived Wells of life without provocation, the correct verdict was guilty of murder, whereas, if they thought that Wells had provoked Turner to use violence towards him, they should find the prisoner guilty of manslaughter. The judge seemed somewhat taken aback by the jury's verdict of guilty of manslaughter and sentenced Turner to be transported for life. He sailed for New South Wales on 2 June 1836 on *Lady Kennaway*.

17 OCTOBER 1897 Seventeen-year-old Ernest Henson Pearce died at the Leicester Infirmary.

Six weeks earlier, he injured his leg while playing football. It appeared slightly bruised and there was a small graze on it but Ernest wouldn't allow his mother to bathe or dress it, saying that he was always getting kicked.

Ernest made no complaints about his leg until 9 October. The previous day, he came home from work apparently suffering from influenza and went straight to bed. When his grandmother was straightening his bedclothes the next morning, he told her that she was hurting his sore leg and, when she looked at the limb, she found it inflamed and swollen. She applied a poultice but the leg got worse and on 13 October the doctor sent Ernest to hospital, where he died four days later from gangrene and blood poisoning.

Ernest's brother and two friends recalled Ernest being kicked but were adamant that the play wasn't rough and that nobody kicked him wilfully, adding that he had played football numerous times since. The inquest jury returned a verdict of 'death from gangrene, from a blow accidentally inflicted', finding insufficient evidence to show how the blow was caused.

18 OCTOBER 1898 Lucy Seal appeared at the Leicester Quarter Sessions charged with unlawfully and maliciously wounding her husband, Albert, at Loughborough.

On 2 July, Albert asked Lucy to fetch his wages of £1 3s 4d, telling her to take £1 for housekeeping and give him the change for spending money. When he later asked Lucy for his money, she told him, 'You won't have a farthing,' and, when he tried to take it, she hit him over the head with a poker, splitting his scalp to the bone.

Lucy gave a significantly different version of events, swearing that Albert was rolling drunk and knocked her out of her chair when she wouldn't give him any money. Believing that he would waste it on drink, she continued to refuse to hand it over, at which Albert grabbed her by the throat and pinioned her to the back door, before pushing her violently away. She grabbed the poker and, when Albert rushed at her again, she hit him in self-defence.

At her trial, Lucy said that she was very sorry for what she had done but had endured a great deal of provocation from her husband, adding that he had been very peaceable and quiet since.

The jury found Lucy Seal not guilty and she was discharged. She fainted on hearing the verdict and was helped from the court by her husband.

19 OCTOBER 1896 Coroner Henry Deane held an inquest into the death of sixty-seven-year-old Eliza Knight, the housekeeper at Rearsby Rectory.

On 10 October, Eliza was unpicking some sewing when she accidentally pricked herself with the scissors, leaving a tiny puncture wound on her finger. Later that day, Eliza complained that her hand was hurting and, three days later, she was in such pain that she sent for the doctor.

The scissors were not rusty and appeared clean to the naked eye, but Dr W.C. Dalley found Eliza's hand very swollen and, over the course of the next few days, the swelling extended up her arm. Dalley diagnosed erysipelas – an acute bacterial infection – and although he immediately began treatment, Eliza died on 16 October.

The inquest jury returned a verdict that death was due to erysipelas, following an accidental puncture of the finger.

20 OCTOBER 1896 When eight-week-old Ada Emily Barsby died at Anstey, she weighed just 3lb – about a third of the normal weight for an infant of her age. An inquest heard that her thirty-two-year-old mother was addicted to drink and had made no preparations for her baby's birth on 19 August. She gave her daughter no food and refused to suckle her.

Sarah Ann and Thomas William Barsby were jointly charged with manslaughter and appeared before Mr Justice Day at the Leicestershire Assizes. Their defence counsel claimed that their neglect of the baby was not intentional, adding that Thomas Barsby had done all he could for the child in the face of his wife's constant drinking and, although the jury found both defendants guilty, they recommended Thomas to mercy. He was sentenced to eighteen months' imprisonment with hard labour, while Sarah was awarded seven years' penal servitude.

21 OCTOBER 1889 Robert Kirkman was suffering from mental depression and melancholia and was also delusional when he walked into the dining room of his home in Cosby, pointed a revolver at his brother-in-law and pulled the trigger. Fortunately, William Blastock was wearing a diamond pin in his shirt front, which miraculously deflected the bullet.

Kirkman was charged with shooting at Blastock with intent to murder him and appeared at the Leicestershire Assizes on 29 November. The court was told that there

Anstey. (Author's collection)

was no quarrel between the two men, who were normally on very good terms. Since there didn't appear to be the slightest possible motive for the shooting, the jury found forty-seven-year-old Kirkman guilty but insane and he was ordered to be detained during Her Majesty's pleasure and sent to Broadmoor Criminal Lunatic Asylum.

22 OCTOBER 1881 An express and a mineral train collided at Desford Junction, killing three passengers and injuring many others. The express driver, John Whitfield, was dreadfully scalded and later died from his injuries in the Leicester Infirmary, as did another passenger, Frederick Astle.

Two inquests were held – the first on the three deceased passengers, Clara Orton, Alice Martha Whetstone and Kate Marion Wainwright, and the second on Whitfield and Astle. Both inquiries returned a verdict of manslaughter against points man Thomas Butler, who moved the points to divert the mineral train into a siding and forgot to move them back again.

Butler was tried for manslaughter at the Leicestershire Assizes in January 1882. However, there were numerous instances of what *The Times* referred to as 'loose management' at Desford. Some of the signals were blown down in a gale more than a week before the accident and had not been replaced, the staff worked excessive hours, and workmen were in the habit of congregating in the signal box and distracting the signalman. In addition, the brakes on the express train were judged to be inadequate. It proved impossible to demonstrate that Butler had acted with criminal negligence and he was acquitted.

23 OCTOBER 1914 Thirty-two-year-old Arnold Warren was tried at the Leicestershire Assizes for the wilful murder of his two-year-old son, James.

Warren's wife left him as a result of his addiction to gambling. Since her husband rarely had any money, Ethel Mary Warren worked to support their son, who was cared for during the day by Warren's mother. In the evenings, Ethel's eleven-year-old neighbour, Edith Skidmore, picked James up and took him for a walk, before taking him home.

On 10 July, Ethel bumped into her husband at the Clock Tower, Leicester. Although magistrates had ordered him to pay ten shillings maintenance every week, Warren told Ethel that he had quit his job and was now trying to make a living as a professional gambler. In fact, he had drawn out his entire savings to bet on one particular horse. He told Ethel that, if the horse lost, he intended to kill himself, showing her a blue bottle labelled 'Poison' in his pocket.

Four days later, Warren met Edith Skidmore with his son in Fosse Road recreation ground. Warren asked Edith to take a note to his wife, telling her that he would look after James while she went, but when Edith got back, there was no sign of either Warren or James. They were later spotted in the park, both drenched in blood. James's throat had been cut and he died from blood loss, while his father had taken laudanum.

After a stay in hospital, Warren was moved to Leicester Prison to await his trial for wilful murder and, found guilty, he was sentenced to death and was hanged by John Ellis on 12 November.

Clock Tower, Leicester.
(Author's collection)

24 OCTOBER 1931 Fifty-five-year-old nurse Annie Robson was tried for wilful murder at the Leicestershire Assizes.

When sixty-five-year-old Mildred Alice Pochin of Barby Hall was convalescing after an illness, her family hired Annie to care for her at home. On 8 July, Annie entered Mrs Pochin's room carrying a jug of water. Shortly afterwards there was a piercing shriek and Annie shouted, 'You damned old cat. This has been going on since you came back.'

'Oh! You're killing me,' replied Mrs Pochin, who then dashed from the room naked apart from her slippers, claiming that her nurse had gone stark raving mad and thrown boiling water over her. Mrs Pochin had a cut on her forehead and was so severely scalded on her breasts and upper arms that she died on 14 July.

At Annie's trial, the prosecution maintained that she had reacted to a groundless idea that Mrs Pochin meant her harm by losing control and giving free rein to her temper. The defence insisted that the only possible explanation for the murder was that Annie was insane, calling medical witnesses to suggest that the killing was done 'in a state of amnesia brought about by psychic epilepsy', which usually occurred as a result of 'brooding on matters of a sexual nature.' Dr Colohan – described as 'the well-known mental specialist' – told the jury that two years earlier, Annie underwent major surgery, which may have interfered with the working of 'certain glands'. Having examined her, he came to the conclusion that she was suffering from delusions.

The defence's explanation proved persuasive and Annie Robson was pronounced guilty but insane and ordered to be detained during the King's pleasure.

25 OCTOBER 1888 A gang of railway labourers were transported to the Syston North Junction of the Midland Railway. It was very foggy and, as the men were about to begin work, they heard an approaching goods train and stepped back out of the way. Unfortunately, they stepped straight into the path of the passenger express from Derby.

William Cheney and John Waring were killed instantly while Henry Drinkwater was seriously injured and taken to the Leicester Infirmary with a broken leg and shock. He later made a statement to say that he saw the express train and was trying to pull one of the other men out of its way.

At the inquest, coroner Henry Deane's first task was to deal with jury member David North, who turned up drunk and was fined 20s and sent home. The inquest then concluded that the thick fog prevented the deceased from seeing the express train and that the sound of the goods train had drowned out its approach. Two verdicts of 'accidental death' were recorded.

26 OCTOBER 1878 At weekends, the schoolrooms at St Matthew's Church School, Leicester, were used by an athletics club. On 26 October, seventeen-year-old clerk Ernest Orill Robinson was swinging on a trapeze at a height of 6 feet from the ground when he slipped and fell, landing head first on the floor. Medical aid was summoned but Ernest was dead from a dislocated neck by the time a doctor arrived.

An inquest held at the school heard that mattresses had been placed beneath the trapeze but Ernest fell beyond them. A verdict of 'accidental death' was returned.

27 OCTOBER 1844 Thomas Berresford was an eccentric recluse, who shared an isolated smallholding near Ratby with his maiden daughter, Ann. The seventy-four-year-old man and his daughter were objects of ridicule to the local youths, who found tormenting them an entertaining pastime.

On 27 October, a gang of eleven young thugs went into Berresford's yard and, in the words of one of the group, 'teased him out.' Berresford came out with a gun and was beaten about the head with a thorny stem of briar. He asked the youths to go away and eighteen-year-old William Harrison said that they would, if Berresford would shake hands with them. This he did and the youths left, but as soon as they reached the lane, they threw a hail of stones at Berresford, who was still holding his gun. It went off and the charge lodged in Harrison's chest, causing him to bleed to death almost instantly.

At the inquest into Harrison's death, the coroner found a verdict of manslaughter against Berresford, who was committed for trial at the Leicestershire Assizes. Berresford's defence counsel tried to persuade the jury that his client either fired in self-defence after extreme provocation or that the shooting was an involuntary reaction to being hit on the arm by a stone.

Mr Justice Patteson conceded that Berresford had been 'ill-used' but pointed out that it did not justify the use of firearms, saying that the old man should have complained to the police rather than taking matters into his own hands. Nevertheless, Patteson instructed the jurors that it was their job to say whether the shooting was accidental or intentional, adding that, if the former, the prisoner was not guilty but if the latter, he was guilty of manslaughter.

Patteson seemed surprised when the jury returned a verdict of guilty of manslaughter, although they added a recommendation for mercy in view of Berresford's age and the undisputed provocation. Patteson told Berresford that even without the jury's recommendation he would have passed a very lenient sentence, settling on four months' imprisonment with hard labour. Patteson then turned to the youths who had given evidence and contemptuously told them that, if it were in his power, he would have them all severely whipped.

28 OCTOBER 1845 Nineteen-year-old Henry Payne was an inmate of the Leicester Union Workhouse and, on 26 October, the governor awarded him twenty-four hours of solitary confinement for refusing to work. When he re-joined his fellow inmates the following day, Payne vowed to get even with governor John Cole.

After breakfast on 28 October, Cole said grace then turned to leave the room. Payne followed him and, from a distance of around 3 yards, suddenly threw a sharp stone weighing around 20oz at the back of Cole's head. The stone cut Cole's scalp to the bone and a surgeon who examined the wound expressed surprise that Cole's skull wasn't fractured.

Payne was charged with having feloniously cut and wounded Cole with intent to kill and main him, with alternative indictments for intent to main, to disfigure, to disable and to do grievous bodily harm. Tried at the Leicestershire Assizes in March 1846, he was found guilty of wounding with intent to do grievous bodily harm and was sentenced to fifteen years' transportation. He sailed to Van Dieman's Land on board the ship *John Calvin* on 9 May 1846.

29 OCTOBER 1895 An inquest was held at the Town Hall in Leicester into the death of thirty-year-old labourer Andrew Morton White, who died at work on 28 October.

White was digging out the foundations for Leicester's new Technical School and was standing in a 7ft 6in deep trench. George Kettle was with him, using a pick to loosen the earth, which White then shovelled into a cart. Suddenly, the trench wall collapsed. The falling earth swept White's legs from under him and he fell backwards, cracking the back of his head on the cart. He began bleeding from his nose and mouth, dying from a fractured skull before the arrival of a doctor.

The excavations foreman stated at the inquest that the collapse occurred nowhere near where Kettle was working, adding that it was not normal practice to shore up the sides of a trench until a depth of 8 or 9 feet was reached.

The inquest jury believed that all reasonable precautions had been taken, returning a verdict of 'accidental death'. White's wife had given birth only weeks earlier and the jury donated their fees to her; the coroner and the school's architect each contributing an additional £1 and the contractor offering to pay the funeral expenses.

30 OCTOBER 1933 Midland Red Bus driver Wilfred Pratt of Nuneaton was starting his bus in Leicester when it suddenly backfired. Pratt was thrown clear over the starting handle, landing on his head on the road. He was taken to the Leicester Infirmary, where he died soon after arrival from a fractured skull.

Coroner Edward Fowler commented at the inquest that he had heard of engines 'kicking' and causing fractured wrists or broken arms, but had never heard of a kick powerful enough to flip a man right over. To Fowler's knowledge, Pratt's was the first fatality of its kind.

The inquest jury returned a verdict of 'accidental death'.

31 OCTOBER 1881 James McNeil, an assistant warder at Leicester Prison, went to collect prisoner John Jarman for exercise at 6.25 a.m. Sixty-year-old John felt unwell and asked to be allowed to remain in his cell, so McNeil double locked the door and left him to rest. When McNeil next checked at 7.50 a.m., Jarman lay on the floor in a pool of blood, his throat cut from ear to ear. The previous evening, he was visited by friends, who brought him tea in a glass wine bottle and the jagged wound in Jarman's throat had undoubtedly been made by the bloodstained piece of glass found by his side.

Jarman was awaiting his trial at the next assizes for the attempted murder of his estranged wife, Maria, who left him after he frittered away their savings of almost £1,000 on drink. At the beginning of July, Jarman rented premises in Market Harborough, with the intention of starting a confectionery business, and was trying to persuade his wife to make a fresh start. When she refused, he plunged a clasp knife into her neck, before attempting to cut his own throat.

When arrested, Jarman seemed deranged and accused his wife of trying to kill him for the past three years. Now, an inquest into his death found that he committed suicide while in an unsound state of mind.

NOVEMBER

Gateway to Leicester Castle, site of the assizes. (Author's collection)

NOVEMBER 1871 William and Sarah Wainwright of Market Bosworth were quarrelling and one of their neighbours called the police to separate them. PC Job Holyoake arrived and suggested that William went out for a while to calm down.

At about 11 p.m., Sarah was standing on her doorstep waiting for her husband to come home when Holyoake came back and told her that he had treated William to a pint of ale. Sarah told him that he shouldn't have done, but, before she could protest any further, Holyoake put his arm round her waist and propelled her indoors, pushing her up against a wall and sexually assaulting her.

Sarah struggled and kicked and called out for her neighbour, Mary Ann Jackson, who arrived and found Sarah crying, her hair down, her elbow bleeding and her clothing disarranged. Holyoake stood less than a yard away and, according to Mrs Jackson, had obviously been drinking.

He left abruptly and minutes later, William arrived home. The following morning, he, Sarah and Mary Ann Jackson went to see Police Sergeant Peberdy to make an official complaint against Holyoake. Peberdy had seen Holyoake some hours earlier and, having then formed the impression that he was drunk, sent him home. After hearing from the Wainwrights, he formally charged Holyoake with assault.

Holyoake appeared at the Leicestershire Assizes before Mr Justice Lush in December 1871, charged with assault with intent and with indecent assault. He was a married man with three children and a former soldier, who had been in the police force for nineteen months and had proved an excellent policeman.

Market Bosworth. (Author's collection)

Holyoake's defence counsel argued every point of the case, reminding the court of his good character and asking them to consider the improbability that he would interfere with Mrs Wainwright, within earshot of Mrs Jackson, when her husband could have returned home at any minute. When the jury found Holyoake guilty of indecent assault, Mr Justice Lush told him that he felt a certain compassion for him, saying he didn't believe Holyoake would have offended if it hadn't been for the drink. Nevertheless, Lush explained, he had a duty to the public and, since Holyoake held an official position as a protector of public morality, he must serve nine calendar months' imprisonment, with hard labour.

Mr Justice Lush. (Author's collection)

2 **NOVEMBER 1863** Edward Thompson, his fourteen-year-old son Charles and Thomas Barnes had about five minutes of their shift at Bardon Hill Quarry still to work.

Steam power was used to break stone at the quarry and the boiler was housed in a large shed, which was open at both ends. The shed was covered by a semi-circular corrugated iron roof and just before 5 p.m., a sudden gust of wind blew the roof off. It fell on the Thompsons and Barnes, who were standing on a railway truck, throwing stones onto the conveyor belt that fed the crushing mill.

Charles Thompson was knocked into the truck and suffered only minor cuts and bruises. His father and Barnes were knocked to the ground and crushed beneath the weight of the heavy metal roof. Barnes was seriously injured but Edward Thompson died instantly.

The roof was estimated to weigh two tons and was fixed to the brickwork of the boiler shed by iron tie pins and rods bolted through the brickwork. In addition, a large 2cwt metal weight hung from the underside of the roof, to further anchor it.

An inquest jury returned a verdict of 'accidental death' on Edward Thompson, while Barnes is believed to have survived, in spite of being in 'a precarious condition' at the time of Thompson's inquest.

3 NOVEMBER 1880 Elizabeth Stacey appeared at the Leicestershire Assizes charged with the wilful murder of her illegitimate daughter, Eliza.

On 19 September, three weeks after giving birth, laundress Elizabeth left her lodgings in Leicester, saying that she was going to her mother's house at Rugby. Soon afterwards, Eliza was found drowned in a pool by the roadside. Elizabeth was apprehended and charged with murdering her child by drowning it. She told the police,

> I have been in great trouble about this since I done it. I do not know what induced me to do it but my sister has got my little girl and my mother has got my boy and I did not like to take this other home with me. When I sat down by the pond I gave it the breast and it went to sleep. I then put it into the water. I went away a little way and then went back but could not see it. I then went home to Rugby. [*sic*]

By the time her case came to trial, Elizabeth had changed her story, now claiming that Eliza died while at the breast and she had merely disposed of her daughter's corpse in the pool. The jury didn't believe her, finding her guilty, albeit with a recommendation to mercy. Her mandatory death sentence was later repealed and she was sent to Millbank Prison in London.

4 NOVEMBER 1886 Twenty-three-year-old Annie Burbank worked as a housekeeper for single farmer William Harding at Cotesbach. Annie was pregnant but when she regained her figure and there was no baby at the farm, tongues began to wag.

The gossip reached the police and Annie was interviewed, admitting that she had given birth to 'a four-month child'. Pressed for more information, she told the police that the baby fell into the farm toilet and was so small that she didn't think its body could be retrieved.

While draining the cesspit, the police spotted some freshly laid turf in the farm garden and Harding explained that he had buried two cats after shooting them. Nothing was found in the cesspit and, when the police asked Annie if her baby was in the garden, she swore that the only bodies buried there were those of three dead cats.

The police excavated the area and found just two cats, along with a dead baby, who had a leather washcloth tied tightly around its head. When Annie heard that an infant had been found, she told the police, 'My master knows, he will tell you all about it,' but Harding denied any knowledge of the tiny corpse.

Both master and servant were arrested after the inquest, Harding still denying any knowledge of the baby's fate, although he admitted to being its father. Realising that she was going to take all the blame, Annie made a new statement, claiming that Harding took the child and smothered it as soon as it was born.

The couple were tried together at the Leicestershire Assizes in January 1887, charged with the wilful murder of their child, on or about 4 November 1886. However, there was disagreement between the medical witnesses as to whether the child ever breathed independently and the judge ordered the case to be dismissed due to lack of evidence. Both Burbank and Harding were immediately tried for concealment of a birth and found guilty, with the jury recommending mercy for Burbank.

Remarking on the fact that no doctor, midwife or neighbour had been called to assist Annie in her confinement, the judge commented that it was almost as if the baby had been 'foredoomed' by the prisoners. He sentenced Harding to twelve months' imprisonment with hard labour and Annie Burbank to six months' imprisonment.

5 NOVEMBER 1854 The village boys of Worthington constructed a bonfire to celebrate Guy Fawkes' night.

The boys were also firing pistols and Sarah Elizabeth Mee became concerned for her son. She sent her thirteen-year-old daughter out to look for him and when she didn't return home as quickly as her mother expected, Sarah went out to look for both children.

Sarah's daughter heard her mother calling her and went towards her. As she did, somebody fired a gun nearby and Mrs Mee shouted 'Oh!' and dropped to the ground.

A doctor was summoned and Mrs Mee was carried home but she was beyond medical assistance. Thinking that she had been shot, the doctor stripped off her clothes but found no external injuries. Mrs Mee was a particularly nervous, timid woman and a post-mortem examination showed that the cause of death was the rupture of several blood vessels leading to her heart. It was determined that the sound of gunfire had so frightened Mrs Mee and induced palpitations of such ferocity that she literally died from fright.

6 NOVEMBER 1839 Railway labourers Charles and Robert Warden were engaged in the construction of Bassett's Hill Cutting at Countesthorpe. The brothers were filling waggons with earth when another labourer, who went by the name of 'Lincoln Bill', began working on a section of the embankment with his pick.

Having loosened the earth, he should have made sure that it was left in a safe condition. Instead, he went to talk to another group of labourers, telling the Wardens that the earth was perfectly safe and could not possibly fall on them.

Sadly, he was wrong and a large section of the embankment – estimated to weigh half a ton – suddenly dropped onto Robert's pelvis. It was at least five minutes before he could be freed and the injuries to his bowels and genitals were so extensive that, in spite of the attentions of a doctor, he died four days later.

When the inquest was held at Willoughby Waterless, 'Lincoln Bill' had absconded. However, the jury were assured that he was not usually careless in his work and a verdict of 'accidental death' was returned.

7 **NOVEMBER** **1880** Thirty-five-year-old Annie Elizabeth Cook was found dead in the bath at her father's home on London Road, Leicester. Annie had complained to a friend that she had previously fainted in the bath, after the installation in the bathroom of a new 'patent instantaneous gas water heater', although she did not mention this to her parents. However, her father – the then 'excursion agent' Thomas Cook – also claimed to have noticed a disagreeable smell when the apparatus was lit.

When Annie took her last bath, the heater had been used only three times before. Dr Henry Lankester found evidence of an exceedingly high temperature in the bathroom which, coupled with the offensive odour, might have induced Miss Cook to faint. He gave drowning resulting from syncope as the cause of her death and the inquest jury found accordingly.

London Road, Leicester. (Author's collection)

8   NOVEMBER 1924   The jury at the inquest into the death of Phoebe Whyman of Griffydam, who died shortly after giving birth to her eleventh child, concluded that her death was due to inattention at childbirth.

The coroner commented on Phoebe's living conditions, which he described as 'deplorable'. The inquest was told that her home was little more than a hovel. Of Phoebe's eleven children, eight survived and all lived with Phoebe and her collier husband, Jack, in a house with just two rooms – one up, one down. At the time of Phoebe's confinement, there was barely any furniture and very little food in the house.

9   NOVEMBER 1846   As the driver of the afternoon train from Derby to London entered the Normanton Cutting between Kegworth and Loughborough, he noticed a man walking along the line. The man was only about 5 yards in front of the train and the driver had no time to stop or even shout a warning. The left buffer struck the man on the back and he fell, hitting his head on the engine's lamp. His body landed on the line and he was run over by the train and cut to pieces.

He was later identified as twenty-nine-year-old John Eden, who had been weeding on the line and was walking to Loughborough to meet his fiancée. The couple were due to marry the following week and Eden also financially supported his mother. An inquest returned a verdict of 'accidental death'.

10   NOVEMBER 1891   Coroner George Bouskell held an inquest at Enderby into the death of Thomas Jones, who died on 7 November.

Cross Street, Enderby. (Author's collection)

Wilhelmina Vesty, who lived next door to his lodgings, went out for a drink with Jones on the night of his death. By closing time, Thomas was intoxicated. It was a very dark, foggy night but Thomas insisted on walking back past the quarry and, when Wilhelmina protested that it wasn't safe, he told her that he was going that way whether she liked it or not. Thinking him too drunk to be left alone, Wilhelmina followed and before long, Thomas put his arm round her waist and began to swing her round.

Wilhelmina grew dizzy and fell onto the bank and, as she did, Thomas disappeared over the edge of the quarry. Wilhelmina ran screaming back to the village and fetched quarryman William Farr, but he could see or hear nothing untoward. He collected a lamp and went down into the quarry with PC Moore and four other men, finding Thomas Jones lying dead at the bottom with serious head injuries.

The inquest should have been straightforward but for an argument between Coroner Bouskell and Mr Turle, the doctor called to examine the body. Turle refused to give evidence without having first received a written summons, whereas Bouskell was adamant that he had been given a verbal summons, which should suffice. The issue developed into a stand-off between doctor and coroner and, eventually, the jury had to rule on the death without hearing the medical evidence. They returned a verdict of 'accidental death'.

11 NOVEMBER 1893 Ellen Conley of Loughborough went upstairs, leaving her baby, Anne, downstairs. After a few minutes, Anne began to cry and when Ellen went to her she found her wicker cradle on fire.

Ellen snatched her baby from the flames and ripped her burning clothes off. A doctor was at the house within fifteen minutes but Anne had horrific burns – her left hand was so charred that it fell off while the doctor was examining it, her left eye fell out and even the inside of her mouth was charred.

In spite of her terrible injuries, Anne lived for two months, nursed day and night by her mother, who simply refused to let her daughter die. Eventually, the baby succumbed to her injuries, the cause of her death given as 'exhaustion'.

Coroner Henry Deane held an inquest at Loughborough and commented that it was a marvel that the child had lived so long, which he put down to Ellen Conley's devotion. However, Deane also remarked that, given her shocking injuries, he believed that it was a mercy that Anne died.

The inquest jury found a verdict of 'accidental death', suggesting that the practice of leaving infants so close to the fire was a dangerous one.

12 NOVEMBER **1864** Sarah Ann North and John Potter of Whitwick had been courting on and off for seven years, although theirs was a turbulent relationship and Potter often beat Sarah. In February 1864, Sarah was granted an affiliation order against him and he was ordered to pay maintenance for their illegitimate child, but by November he had fallen behind with the payments and Sarah went back to the magistrates.

On 12 November, the couple met by chance at Thringstone and as they walked back towards Whitwick, Potter tried to put his arm around Sarah who objected, saying that her stepfather would throw her out if she was seen with him. Potter walked off in a huff but some time later, he caught up with Sarah and her companion, Mrs Goff, and asked Sarah to go for a walk with him.

Sarah refused, saying that she wanted nothing more to do with him until he was steady and sober. She and Mrs Goff continued walking but Potter followed and put his hands on her shoulders as if to kiss her. Instead he tried to cut her throat with a razor, although fortunately he only cut her chin.

Twenty-two-year-old Potter was charged with feloniously cutting Sarah with intent to kill and murder her. When he appeared at the Leicestershire Assizes in December, his defence counsel called character witnesses to testify that Potter was normally a quiet, inoffensive man.

Although Potter went looking for a razor after first leaving Sarah at Thringstone, the defence contended that he never intended to murder her, adding that if he had, he would have chosen somewhere more private on the road back to Whitwick. Admitting that Potter was very drunk at the time, the defence suggested that he just intended to frighten Sarah. Mr Justice Mellor's summary of the case seemed very favourable towards the prisoner and the jury found him guilty of the lesser offence of unlawfully wounding. He was sentenced to twelve months' imprisonment with hard labour.

13 NOVEMBER **1899** Three-year-old Harold Benford died at the Leicester Infirmary from internal complications, following a chemical burn. Harold's father, James, was a fishmonger and, a couple of weeks earlier, he was carrying a bottle of disinfectant in his breast pocket. While holding Harold in his arms, James bent over, causing the stopper to come out of the bottle and the contents to spill down the child's back.

The disinfectant was caustic and caused a chemical burn that ran the length of the boy's back from top to bottom. Although Harold initially didn't seem badly hurt, the burn didn't heal and he gradually grew weaker until his death, which the inquest jury ruled was accidental.

14 NOVEMBER 1863 Hawker James Wells was a convict at the Leicester County Gaol and had been reported to the visiting justices for a misdemeanour, for which he was punished. After his prescribed punishment, Wells was put back in his cell, where he began to shout and curse.

Warder Thomas Hall went to quieten Wells down and, as he opened the cell door, Wells attacked him with a piece of lead piping. Another warder nearby saw Hall fall and rushed to help him, finding him bleeding heavily from two wounds on his head.

Twenty-two-year-old Wells was indicted for unlawful wounding and, having been found guilty at the Leicestershire Assizes on 7 December, was sentenced to three years' imprisonment to commence at the end of his current sentence. On leaving the dock, Wells threatened to kill every one of the warders and then himself, saying that he was tired of living.

15 NOVEMBER 1857 The body of twenty-three-year-old Richard Shirley Harris was discovered on farmland in Newfoundpool.

Harris left his home in the afternoon of 14 November, intending to go shooting. When he didn't return a search was made for him, but he wasn't found until seven o'clock the next morning. A post-mortem examination revealed that he had been shot in the right-hand side of his chest, severing a large artery, and had undoubtedly died almost instantaneously from haemorrhage.

An inquest deduced that Harris was climbing over a stile when twigs from the adjacent bushes touched the trigger and caused the gun to fire. The jury returned a verdict of accidental death on Harris, who had been married for only a year.

16 NOVEMBER 1835 Mr and Mrs Harrap kept the village pub in Frolesworth and occasionally employed twenty-seven-year-old Thomas Manning to do odd jobs. When sober, Manning was a good workman but when he came into the pub on the evening of 16 November, he had already been drinking quite heavily.

He ordered half a pint of ale and, as soon as he had drunk it, he walked behind the door of the bar and relieved himself inside the pub. The Harraps were outraged, saying that they had never seen such beastly conduct and refused to serve him any more drink.

Unashamed, Manning sat down, his shotgun between his legs. While Ann Harrap went to fetch someone to help evict Manning, her husband watched as Manning pretended to load the gun, swearing that he would shoot the devil or any other person who might come in. Mrs Harrap stood outside the bar and shouted through the open window, pretending to be Manning's mother calling him home, but Manning didn't move until she came back inside, when he raised his gun and shot her in the shoulder.

She died a few days later and Manning was tried for her wilful murder at the Leicestershire Assizes in March 1836. The judge told the jury that, if Manning knew that the gun was loaded when he fired it, he was guilty of wilful murder. However, the fact that he only pretended to load it suggested that he intended to frighten rather than injure Ann Harrap and, if this were the case, Manning's crime was manslaughter.

The jury found him guilty of manslaughter and the judge sentenced him to be transported for life, saying that he was much too dangerous a character to be allowed to remain in this country.

17 NOVEMBER 1900 Sixteen-year-old Richard Tunbridge appeared at the Leicestershire Assizes charged with wounding Florence Scarfe at Loughborough with intent to do her grievous bodily harm.

Richard and thirteen-year-old Florence were both members of a travelling fair – Florence helped her uncle run the coconut shies while Richard was a general labourer. On 22 October, Richard was assembling the shooting gallery and taking the guns out of their box. He took exception to Florence, who was standing watching him while nursing a baby and told her to go away otherwise he would shoot her. Florence left but Richard shot her anyway, the pellet hitting the back of her head.

Because of Richard's youth and as a result of what the judge described as 'the straightforward way in which the accused behaved after the thing happened', he was not penalised but was bound over to come up for judgement if called upon in the future.

18 NOVEMBER 1882 When forty-five-year-old Louis Padley of Hugglescote was widowed, he waited precisely three weeks before taking his fourteen-year-old daughter Jane to a public house and trying to force her to drink gin. Jane disliked the taste and refused, hence she was still sober when her father raped her, threatening to kill her if she told anyone.

On 18 November, Jane's eighteen-year-old sister, Emma, came to visit and, as she lay in bed, she heard her father abusing her sister. When Jane came to bed crying soon afterwards, Emma confronted her and, the following day, took her sister to the police station and lodged a complaint against their father. Medical evidence confirmed Jane's account of her father's actions and he was charged with 'feloniously and against her will carnally knowing Jane Padley, his daughter, at Hugglescote on 18 November 1882.'

When Padley was found guilty at the Leicestershire Assizes in January 1883, the judge commented that his crime was particularly heinous since he had a special duty of care towards his daughter. He was sentenced to ten years' penal servitude.

19 **NOVEMBER** **1940** During the night of 19/20 November, Leicester saw its worst air raid of the Second World War, in which 108 people were killed and a further 284 were injured. Approximately 255 homes were flattened, along with fifty-six factories and industrial premises.

The first bomb fell at Kirby Muxloe at 8 p.m. and eighty-six-year-old Eliza Worker later died from injuries received. More than forty people died when bombs hit the junction of Highfield Street and Tichbourne Street and a further thirteen perished when bombs fell at the junction of Saxby Street and Sparkenhoe Street.

Officers from Charles Street police station were setting up a command post on the corner of Stoughton Street when a bomb fell directly onto them. DS Leonard Norman and DC Edwin Trump were killed instantly and DC Brian Hawkes was mortally wounded, dying later at the Infirmary.

Shortly after midnight, a bomb demolished a shelter under a needle factory in Queen Street, killing five people, and eight more died when a parachute mine fell at Oadby.

20 **NOVEMBER** **1896** At the Town Hall in Leicester, itinerant hawker Charles Lester, aged forty-three, was tried at the Borough Assizes for a criminal assault on a nine-year-old girl, Alice Webster. His guilt was never in doubt, since in the course of his sexual assault on the child he infected her with venereal disease.

Presiding judge Mr Justice Day described Lester and men like him, who 'prowled about seeking to ruin little children', as 'a pest to society'. When the jury returned a guilty verdict, Day sentenced Lester to seven years' penal servitude.

21 **NOVEMBER** **1892** The passenger train from Birmingham to Leicester reached Knighton four minutes late but, since the signals were all in its favour, it was able to proceed at a speed of forty miles an hour. As the train went through Knighton Junction, the fireman remarked that he thought they might have hit something. He looked back and saw a man's body lying at the side of the line and, when the train arrived at Leicester Station, traces of blood and flesh were found on the front.

The deceased was twenty-four-year-old Frederick Knifton, a flagman for the Midland Railway Company. Two of his fellow employees witnessed his death and related at the inquest that he seemed deep in thought when he was hit by the train. Both witnesses tried to alert Knifton to the oncoming train – one said that he was unable to attract his attention and the second saying that Knifton appeared to realise that he was going to be hit too late to take any avoiding action.

In recording the jury's verdict of 'accidental death', coroner Robert Harvey put the fatality down to 'a moment's inattention', saying that he could find no evidence of negligence on the part of anyone but the deceased.

22 NOVEMBER 1866 The train from Burton-on-Trent to Leicester left Moira and accelerated to thirty miles an hour when driver William Jardine thought he saw something on the track. He was unable to stop and, as the engine went over the obstruction, Jardine clearly saw a dog jumping out of the way.

When the train reached Ashby-de-la-Zouch, Jardine found spots of blood and what looked like human hair on the front. He alerted the stationmaster and, walking back towards Moira, they found a man lying dead on the line, his faithful dog sitting next to him. The man's entire face had been completely knocked off and lay 10 yards further down the line.

He was later identified as forty-four-year-old gamekeeper Joseph Fairbrother, who met with his death while walking home after a day's shooting, leaving eleven children fatherless. An inquest held by coroner Mr J. Gregory returned a verdict of 'accidental death'.

23 NOVEMBER 1890 A group of children amused themselves at Loughborough by hauling a small milk cart up a hill and then riding down again. On their third run, eleven-year-old John Heathcote Caldwell was between the shafts when the cart suddenly flipped over.

John, his younger sister and another boy were thrown out of the cart but two boys were trapped beneath it. When the cart was lifted, Reginald Upton got up and walked away but seven-year-old Robert Caldwell gasped once and died. The children ran for a doctor but there was nothing he could do for Robert, who had fractured his skull.

Coroner Mr Henry Deane held an inquest at which the jury returned a verdict of 'accidental death'. It was only fourteen months since Deane held an inquest on two more children from the Caldwell family, who accidentally drowned.

24 NOVEMBER 1933 As twenty-one-year-old Elizabeth Mary 'Betty' Hill rode out with the Fernie Hunt at Market Harborough, her horse slipped, unseating her as it tried to regain its feet. Betty, who was an excellent horsewoman, died soon afterwards from a fractured skull.

Tragically, the source of the injury was the hard bowler hat that Betty was wearing to protect her head, the rim of which was driven into her forehead when she hit the ground. 'A bowler cuts like a knife,' explained the doctor who gave evidence at her inquest, where a verdict of 'accidental death' was recorded.

25 **NOVEMBER** **1855** Farmer John Fowkes of Snarestone had three sons and two daughters, including Elizabeth, who moved back to live with her father after being widowed in 1845. Before her marriage Elizabeth gave birth to several illegitimate children, two of whom worked on the family farm – John Acres managed the accounts and Thomas Atkins worked as a labourer, as did two of John senior's sons, William and John junior, known as Jack.

Fowkes was in poor health and Jack became concerned about arrangements for distributing the estate after the old man's death. Believing that his father was favouring his grandsons over his sons, Jack grew very agitated and was convinced that Acres was to get £700. Although William assured him that this was not the case, Jack believed the local gossips over his brother and threatened to do something to redress the situation.

On 25 November, John Fowkes, William, Elizabeth, John Acres and Thomas Atkins were at home with a friend, PC Cooper. Elizabeth and Thomas retired for the night, after which John senior opened the window to get some fresh air into his lungs. He closed it after a couple of minutes and, seconds later, Jack thrust the barrel of a gun through the glass and shot John Acres in the face, killing him almost instantly.

Jack was charged with wilful murder but the evidence against him was purely circumstantial and, at the assizes, the mainstay of the prosecution was William's assertion that he had seen his brother at the window. Jack swore that William was lying but even so, it took the jury less than fifteen minutes' deliberation to find him guilty of wilful murder.

'I am innocent of the job that's brought against me, suffer what I may,' Jack shouted, as the judge tried to pronounce the death sentence. His protests fell on deaf ears and he was hanged at Leicester on 19 March 1856.

26 **NOVEMBER** **1933** Three-year-old Derek Archibald Robb vanished from near his Leicester home and the next morning, his body was found in a canal.

Police didn't believe that the little boy had fallen into the water accidentally and Derek's mother was equally convinced that her son had met with foul play. Derek's coat, hat and boots were on the canal bank and his mother told the police that he was unable to undress himself or unfasten his boots. In addition, the little boy was afraid of the dark and would have had to walk some distance and cross a busy main road to get to the canal.

A post-mortem examination showed that Derek died from drowning but there was not a mark on his body and nothing to suggest how he might have ended up in the water. At the inquest, the coroner advised the jury to return an open verdict, which would not hamper the police if they apprehended a suspect.

In fact, the police already had someone in custody. In trying to locate anyone who saw Derek on 26 November, they interviewed twenty-two-year-old William Hubert Allen, who confessed to asking Derek to go for a walk. When the child agreed, Allen related that he took him to the 'river' and removed his trousers and overcoat, although he denied 'interfering' with Derek or putting him into the water, claiming to have left the boy sitting by his clothes on the bank.

Allen was charged with wilful murder but by the time the case reached the Leicester Assizes in February 1934, he was judged unfit to plead. According to Dr A.H. Grierson, the senior medical officer at Brixton Prison, Allen was 'an imbecile', who could not read, write or count and had a mental age of six. He was ordered to be detained during His Majesty's pleasure.

27 NOVEMBER 1923 Colliery carpenter Frederick Kenniwell (or Kennewell) went for an evening bicycle ride and didn't return. He was found dead on the roadside at Ellistown on 29 November.

The cause of his death was deemed to be exposure and, at the inquest, the coroner deduced that Kenniwell's bicycle skidded in the icy conditions, throwing him onto his head and knocking him unconscious. Soon afterwards, there was a heavy snowfall, which buried fifty-four-year-old Kenniwell, effectively hiding his body until the snow melted. The jury returned a verdict of 'accidental death'.

28 NOVEMBER 1908 As collier John Darker drove a small cart towards Loughborough, he met with a car travelling in the opposite direction on a bend at Whitwick. The car and the cart collided, killing the pony instantly. John Darker was also killed and his wife Emma died minutes later. Two of the couple's sons and the occupants of the car escaped with minor injuries.

At the inquest held by coroner Henry Deane, there was a difference of opinion about the cause of the accident. Lewin Darker stated that his father was on the correct side of the road and driving at no more than four miles an hour. The car driver, Charles Z.M. Booth, and his passengers argued that Darker was on the wrong side of the road and that the pony was proceeding at 'a smart trot', much faster than four miles an hour.

Eyewitnesses and medical evidence supported Booth's version of events and the inquest jury found that the collision was caused by a want of care on Darker's part, in not allowing sufficient room for the car to pass.

Booth was the son of philanthropist and social reformer Charles Booth, who intimated to the coroner that he would be compensating the several children orphaned by the deaths of Mr and Mrs Darker.

29 NOVEMBER 1842 An inquest was held into the death of eighteen-month-old Sarah Ann Cook of Leicester, who, on the morning of 24 November, got hold of some Lucifer matches, which were carelessly left within her reach.

The toddler sucked the tips off several of the matches but showed no ill effects until later that evening, when she began to vomit, dying shortly afterwards. The cause of death was determined to be poisoning from the phosphoric acid, into which the tips of the matches were dipped. The inquest jury returned a verdict of 'accidental death'.

30 NOVEMBER 1869 Poultry dealer William 'Nutty' Miles went into a public house at Rearsby. He was already very drunk and, for some reason, took exception to a little dog, which lay on the rug in front of the fire. Before anyone could stop him, he picked the dog up and tossed it onto the flames.

The dog was quickly rescued and the pub landlord and customers rounded on Miles and berated him for his cruelty. Miles stated that he would quite happily burn all such animals to bits and, to prove his point, when the landlord went out of the room Miles lifted the lid of a copper and dropped a kitten into the boiling water, holding the lid down. The other customers fought to rescue the animal but were too late.

When Miles was brought before magistrates at Leicester Police Court on 4 December, Mr Haxby, who prosecuted the case on behalf of the Society for the Prevention of Cruelty to Animals, begged them to send Miles to gaol, without the option of a fine. The magistrates were only too pleased to oblige, sentencing Miles to six months' imprisonment with hard labour.

DECEMBER

HM Prison Leicester. (Author's collection)

1 DECEMBER 1881 When the gas was turned on to light the boilers for the very first time at the newly constructed blast furnaces at Asfordby, there was a sudden explosion.

Something struck foreman fitter Mr Jones on the forehead, fracturing his skull and causing his almost instant death. Another man was burned, although he is believed to have survived the accident, and several others sustained minor injuries.

Jones left a wife and seven children and, at the inquest, his employers announced that they would provide for the deceased man's family. Having heard all the evidence, the jury could attribute no blame for the explosion, and asked coroner Mr Oldham to record a verdict of 'accidental death'.

2 DECEMBER 1895 Eighteen-month-old Clarence Bertram Lane of Leicester threw a tantrum when his older brother took away one of his toys. Clarence screamed with rage for some time then held his breath until he went black in the face.

The boy's mother picked him up and shook him, and threw cold water on his face, but nothing had any effect. Mrs Lane then rushed Clarence to her neighbour's house and left him there while she went for a doctor but, although she returned within minutes, Clarence had died in her absence. Surgeon Mr Emmerson passed an opinion that death was due to spasms of the glottis, causing asphyxia.

Mrs Lane told the inquest that Clarence had a habit of holding his breath when he got into a passion and the jury returned a verdict of 'death from natural causes'.

3 DECEMBER 1885 Forty-year-old widower Thomas Bailey of Whitwick had been the sole parent to his seven children since his wife died four years earlier, although much of the responsibility for her younger siblings fell on the oldest daughter, Sarah Jane.

In summer 1885, Sarah Jane became seriously ill but Thomas did nothing about his daughter's condition until 3 December, when he consulted his sister. Ann Morley went to visit her niece and found her sitting by the fire wearing a tweed dress tied up with string and a tattered chemise. Sarah asked her aunt if she could go home with her, claiming to be hungry, but while Ann was there, Thomas gave his daughter some roast mutton and beer, after which she said she felt much better.

When fourteen-year-old Sarah died on 5 December, a doctor called to the house was so appalled by the child's living conditions that he notified the police. The only food in the house was half a loaf of bread, two ounces of sugar and a spoonful of tea. There was no bed or bedclothes, apart from a soaking wet, rotten mattress, and the younger children were dirty and neglected.

Sarah died from heart disease and dropsy but, in the opinion of the surgeon who conducted the post-mortem examination, a lack of proper nourishment and appropriate medical treatment were contributory factors. Although Sarah died from natural causes, the surgeon believed that an absence of nourishment actually caused her heart to stop beating.

The inquest into Sarah's death returned a verdict of 'manslaughter' against her father, who spent most of his earnings on drink and had tried to persuade his son to testify that Sarah refused to allow him to call a doctor.

He appeared at the Leicestershire Assizes in January 1886. The jury found him guilty of neglecting to provide 'necessaries and comforts' for Sarah and, when Mr Justice Denman asked if they believed that her death was caused or hastened as a result, they stated that they left that to the medical gentlemen. When Denman pressed them for a decision, they conceded that it was their belief that with earlier attention, Sarah might have lived a little longer.

'Then it is a verdict of guilty,' stated Denman, sentencing Bailey to twelve months' imprisonment with hard labour.

4 DECEMBER 1926 Twenty-year-old James Gimson of Cosby borrowed a shotgun and several cartridges, with the intention of shooting sparrows in his garden.

Unfortunately, as he was raising the gun to his shoulder to fire the last cartridge, it went off accidentally. The shot went through the living room window of his home, where his mother and sister were entertaining friends.

Forty-nine-year-old Mary Ann Gimson was hit in the head by the shot and although she was rushed to Leicester Infirmary, she died there shortly afterwards – an 'accidental death' according to the inquest.

5 DECEMBER 1864 Wheelwright Timothy Baum of Syston appeared at the Leicestershire Assizes charged with two counts of wilful murder.

Baum had been suffering from inflammation of the covering of the brain and on 25 November, his doctor advised rest and prescribed an opium sedative to be taken nightly. That night, Baum's mother-in-law, Ann Shelton, took him his medicine, which he drank while chatting pleasantly to her. She then left the room to prepare for bed and, minutes later, heard squealing from Baum's bedroom. She rushed back and saw him standing by the side of the bed, a knife in his hand and blood soaking his nightshirt.

When Mrs Shelton questioned him, he told her that he was going downstairs to fetch another knife to 'do for himself'. After he left the room, Mrs Shelton found her daughter Jane (Baum's wife) dead in bed, with the couple's eleven-month-old baby,

Emma, dying in her arms. Neighbours responding to Mrs Shelton's hysterical screams burst into the house and seized Baum as he was rummaging through the kitchen drawers, preventing him from carrying out his threat.

At his trial, Baum told the court, 'I don't remember anything of it.' The question for the jury was not whether twenty-seven-year-old Baum killed his wife and child, but his mental state at the time. He was sober, steady and hard-working, known as a man of excellent character, who was a devoted husband and father and there seemed no motive whatsoever for his actions. The jury found him not guilty by reason of insanity and he was sent to Broadmoor Criminal Lunatic Asylum, to be detained during Her Majesty's pleasure.

Broadmoor Lunatic Asylum. (Author's collection)

6 DECEMBER 1897 Shortly after midday, a man working at the Brush Electrical Engineering Company, Loughborough happened to look up and saw that William Bray had his head caught in the machinery. Before anyone could react, Bray was sent spinning head first over his lathe and crashed into the pit below. His colleagues rushed to him but he was already dead, the top of his skull almost completely severed.

An inquest held by coroner Henry Deane heard that Bray had worked at the plant as a lathe turner for ten years. His lathe was so large that he needed to stand on a metal platform to use it, although the platform was quite secure and could not have caused the accident. Nobody had seen precisely what happened but the most plausible theory was that thirty-four-year-old Bray bent down to see how his lathe was working

The Brush Works, Loughborough. (Author's collection)

and completely forgot about a protruding clip on the revolving face of the lathe, which caught him on the head and knocked him into the machinery.

The inquest jury returned a verdict of 'accidental death'.

7 DECEMBER 1874 Coroner George F. Harrison held an inquest into the death of Sarah Bigley.

Sarah and her husband George, of Leicester, were happily married but both enjoyed a drink and whenever they drank they became quarrelsome. On 7 November, George arrived home very drunk indeed and began cursing Sarah, eventually picking up a lighted paraffin lamp and swinging it at her. Sarah jumped out of the way, tripping over her own feet and falling backwards into the pantry. She got up and tried to take the lamp from George but he swung at her again, hitting her on the bosom. The lamp shattered, spilling paraffin down her front and, within seconds, she was on fire.

George and the couple's lodger, William Sharp, tried to beat out the blaze with their bare hands, eventually smothering the flames with blankets. Sarah was taken to hospital, where her condition was judged so serious that a magistrate was called to take her deposition. In the knowledge that she was dying, Sarah told the magistrate that the lamp glass fell off and broke, spilling paraffin down her dress. 'I have three children and I hope you won't prosecute my husband for their sake,' she said.

After giving her deposition, Sarah rallied and lingered until 6 December, before dying from inflammation of the lungs. The coroner admitted that the case was somewhere between an accident and manslaughter. 'I did not strike her with the lamp,' Bigley insisted. 'We were differing at the time and I picked the lamp up, she reached forward to me and the glass fell out of the lamp and the oil fell onto her bosom. I tried to put the flames out as well as I could and called out for assistance.'

Bigley was charged with his wife's manslaughter although, having heard that the lamp glass was cracked long before the incident that cost Sarah her life, the jury at the Leicestershire Assizes found him 'not guilty'.

8 DECEMBER 1857 As Mr Bailey was walking through Melton Mowbray he accidentally bumped into Elizabeth Hawley, knocking her over. A doctor was called to attend to her but she went into a decline and died on 12 December.

The surgeon who cared for her performed a post-mortem examination, confirming his suspicions that she had no injuries whatsoever, either internal or external, and the cause of death was shock to the nervous system occasioned by the fall.

At an inquest held by coroner Mr Latham, the jury were told that it was a very dark night and Mr Bailey just hadn't seen Elizabeth. The jury returned a verdict of 'accidental death', absolving Bailey of any blame and recommending that more gas lamps were erected in the darker parts of town.

9 DECEMBER 1899 Alice Sills ran a small shop from the front room of her Leicester home. On 9 December, she had a hospital appointment, so left her two-year-old daughter Ivy Maud in the care of her older siblings, John, Violet and Sissy. Before leaving, Mrs Sills gave each child an orange and some sweets.

Shortly after Mrs Sills returned home, Ivy began vomiting and before long her sisters followed suit. Mrs Sills put the children to bed and called for a doctor, who treated them for sickness, diarrhoea and stomach pains. The two older children quickly recovered but Ivy continued to be sick and her mother sent for the doctor again that evening. During the night, the toddler suffered from convulsions and she died the next morning, with the doctor in attendance.

At the inquest, Mrs Sills insisted that there was nothing in the living room that the children could have eaten, adding that the door to the shop was locked. The children denied having eaten the sweets, although Mrs Sills had been unable to find them. The specially made Christmas sweets came from London and Mrs Sills said that she had already sold a great many at four for 1d and had no complaints from any of her customers.

The doctor who treated the children believed that Ivy's death was due to exhaustion from vomiting and that the sickness in all of the children was caused by the ingestion of some kind of irritant poison. However, it had not proved possible to isolate a particular poison from analysis of Ivy's organs or bodily fluids, nor to determine how or when the poison was ingested.

It seemed apparent that Ivy and the other children had eaten something in their mother's absence, although all of the children denied having done so. Eventually, the inquest jury decided that 'death was due to exhaustion from vomiting, brought on by some irritant poison, although there was no evidence to show how or where the poison was obtained.'

10 DECEMBER 1802

At about 10 p.m., Elizabeth Tebbutt left her mother's house to return to her brother William's house in Kegworth, where she acted as housekeeper. She was found battered and bruised on her route home the next morning, her disturbed clothing suggesting that she had been raped. She died within the hour, although a post-mortem examination showed that none of her injuries was life-threatening – Elizabeth died from exposure, having been rendered incapable of movement and abandoned to the elements.

On 29 April 1836, sixty-five-year-old Henry Roper was ill and his daughter called in a neighbour to help. Mr Murden was a lay-preacher and, although in severe pain, Roper seemed keen to unburden his conscience, telling him, 'I have done murder.' When Murden questioned him, Roper confessed to having 'ravished Miss Tebbutt and left her to die in the cold.'

Kegworth High Street and church. (Author's collection)

Elizabeth's second brother, Edward, was told of Roper's statement and visited him on 5 May, at which time Roper repeated his confession. He went on to make similar statements to the police, magistrates and the gaol chaplain. However, when he appeared before Mr Justice Park at the Leicester Assizes on 29 July, he had changed his mind and denied having made any statement of guilt.

Two of the indictments against Roper specifically stated that he raped or intended to rape Miss Tebbutt. The doctors who performed the post-mortem were long since dead and Park disallowed their evidence given at the inquest, leaving no proof of rape. Roper was left facing just one charge, that, having thrown Miss Tebbutt down and struck her several blows, he left her exposed to the inclemency of the weather.

In his confession, Roper said that Miss Tebbutt was carrying a bottle of gin, which he drank. It was improbable that the victim, who was described as 'the most discreet, temperate and virtuous woman in all of Leicestershire', would have been carrying gin. Mr Justice Park told the jury that they must give Roper the benefit of any doubts they might have, reminding them that he was a man of good character, who married only eleven days after Miss Tebbutt's death and had lived in the village ever since, without provoking the slightest suspicion. Park seemed to believe that Roper's guilt was simply a delusion prompted by his illness and, when the jury acquitted Roper, he commented that he considered their verdict the correct one.

11 DECEMBER 1870 Coroner Mr J. Gregory held an inquest at Whitwick into the death of thirteen-year-old Hiram Allen.

In the brickyard at the Whitwick Colliery Company was a well, into which hot water from the boiler was piped for use in the brickmaking process. The well was reached by descending some steps and the opening at the top was only large enough to admit a bucket, but, at 8 a.m. on 10 December, labourer Harry Ward heard somebody shouting, 'Fetch me out!'

Realising that the shouts were coming from the well, Ward went to check and found Hiram in the water. Ward pulled him out and he was stripped of his wet clothes and taken home in a cart. A surgeon was called but, later that afternoon, Hiram began convulsing and died at around 5 p.m. In his lucid moments, he explained that he slipped into the well while trying to wash out a tub.

In returning a verdict of 'accidental death', the jury recommended that a guard should be erected around the hole.

12 DECEMBER 1898 Coroner Henry Deane held an inquest into the death of thirty-one-year-old farm labourer Arthur Spencer, from Ragdale.

On 10 December, threshing was about to commence and Spencer was on top of the steam threshing machine, ready to begin feeding it with bundles of corn. Suddenly, a gust of wind caught him and blew him into the rapidly revolving machinery. Although his fellow labourers immediately stopped the engine, when Spencer was extricated one of his legs had been torn off at mid-thigh.

The stump was bandaged and he was driven by cart to Loughborough Hospital, where he underwent a further amputation of his leg, but died on 12 December from shock arising from his injuries. The inquest jury returned a verdict of 'accidental death'.

13 DECEMBER 1892 Benjamin Weaver appeared at Melton Mowbray Petty Sessions charged with cruelty to a dog.

The charge arose from an incident at Asfordby on 29 August, when two young boys saw Weaver, Charles Marsh and John Hatfield treating one of the Cottesmore Hunt's foxhounds with abominable cruelty. Hatfield and Marsh appeared before magistrates on 6 November. Hatfield was convicted and sentenced to one month's hard labour, while Marsh, who had spent five days in prison awaiting his trial, was discharged due to lack of evidence against him.

Weaver absconded and was not apprehended until 8 December, when he was arrested by the Lincolnshire Police and handed over to the Melton force. Now magistrates heard that Weaver had thrown bricks at the hound, dragged it along by its ears and then cut its throat.

Weaver admitted dragging the dog by its ears but denied having cut its throat, arguing that the seven-year-old witness was too young to be reliable. Magistrates believed the child's words over Weaver's and sentenced him to two months' imprisonment. As he left the dock, Weaver literally danced a jig for joy, saying that he had fully expected a sentence of at least six months.

14 DECEMBER 1839 Angus McKie was one of a number of Scottish labourers on the Midland Counties Railway who frequently congregated at The Bell Inn, Syston, where their favourite occupation was a game called 'weighing'.

The game involved two men standing back-to-back with their arms locked. One man then bent forwards, lifting the other on his back, and the object of the game was for the man being lifted to stretch up and touch a beam with his legs. As McKie was being lifted, he stretched out his legs towards the beam but lost his balance and fell, hitting the ground head first. He died a few days later from what was described by doctors as 'a concussion of the brain and compression of the spinal cord.'

An inquest on 21 December ruled that his death was accidental.

15 DECEMBER 1891 Robert Haynes of Markfield had a cold, so his mother left him by the fire where it was warm, while she went upstairs to deal with her baby. Hearing screams, she ran downstairs to find three-year-old Robert's nightshirt on fire.

Fanny Haynes treated her son's burns but didn't call a doctor and when her husband Thomas came home from work, Fanny told him about the incident but didn't reveal the full extent of Robert's injuries. Thomas looked at his son and, seeing a small burn on his face, wrongly assumed that the child was not badly hurt. Had he checked beneath Robert's clothes, he would have discovered severe burns on his chest, right arm and the front of his neck, and extensive scorching on his left leg. Robert's mouth and throat were so blistered and ulcerated that he was unable to eat, but Fanny continued to treat the boy's burns and to reassure her husband that Robert was fine.

No doctor was called until 23 December, when Robert began to make a strange rattling noise in his throat. Surgeon Mr A.J. Wright found the house in a filthy condition. Robert's burns were swathed in dirty rags and, in spite of the surgeon's best efforts, he died from exhaustion on 24 December.

Coroner George Bouskell held an inquest on 28 December, where Mr Haynes told the jury that he relied on his wife to look after the children and had accepted her assessment of his son's injuries without question. Asked about his financial situation, Haynes agreed that he earned good wages working as a collier but said he was a little short of money to pay doctor's bills, having recently bought a dog and paid for its licence.

Bouskell was furious that Haynes could keep a dog but not give his son proper medical attention. Although the jury found that Robert's death was the result of 'accidental burns', the coroner stressed to his parents that they had come very close to being committed for manslaughter.

16 DECEMBER 1899 Thirteen-year-old Thomas Spencer of Leicester died after being shot with a toy pistol.

When neighbour James Taylor and his wife were invited to the Spencers' house for a drink on 4 December, he suddenly remembered a toy pistol in his coat pocket, which he had confiscated from a child who was shooting it on the street. Taylor showed Thomas the gun, firing a couple of 'caps' at the door, before Mrs Spencer asked him to put it away.

Taylor decided that it might be amusing to frighten the cat, which was sitting on the hearthrug. 'I'll shift the cat,' he announced, taking out the pistol, intending to fire into the air and make a bang. However, Thomas mistakenly thought that he was intending to shoot the animal and rushed to rescue it just as Taylor fired.

'Mother, it's gone in my leg,' Thomas complained.

Thomas had a lead pellet removed from his leg but developed tetanus and died. At the inquest into his death, coroner Robert Harvey told Taylor that he was fortunate that statements given by Thomas before his death confirmed his account of events. It was obvious that Taylor wasn't aiming at the cat but was firing at the corner of the room and either Thomas got in the way or the pellet ricocheted off a wall into his leg.

Harvey commented that the case was on the borderline between accident and manslaughter, since Taylor showed recklessness and a want of care in firing the pistol. Yet the coroner believed that Taylor had not crossed the line and led the inquest jury towards a verdict of 'death by misadventure'. The jury asked the coroner to severely reprimand Taylor for his actions and the coroner replied that having a child's death on his conscience for the rest of his days should be punishment enough.

17 DECEMBER 1861 Coroner John Gregory held an inquest into the death of Caroline Barnes, who died the previous day while working at a factory in Belgrave Gate, Leicester.

Thirty-five-year-old Caroline turned buttons on a lathe powered by a 10hp steam engine. At midday, her skirts became entangled in a shaft, which was revolving approximately 200 times a minute. Although the engine was stopped, Caroline's clothes were ripped from her body and portions of her skull were scattered around the room in all directions.

The inquest jury were told that a permanent screen would be inconvenient as it would prevent access for maintenance. Caroline had been provided with a portable

Belgrave Gate, Leicester. (Author's collection)

screen to place between herself and the shaft, to prevent her clothing from coming into contact with the moving parts, but she had neglected to put it in place.

Returning a verdict of 'accidental death', the jury agreed that Caroline's neglect was a contributory factor but asked the factory owners to ensure that all machinery was properly guarded in future.

18 DECEMBER 1913 A person walking through Cosby heard the unmistakeable sound of a baby crying and further investigation revealed the infant lying partially immersed in a culvert running under the main road.

The three-week-old baby girl had been seen earlier in the day with a woman named Alice Riley, who had travelled to the village from London. When the baby was found, thirty-six-year-old Alice had disappeared. Police enquiries traced her to Queenstown, Ireland, where she was arrested on 5 January 1914 aboard the ship *Lusitania*, having booked a passage to America.

Lusitania, 1909. (Author's collection)

Alice blamed the abandonment of her daughter on her husband, who she claimed had deserted her while she was in hospital. She appeared before Mr Justice Channell at the Leicester Assizes on 22 January 1914, where she was acquitted on a charge of attempted murder but found guilty of abandoning her baby and sentenced to six months' imprisonment.

19 DECEMBER 1856 The day after a robbery at Croft, Sergeant Edward Parkes came across two men at Braunstone. The men carried a basket and, knowing that a similar basket had been stolen, Parkes stopped them. The men denied ever having been to Croft but when their basket was searched it was found to contain spoils from the robbery.

Parkes asked the men to go with him to a nearby house, which they consented to do. However, Thomas Bromley suddenly broke away and started running towards Leicester. Parkes followed and caught him but as they struggled, Bromley pulled out a pistol, which he fired so close to Parkes's face that his whiskers were singed. (When Parkes later took off his coat a bullet fell to the floor, having passed through his thick coat collar and struck the metal number.)

Eventually, members of the public responded to Parkes's cries of 'Murder' and Bromley was subdued and arrested. He was charged with shooting at Parkes with intent to murder him and additionally with intent to resist lawful apprehension, and tried at the Leicester Assizes in March 1857.

In his defence, Bromley denied ever having removed the pistol from his pocket, saying that it must have gone off when Parkes grabbed his coat. He also claimed to have bought the items stolen from Croft from a man he met on the road.

The judge instructed the jury that there wasn't enough evidence to support the indictment for intent to murder, but Bromley was found guilty of the second count of shooting with intent to resist arrest. As he already had two previous convictions, he was sentenced to transportation for fifteen years.

20 DECEMBER 1887 Coroner George F. Harrison held an inquest into the death of seven-year-old Annie Harriet Day.

On 17 December, Annie was standing inside the gate of the level crossing nearest to South Wigston. A goods train passed by and, knowing that the St Pancras to Manchester express train was due at any minute, a porter told Annie to get to the other side of the gate. Annie misunderstood the porter's instructions and immediately started crossing the line to get to the other side. She was hit by the express train and killed instantly.

Annie was the second child to die at the same spot, the previous fatality having occurred twelve years earlier. In returning a verdict of 'accidental death', the jury strongly suggested that the crossing should be permanently manned or alternatively replaced with a subway or a footbridge.

21 DECEMBER 1877 Annise White died in the Leicester Infirmary as a consequence of injuries received during an argument with her husband at Leicester on 15 December.

Fifty-nine-year-old builder's labourer William White was charged with wilful murder and appeared at the Leicestershire Assizes in January 1878. The chief witness for the prosecution was a close neighbour named James Woodfield, who told the court that on the night in question, he heard the Whites quarrelling about the fact that William was blind drunk.

William threatened to throw a lamp at his wife, who dared him, 'Just do it.' Woodfield then heard a smashing sound and saw a flash of bright light and, when Annise screamed 'Murder!' he rushed into the house to find William standing watching his wife, who was completely enveloped in flames on the opposite side of the room. White did nothing to help as Woodfield ran for a bucket of water then, with the aid of other neighbours, dragged Annise to the communal pump.

'I did not throw it,' was White's only comment on his arrest, apart from asking whether he would be allowed bail.

Annise was a respectable woman, who worked as a laundress to support the family, since William spent his wages – and most of hers – on drink. At his trial, White's defence was that his wife's death was the result of a tragic accident and numerous character witnesses were called, among them a former MP for Leicester. The jury were not impressed and eventually found White guilty of manslaughter. He was sentenced to twenty years' penal servitude.

22   DECEMBER 1888   After kissing his wife and children goodbye, Leicester plumber George Henry Middleton went to work as normal. His wife, Jane Ann, asked him to bring his tools home with him to mend a broken window and, when he got home at lunchtime, he sent one of the couple's eleven children to buy a pane of glass.

Jane was making pastry when, without any warning, her husband suddenly hit her repeatedly over the head with his hammer, inflicting ten scalp wounds, as well as injuries to Jane's face and hands. Three of the hammer blows were hard enough to leave dents in the bone and one actually fractured the skull. Jane knew nothing more until she woke up in hospital on Christmas Day.

The couple's twelve-year-old daughter, Norah, witnessed the attack and raised the alarm but, meanwhile, a policeman living nearby heard screaming and went to investigate, finding Middleton with his throat cut. Both he and his wife were taken to the Infirmary.

Jane underwent trepanning to relieve the pressure on her brain. She later made a statement that her husband had been behaving strangely since September 1888, when he suffered from a bout of asthma and bronchitis.

Middleton left a lengthy handwritten note in which he accused his wife of having an affair with a man. 'Dear friends,' began the letter. 'Forgive me for this cruel act as you know my trouble. I know it is hard for you to believe but she is deceiving all of us. It appears hard but it is so. Her bad ways have been going on ever since we have been married. I have had to bear it; my greatest trouble . . .' [sic]

There was nothing whatsoever to support Middleton's suspicions about his wife and, according to Norah, there was no quarrel between them before her father attacked her mother. Jane Middleton stated that her husband had threatened her several times since his illness, saying that only the thought of 'dear little Rosy' (the couple's youngest child) had prevented him from killing them both.

Middleton was tried at the Leicestershire Assizes in February 1889, charged with attempted murder and with wounding with intent to inflict grievous bodily harm. Found insane and ordered to be detained during Her Majesty's pleasure, he was sent to Broadmoor Criminal Lunatic Asylum but is believed to have eventually returned to his family in Leicester.

23 DECEMBER 1893

Although John and Daisy Tolley of Leicester had been married for less than a year, their union was far from happy and Daisy had twice taken her husband before magistrates for beating her. The most recent occasion was in December 1893, when magistrates dismissed the case, believing that there was fault on both sides. However, the Tolleys decided to separate and Daisy moved back to her parents' home.

Tolley made a couple of visits to talk about what should be done with the couple's possessions and on 23 December he arrived at the house to find his wife and her mother, Mrs Kendall, doing housework. He seemed to want to discuss some blankets but after a few minutes, the conversation grew heated and Tolley suddenly seized his wife's throat, putting a pistol to her head and firing.

'He's killing my Daisy,' Mrs Kendall shouted, as Tolley fired a second shot into the back of his wife's head. Tolley left his wife lying on the floor and walked into the front room, closing the door behind him. While neighbours debated what to do next, someone outside noticed splashes of blood on the window blind of the room into which Tolley had fled. The door was barricaded with chairs from the inside but when it was forced, Tolley was found dead, his throat cut.

Although comatose, nineteen-year-old Daisy Tolley was still breathing and a doctor advised her removal to the Infirmary, although she was dead on arrival from gunshot wounds to the head.

Coroner Robert Harvey opened an inquest into the two deaths that evening, which he adjourned after hearing the medical evidence. When it resumed five days later, the jury were told that Tolley was a former soldier, having served six years in India before his honourable discharge two years earlier, after which he worked as a dyer's labourer until three weeks before the shooting.

At thirty, he was much older than his wife and was acutely jealous. The separation, coupled with his inability to find a job, seemed to have made him despondent and, on the morning of the shooting, he borrowed a revolver from a friend.

The inquest jury needed only a few minutes to return a verdict of 'wilful murder by John Tolley' in respect of Daisy Tolley's death, with *felo de se* – an archaic term meaning murder of oneself – in respect of Tolley's own demise.

24 DECEMBER 1928 Emma Black left her three children alone at home in Anstey while she popped out to do some last minute Christmas shopping. When she returned twenty minutes later, she found the house in darkness, the couch smouldering and the living room full of thick smoke. Three-year-old Margaret and two-year-old Avice were dead on the couch, while the baby was crawling on the floor.

An inquest into the deaths of the two girls surmised that the gas-powered lights had run out and the children were unable to put a penny in the slot meter to restore the supply. In darkness, they lit a piece of paper at the fire and accidentally set the Christmas decorations alight.

The two girls were suffocated by the smoke, the baby escaping because it was at floor level and, since the smoke rose, it was still able to breathe fresh air.

25 DECEMBER 1926 At the ancient Cistercian Monastery of Mount St Bernard, twenty-three-year-old Irish monk Edmund Lonergan tried to light a fire in the monastery's tailor's shop. He was in rather a hurry and was trying to speed up the process by using paraffin and petrol as accelerants when they exploded, setting fire to his robes. Although his fellow monks did what they could for him, Lonergan died from terrible burns almost all over his body.

For the first time ever, an inquest was held at the monastery on 27 December, at which the jury returned a verdict of 'accidental death'.

Mount St Bernard Abbey. (Author's collection)

26 DECEMBER 1870 George Holt and Samuel Loomes went out shooting birds at Lutterworth. Holt took aim at a fieldfare in the hedgerow but missed and, ignoring the fact that one of the barrels of his double-barrelled shotgun was still loaded, he began to re-load. He was holding the gun upright when the loaded barrel fired, almost literally blowing his head off. Only the back part of his skull was left intact and, according to contemporary newspaper accounts of the tragedy, 'his brains were strewn about the greensward on the roadside.'

Loomes was standing about 3 yards away at the time and was liberally splattered with blood and gore. Realising that he could not help his friend, he ran to alert the police and Holt's body was taken home in a cart to await the attentions of the coroner. The inquest jury returned a verdict of 'accidental death', blaming twenty-four-year-old Holt's carelessness with his gun for his tragic demise.

27 DECEMBER 1886 A young boy tried to walk across the frozen canal at Stoke Golding but at roughly the halfway point, the ice gave way and he went into the water. His two friends immediately jumped in to try and rescue him but soon they too were flailing around helplessly.

John Shilton took off his jacket and, keeping hold of one sleeve, threw it to the boys. In this fashion, he managed to drag two of the three to safety but by the time he had done so, their companion had vanished.

Eleven-year-old Charles Quinney's body was recovered using drags two hours later. At an inquest held by coroner Mr G.F. Harrison, the jury returned a verdict of 'accidental death', paying tribute to John, without whose presence of mind two more boys would almost certainly have died. They also acknowledged Quinney's bravery, since he unhesitatingly tried to save his friend, losing his own life as a result.

28 DECEMBER 1842 Until 1846, English law allowed for inquest juries to award something known as a Deodand. In other words, in the event of an object causing a person's death, the jury could demand its forfeiture and sale, the profits to be 'given to God', or applied to some pious use. In reality, most juries demanded a sum of money as a Deodand.

On 28 December 1842, an inquest was held into the death of sixty-seven-year-old Sarah Smith. The jury heard that, on a dark, moonless night, Thomas McDowall of Loughborough and two companions were returning home from Ashy-de-la-Zouch market when the wheel of their cart went over a bump at Coleorton. McDowall stopped and found Sarah lying in the middle of the road, complaining that her leg was broken.

She was taken to the Coleorton surgeon, Mr Orton, where she stated that the cart in front of McDowall's knocked her down and, as she was trying to get up, McDowall's cart ran over her. However, John Morris of Loughborough, whose cart was only yards in front of McDowall's, denied having hit anything.

When Sarah died from her injuries, the argument about who knocked her down began in earnest. Surgeon Mr Orton and his daughter, Sarah's daughter, Morris, McDowall and his three passengers had all apparently heard Sarah giving different explanations of how the accident occurred. Orton and Sarah's daughter understood her to say that Morris's cart passed her and McDowall knocked her over as she was trying to get out of the way. McDowall, his passengers and Orton's daughter were sure Sarah claimed to have been knocked over by Morris and then run over by McDowall.

Both drivers were perfectly sober at the time and the inquest jury ruled that neither was to blame, returning a verdict of 'accidental death'. In the matter of Deodands, the jury hedged their bets, claiming the sum of £2 on Morris's cart and £1 on McDowall's.

29 DECEMBER 1858 Labourer Thomas Gilliver (or Gilbert) of Groby became so intoxicated at a wedding on Christmas Day that he was unable to walk. His nephew

and another man escorted him home, unlocking the door of his house for him since he was incapable of doing so himself.

Nothing more was heard of Gilliver until 29 December, when, not having seen him about, his neighbours went to check on him. They found him sitting cross-legged in his fireplace, which he had apparently mistaken for a chair.

He had slumped forward and his mouth and nose where tightly pressed against one of his thighs, stopping him from breathing. Doctors found that he had suffocated 'while in a state of helpless intoxication' and an inquest jury later returned a verdict in accordance with the medical evidence.

30 DECEMBER 1895 An inquest was held at Buckminster into the deaths of three youths from the village. The evening before, a number of youths were skating on ice at a pond at the local brickyard, when thirteen-year-old Frank John William Allen fell over. The ice was only an inch thick and Allen's weight broke it, plunging him into the freezing cold water, which was at least 17 feet deep.

Brothers Ernest Richard and Arthur Henry Thurlby, who were aged fifteen and thirteen respectively, went to his assistance but they too fell into the water and immediately disappeared. It was forty-five minutes before the first body was pulled from the water and the inquest jury returned verdicts of accidental death on all three boys.

31 DECEMBER 1895 Forty-six-year-old Fanny Rogers appeared at Leicester Borough Police Court charged with wilfully neglecting her six children, who ranged from three to thirteen years old, between 24 June and 20 December.

Mr Simpson, who represented the NSPCC, told the magistrates that the defendant was the wife of a respected Leicester tradesman and had been addicted to drink for many years, to the detriment of her family life. Simpson stressed that the ill-treatment of the children was more mental than physical, since the effects of having a mother who behaved like a maniac at times was terrible. The children were frightened and horror-stricken and were in danger of losing their reason, due to their mother's addiction.

Mr Rogers had done everything in his power to get help for his wife but it now appeared that the only way forward was to separate Mrs Rogers from her children, before she did them permanent damage.

The sole object of prosecuting Mrs Rogers was not to punish her but to protect the children and magistrates granted a separation order for the couple, awarding Mr Rogers sole custody of the children and making adequate provision for his wife's maintenance.

BIBLIOGRAPHY

Coalville Times

Derby Mercury

Guardian / Manchester Guardian

Hinckley Times

Illustrated Police News

Leicester Chronicle

Leicester Daily Post

Leicester Journal

Leicester Mercury

Loughborough Echo

Morning Chronicle

Nottinghamshire Guardian

The Era

The Times

Torquay Times

INDEX

Because they are mentioned so frequently throughout the text, Ashby-de-la-Zouch, Loughborough, Hinckley & Leicester have been omitted from the index.